Food that Really Schmecks

FROM THE BOOKS OF

Elaine Heinz

Food
that Really 🌼
Schmecks

Mennonite Country Cooking as Prepared
by My Mennonite Friend, Bevvy Martin,
My Mother and Other Fine Cooks.

EDNA STAEBLER

THE RYERSON PRESS

© EDNA STAEBLER 1968
Printed and bound in Canada by
The Ryerson Press Toronto

7700 0065 7

Contents

Introduction

Before you read any further I must warn you: I have absolutely no qualification for writing a cookbook except that (a) I love to eat, (b) my mother is a good cook and (c) I was born, brought up and well fed in Waterloo County, Ontario, where the combination of Pennsylvania Dutch-Mennonite, German, and modern cooking is distinctive and "wonderful good."

Like most older Waterloo County mothers, mine made sure her three daughters would not be helpless in a kitchen. She told us what to do and we did it. Mother cooked as her grandmother did and when we three were married we cooked the same way. Our husbands seemed to think it was fine — thrifty, appetizing and plentiful. But whenever company was coming we frantically scrambled through cookbooks to find recipes we thought more impressive than our accustomed, easy-to-make local dishes.

I was in a panic the first time I invited some rather special people from Toronto to have dinner at our cottage on Sunfish Lake, near Kitchener-Waterloo. They were prominent writers and editors—with their wives—who frequently travelled all over the world, ate in sophisticated dining rooms, talked and wrote columns about fabulous foods and were proud of their own gourmet cookery.

What could I serve them that they would find tasty and interesting? I went through all the recipes I had collected; I spent hours reading French and American cookbooks borrowed from the Kitchener Public Library. What? What? What in God's green bounteous earth could I feed them?

"Why don't you give them bean salad with a sour-cream dressing?" suggested a friend. "It's tremendous, and I'll bet they've never tasted it; I hadn't until I moved to this area," she said. "And how about a schnitz pie for dessert?"

1

Bean salad? Schnitz pie? Ordinary, everyday food for company? Unthinkable! I pondered. But why not? Why not a typical North Waterloo County meal—my own way of cooking, my mother's, my neighbour's, my Mennonite friend Bevvy Martin's? My distinguished guests couldn't get that in a flossy restaurant anywhere, or even find the recipes in their epicurean cookbooks.

My dinner would not be elaborate, or exotic, with rare ingredients and mystifying flavours; traditional local cooking is practical: designed to fill up small boys and big men, it is also mouth-wateringly good and variable.

My guests from Toronto arrived. I served them bean salad, smoked pork chops, shoo-fly pie, schmierkase and apple butter with fastnachts. At first they said, "Just a little bit, please," but as soon as they tasted, their praise was extravagant—lyrical to my wistful ears. They ate till they said they would burst. They ate till everything was *all* (nothing left).

For the past fifteen years they have been coming back to my cottage for a weekend in August, and each time I invite them they say they hope I'll give them another old-fashioned Mennonite meal.

"Why don't you write a cookbook?" they ask me whenever they come, and I tell them I couldn't, I'm just a sporadic amateur in the kitchen, not a trained home economist.

"That doesn't matter," they say. "All you have to do is write down how you make your bean salad; how your mother makes her pahnhaas, potato dumplings and divine coffee cakes; how Bevvy Martin makes drepsley soup; and you need only copy your sister Norma's gorgeous cookie recipes and your Peterborough sister's way of making nine-day pickles and relishes."

So, that's what I've been trying to do in this book. I've put down recipes from my sisters', my neighbours', and my own collections; some traditional ways I've learned from Mennonite vendors at the Kitchener market; some German ones from local I.O.D.E. and Ladies' Aid cook-booklets; two from the Walper Hotel; a few of my own originals, adaptations and modern favourites that I can't resist sharing. I've called my mother innumerable times to find out how she made some of the dishes that brought bliss to my childhood; I've gone many times to Bevvy Martin's ancestral stone farmhouse to eat myself full, to talk about food and watch her prepare it.

I borrowed my mother's and Bevvy's little old black-covered notebooks with the handwriting faded and often obscured by splashes of batter or fat. There were recipes for cakes, puddings, cookies — and, in Bevvy's, how to make soup, cheeses, sours, candies and wine. Only the ingredients were listed, no directions for putting them together—any woman should know how to do that! When I asked Mother and Bevvy how they made their soups, salads, pies and cooked their memorable meat and vegetable dishes, they said they didn't have recipes, they just made them; they learned from experience and tasting.

I've used the vague instructions Mother and Bevvy have given me and tried to translate them into definite measurements and methods by making the dishes myself. Some of them were successful, others were flops, and I've had to try them again and again—to the lasting detriment of my waistline. Forgive me, please, if you find some of my directions inadequate. If you test and taste for yourself, you might achieve something fantastic; anyway you'll have fun and a feeling of enthusiastic adventure—integral components of Waterloo County cookery.

Every good local cook of pioneer stock has her own variations of standard recipes: she substitutes an ingredient she likes for one that she doesn't; she improvises, adapts and invents with daring and zest: sometimes to suit an occasion, to use up leftovers or a surplus, or simply to see how a mixture will taste.

This jolly, creative cookery is a heritage from the Mennonite pioneers who, in 1800, came in their Conestoga wagons from Pennsylvania to Waterloo County and devised palatable ways to cook whatever they found in the wilderness or could grow on the land they were clearing, using the cherished little handwritten recipe books they had copied from the similar books of their forebears who came to America from Switzerland, Alsace, and the Rhineland of Germany.

When Roman Catholics and Lutherans from the same parts of Europe settled amongst the Mennonites in North Waterloo, they too schnitzed and made sausages, schmierkase, and sour-cream salads. Throughout the county recipes were generously swapped and invented till a way of cooking developed that is unique and indigenous to this heaven-blessed area that rejoices in its cultivation, preparation and tranquil digestion of irresistibly good-schmecking (tasting) food.

I do not exaggerate. That's the way it really is here in our beautiful pastoral Waterloo County.

But there is a paradox: we talk and we talk about our bountiful food; we copy out recipes, we cook and we bake and we sniff the good smells; we taste, we savour, and we eat; we eat till it's all; then we look at each other—or at ourselves in a mirror—and we say tomorrow we really must start to eat less. Tomorrow, tomorrow—it is always tomorrow—until the next day when again we cook some more lovely fat, good-schmecking food, and again we eat till it's all.

Those
Mouth-watering
Mennonite Meals

One of the joys of my life is to visit my Old Order Mennonite friends, the Martins, in their sprawling fieldstone farmhouse near the Conestoga River in Waterloo County. Their large old-fashioned kitchen, warmed by a big black cookstove, always has a homely fragrance of wonderful things to eat. Sometimes there is an apple smell, sometimes an aroma of rivel soup, roasting meat, baking cinnamon buns or spicy botzelbaum pie.

Bevvy, the plump little lady of the house, is always busy schnitzing (cutting up apples for drying), canning or cooking. With the wings of her soft brown hair smoothly parted under her organdie prayer cap she wears a plain navy-blue dress with a skirt almost down to her ankles. She greets me with a smile and a handshake: "Of course you'll stay for supper," she says as she hangs up my coat on a nail. "You know we feel real bad if you come for a visit and don't make out a meal."

I readily accept, always and often.

The food Bevvy cooks has such mouth-watering savour that no one can resist it. Like all Mennonite cooking it is plain but divinely flavoured and different from any other. You don't have to belong to the Mennonite faith to enjoy it: everyone who has grown up in Waterloo County is devoted to sour-cream salads and the richness of Dutch apple pie. Visitors and newcomers beg for recipes that have passed from generation to generation of Mennonite housewives without being printed in a cookbook. Everyone who tastes schnitz und knepp, crusty golden pahnhaas and luscious shoo-fly pie wants to know how to prepare them.

Simplicity, economy and experience are the keynotes of Mennonite cooking. Recipes are invented to make use of everything that is grown on Waterloo County farms. Fruits are canned and pickled and made into juicy pies. Beef and ham are cured with maple smoke, pork scraps become well-seasoned sausages. Sour

5

milk is made into cheeses, sour cream is used in fat cakes and salads. Stale bread is crumbled and browned with butter to give zest to vegetables, noodles and dumplings. Nothing is ever wasted and every meal is a feast.

"Today it gives endive salad and fetschpatze (fat sparrows)," Bevvy tells me as she puts on a clean print apron, tying it first in front to be sure the bow is even, then pulling it round and patting it over her stomach. I sit in the rocker by the kitchen window while she bustles between the sink, the stove and the big square table covered with bright-figured oilcloth. "You don't mind if I keep on working while we wisit," she says. "The curds are getting that smell I don't like round the house and I have to quick make my kochkase (cook cheese)."

She melts butter in a granite-ware kettle and into it pours sour-milk curds which have been scalded, crumbled and ripened for three or four days. She stirs the mass till it melts to the colour of honey, adds cream and keeps stirring till it comes to a boil that goes "poof!" then pours it into a crock and sets it away in the pantry. "Do you want to lick the dish?" She gives me a spoon and the kettle to scrape. "Some like it better with caraway seed in but we rather have it chust plain." Sampling its mild mellow goodness, I agree that it couldn't be better.

As she works at the kitchen sink Bevvy glances through the window above it. "I look up the lane every once in a while to see if there's a horse and rig coming for supper," she says. "We love to have company drop in."

"Does it happen often?"

"Not so much during the week but every Sunday when we have service in the church nearest us people come here for dinner. Sometimes there's not so many, maybe chust a family or two but sometimes we might have thirty-five. We never know, they chust come."

"Without being specially invited?"

"Ach, our people are always welcome. They know we have plenty to eat and it don't take long to get ready when everyone helps. Come once and I'll show you."

In a dark pantry off the kitchen she shows me crocks of cheese, elderberries, lotvarrick (apple butter), bags full of schnitz (dried apple segments), dried corn and beans, pails of maple syrup, and sacks of sugar and flour.

The cellar looks like a store. A room twelve feet square has shelves all around it from the floor to the ceiling filled with quart and half-gallon jars of fruit, vegetables, jam and pickled things. On a larder that hangs from the ceiling in the centre of the room are pies and buns and cake. On the floor there are crocks of head cheese, jars of canned beef and chicken, and pork sausage sealed in with lard.

In another room smoked meats and sausages hang from the beams above us. There are great bins of potatoes and turnips. Other vegetables are stored in boxes of leaves and there are barrels full of apples.

"This is our work for the summer and fall," Bevvy says. "We like preserving and it makes us feel good when we have it away in the cellar."

When Bevvy's children come from school and their chores in the barn are all done, Amsey, aged ten, the very shy youngest in black stove-pipe pants and a collarless jacket, shines up a basket of apples, then happily makes a bowlful of popcorn because there is company to treat.

Bevvy's merry pretty daughter Lyddy Ann, who is fifteen and dressed in the same style as her mother—except that she doesn't wear a cap—sets the kitchen table with ironstone china and the staples that are on it for breakfast, dinner and supper. There is bread, butter, and jam: "We were taught we'd be sick if we didn't eat jam-bread at the front part of every meal," Bevvy says. There are pickles and dishes of sours; "We may never leave anything on our plates and sometimes a little relish on a piece of schpeck (fat meat) helps to make it swallow," Lyddy says. For every meal there are potatoes and coffee.

At least twice a day there's a plateful of summer sausage. For breakfast there is, in addition, coffee cake, porridge or cornmeal mush and a bowlful of schnitz and gwetcha (dried apples and prunes cooked together). For dinner and supper there is always a bowl of fruit, a plateful of cookies or cake, pudding and pie—besides soup and the main course. When I tease Bevvy about having three desserts she says, "Canned peaches are not dessert, they are chust fruit. Pudding is not dessert neither, it is only for filling the corners, and cookies and pie are chust natural for anybody to have."

On the stove there's a kettle of simmering beef broth; a pot of potatoes is boiling, ham is frying in an iron pan, a sauce for the salad is thickening; and in a pan of hot lard the fetschpatze are becoming a tender golden brown.

Bevvy's great handsome husband, David, wearing a plaid shirt and overalls, and her twenty-year-old Salome, dressed like Lyddy Ann, come in from their work in the barn. They greet me with hearty handshakes, then wash and "comb themselves" at the sink.

At the stove there's a clatter of action. Bevvy puts the baked fetschpatze into the warming closet. Lyddy mixes the salad. Salome mashes the potatoes and spoons them into a bowl. Bevvy puts the meat on a platter.

We sit around the bountiful table and bow our heads in a long silent prayer.

Everyone reaches for a piece of bread. David helps himself to the meat, potatoes, vegetable and salad, then passes them on to me. I fill up my plate and pass the dishes to Amsey. As we eat the curly, crisp endive salad Bevvy tells me exactly how she has made its thick, warm sour-cream sauce.

"I never seen you measure exact that way yet," Lyddy Ann says to her mother.

"Ach, I made it so often already I chust put in what I think. Like for most things, I tell by the feel or the taste. Since I was a little girl I helped my mam and I learned from her chust like my girls learn from me. That's why it's hard to give the amounts of a recipe to a stranger."

Salome says, "She tells us, 'Put in a little handful of this, or a big handful of that, a pinch of one thing, or half-an-egg-shell of something else, or a lump the size of a butternut'. It's always 'flour to stiffen or enough to make a thin batter'. And for soup and the like of that it's 'put in milk or water up to the second scratch in the kettle'."

Bevvy laughs, "Ach, well, so it must be. How much you make depends on how many people you cook for. We don't like to run short on anything but we don't like to waste nothing neither."

"She usually guesses chust right," Amsey says, "except when it's brown sugar sauce for the apple dumplings and I could eat extra."

Bevvy cooks all her meats and vegetables without consulting a guide and their flavour is magnificent. She makes potpie of pigeons and rabbits and veal. She roasts beef, pork and lamb. Her gravies are brown and shiny. She fries chickens in butter and, dipped in egg and bread crumbs, the little fresh fish that Amsey catches in the river. She cooks sauerkraut with succulent spareribs. In an iron pot she makes stew and pot roasts browned with onions and bay leaves. Sometimes she has duck or roast goose bursting with savoury dressing.

"But we don't always have fresh meat in the country," Bevvy says. "Only right after we butcher. We have to cure it to keep it. Some we make into sausage, some we pack solid in jars and steam it; we smoke beef and ham. What we like best is the summer sausage: it is beef and pork ground real fine with seasoning and salt-petre, then stuffed tight in cotton bags the size of a lady's stocking and smoked for a week with maple smoke."

"We eat that every day; we never get sick of it," David says.

"We couldn't live without summer sausage," little Amsey says as he slaps a slice on a piece of bread and butter.

"Ach, we could live without only we rather wouldn't," Bevvy says. "We got all other kinds yet, like schwadamahga sausage and liverwurst and head cheese: they're mostly made from the pork scraps but they go good with fried potatoes and pickles, or beet and red-cabbage salad."

Salome says, "I rather have schnitz und knepp (dried apples boiled with a ham bone and dumplings)."

"Me too," says Lyddy Ann.

"You should see these women," David says to me, "how they sit sometimes all day schnitzing apples and drying them for the winter. Or making lotvarrick from cider and apples and cin-namon boiled and stirred half a day till it is brown and thick enough to spread with schmierkase on bread." He licks his lips and shakes his head, "Oh my, but that is good."

"She'll think we're a pig the way we make so much of our food," Salome says.

Bevvy smiles at me calmly, "She knows we work hard and we need it and never throw nothing away."

Not even a piece of bread. Before it's too stale Bevvy uses it for pudding or stuffing in tenderloin, spareribs, or fowl. She breaks pieces of bread into milk soups. When it is hard as a cracker she grinds it and keeps it in jars to mix with cheese on a casserole or to brown with butter and sprinkle over cooked vegetables, brown buttered dumplings with onions, and anything made with a cream sauce.

"One of our strictest rules is never to waste a thing," Bevvy says. "When the Mennonites were over in Switzerland yet, they got chased around by those that didn't like their peace-loving reli-gion and I guess they had to eat whatever they could get. Then in

1683 they started coming to Pennsylfawnie and gradually had things a little easier. But those that came up here to Ontario after the American Revolution had it hard again. Even if they had money they couldn't buy anything yet because there was nothing here but bush till they cleared the land and started to grow things.

"It's only lately since I grew up that we bought food in the stores, except sugar and spices, molasses and salt. We only used what we grew in our own fields and garden and made recipes up to suit."

From a drawer in the cupboard Bevvy brings me her most treasured possession: a little handwritten black notebook in which she has copied recipes, swapped and inherited. It is well-worn and some of its pages are spattered with lard. At the top of each page is written the name of the recipe's donor. There is Aunt Magdaline's Hurry Cake, Grossmommy Martin's Kuddlefleck and Cantaloupe Pickle, Melinda Gingerich's Groundcherry Preserve. "When I see those names," Bevvy says, "I know chust how it tasted because most of the recipes I got when I ate at their places."

"This is Cousin Katie's recipe for fetschpatze; we eat them hot and dunked in maple syrup," Bevvy says as the deep-fried golden balls are passed around the table. And we all eat so many that David says, "It wonders me that we'll have room after this for the pie. But we will."

Every plate on the Martin's table is as clean as if it had not been used when we finish eating our dinner. David sits back in his chair with a grunt of great satisfaction and dexterously uses a toothpick. Salome glances at me and laughs, "You look like you have afraid you'll bust your buttons."

"I am; I think I've gained five pounds since I sat down."

"Ach, not chust from one meal," Bevvy says.

David's eyes have a teasing twinkle, "If she eats with us for a week she'd be wonderful fat."

"Like Aunt Hannah," says Amsey.

"Shame on youse," Bevvy chides, "she ain't got the frame to sit that broad."

"I'd certainly lose my waistline if I ate much of your wonderful cooking."

David grins and pats his well-rounded belly, "I'm glad our people ain't so stylish that they care about getting fat. We chust eat ourselves till we're full."

Bevvy has told me, "Our Mennonite and old-time Waterloo County language is kind of like it but still not the same yet as the Pennsylfawnie Deutsch they talk in Pennsylvania."

Originally a Rhineland dialect that was transplanted to America in 1683, Pennsylvania Dutch speech has developed in its own delightful way, liberally borrowing English words or slightly "deutchifying" them and creating new words for modern ideas or inventions. (For example: the German word for railway is *Eisenbahn*, the Waterloo County word is *rigglevake*.)

Because it is a spoken dialect there are no rules for writing it. I have tried to spell Bevvy's words as they sound to me.

The Twin Cities with Schmecks Appeal

Kitchener and Waterloo consider themselves the finest pair of cities ever raised on sauerkraut and enterprise. Waterloo, with two dynamic universities and the head offices of six insurance companies, boasts that its older housewives make hasenpfeffer that is unexcelled in the Commonwealth. Kitchener, the most highly industrialized community in Canada, claims that good-schmecking regional cooking has moulded its history.

When the Mennonite pioneers came to the wilderness of Waterloo County in 1800 there were land-clearing bees and building bees till each family had a log cabin with a fireplace in which to bake bread. People from Germany came to the Mennonite hamlet in 1824 and Ben Eby, the Mennonite bishop, changed its name from Ebytown to Berlin to make them feel at home.

Canada's first lager beer brewery was opened in Berlin (now Kitchener) in 1840. Wilhelm Kaiser opened a beer garden where citizens enjoyed their ale on summer evenings and listened to the playing of Berlin's first German band.

When the County of Waterloo was organized in 1850 Berliners organized a campaign: with music, parades, plenty of beer and good cooking they entertained the member of Parliament for the district and convinced him that Berlin should be made the County Town.

Waterloo wasn't doing so well until an enterprising citizen persuaded a Mennonite farmer to sell his pioneer holdings along the main street. The acres were staked off into building lots and a public picnic was advertised. A wagon drawn by an ox team was loaded with refreshments—liquid and solid; an auctioneer took his stand in the middle and was moved from lot to lot while a crowd of people followed—eating, drinking and bidding till all the drinks were gone and all the land was sold.

Waterloo's population was doubled within a year. It boasted thirteen taverns, the Orpheus and Harmony Halls where members gathered on weekly evenings and drew beer from a barrel. On Sundays after church they took their round-cheeked families and their picnic baskets filled with "levavascht," "bretzels" and home-made brew to a grove on Buck's Hill where the singing masters led them in a joyful "saengerei" (sing-song).

Joseph Seagram came to Waterloo in 1857 and bought the grist mill whose side line was Alte Kornschnapps. J. M. Schneider, who worked in a button factory in Berlin, began making sausages at night in the basement of his cottage home.

The two towns grew closer together: They attended each other's balls and joined one another's Vereine (societies). The Gesang-vereine sang cantatas and held international saengerfests: cedar arches decorated the streets, bands and choirs came from faraway cities, and thousands of people in costume paraded to the park where they "ate themselves full" of frankfurters, schnitz pies and wine punch made by the frauenleit (ladies).

The population of Berlin and Waterloo almost doubled during the eighties; young Mennonites from the country came to work in the towns; more Germans and British moved in. MacMahons, Evanses and Jacksons married Schnitzlers, Lingelbachs and Ebys; Englishmen ate sauerkraut and Germans learned to play bagpipes.

In 1910, during a sumptuous banquet in the skating rink, Berlin was the first distant municipality to be flooded with electric light from Niagara; the town celebrated for three days. Two years later Berlin was declared a city: citizens cheered and embraced one another, the band played, church bells rang, giant firecrackers exploded, beer flowed freely, people danced up and down the main street till roosters in the back yards started to crow. In 1916, during World War I, Berlin was renamed Kitchener.

Kitchener and Waterloo grew larger and larger as their many factories expanded and became more diversified. The vast local meat-processing industry developed a specialty that has brought them renown and the praise of a grateful populace: pigs' tails— roasted, shiny and succulent—are eaten with lip-smacking, finger-licking delight at local banquets, picnics, and gatherings for great celebrations.

Though Kitchener and Waterloo are now building skyscrapers and planning for a metro population of half a million people, they happily preserve their gemütlichkeit (geniality) and the tradition of good eating along with good drinking. Visitors never forget

Twin City parties and come back again and again. Hard-headed citizens drink beer in their shirt sleeves as their wives bake schnitz pies, fanatically clean their houses and prefer a cooking school to a fashion show. And every Saturday morning they all crowd into the old red market building behind the City Hall where farm women, wearing the bonnets and plain clothes of the various sects, come—as they have done for 130 years—to sell tiny cobs of pickled corn, apple butter, crocheted doilies and schwadamahga sausage.

Some Drinks, Wines and Punches

The Old Order Mennonite farmers of Waterloo County have never taken part in urban festivities, but they like to drink mellow brown cider and dandelion wine when they gather together. Bevvy tells me, "But our preachers warn us, *'Drink net tzu fiel'* (Don't drink too much)."

All of the following recipes are from Bevy's little black cookbook.

ELDERBERRY BLOSSOM WINE

1 quart elderberry flowers	1 pound raisins
4 pounds sugar	1 gallon boiling water
3 lemons	1 package yeast

Pour the boiling water over the blossoms, sugar, lemons and raisins. Let stand for a day then add yeast. Let stand in the crock for 6 or 7 days. Strain and bottle, cork loosely.

EMANUEL'S DANDELION WINE

One day in May I decided to get rid of some of the millions of dandelions on my lawn by making Emanuel's wine. I simply sat on the grass, picked off all the yellow flowerheads as far as I could reach around me, moved to another thickly flowered spot and kept moving and picking until I had two quarts of blooms (half the recipe). The wine-making was easy and fun; it filled two small Chianti bottles with rather murky yellow liquid—until my friends started sampling.

4 quarts dandelion flowers	2 tablespoons yeast
4 quarts cold water	3 pounds white sugar
3 lemons	1 piece of bread
2 oranges	

Pour water over flowers, add lemons and oranges, juice and rind. Let stand for 2 days, then bring to a boil. Let cool. Dip a piece

15

of bread in yeast dissolved in lukewarm water; put the yeast-soaked bread into the dandelion mixture. Let stand a few days then strain and add sugar. Let stand in crock a little while longer —several days—then bottle but don't cork tightly.

So far mine has not been intoxicating.

MAGDALINA'S DANDELION WINE

6 quarts freshly-picked flowers	4 pounds white sugar
4 quarts water	3 sliced lemons
	2 tablespoons yeast

Pick the dandelions. Pour water over them and let stand 3 days and 3 nights. Strain through a cloth and add white sugar, lemons, yeast. Let stand 4 days and 4 nights. Strain again and pour into bottles. Cork lightly and let stand—till your curiosity gets the better of you.

LIZZIE'S UNFERMENTED DANDELION WINE

Let your children try this.

2 quarts dandelion blossoms	4 lemons, juice and rind
4 quarts hot water	2½ pounds white sugar

Put the blossoms and hot water in a crock and let stand for 2 days and 2 nights. Remove most of the blossoms, boil the rest with the lemons for 15 minutes. Cool, strain, and put in the sugar. Next day strain again and bottle.

MENNO MARTIN'S GRAPE WINE

No harm in trying—it sounds very simple.

4 quarts grapes—or any kind of berries	1 pound brown sugar
2 dipperfuls of water (about 2 quarts)	1 quart white sugar to every quart of mixture

Smash the grapes or berries and put them into a crock with 2 dipperfuls of water. Let stand 3 days and 3 nights, then press through a cloth. Put the juice in a crock and add 1 pound of brown sugar. Stir well. Let stand for 2 weeks. Skim every day but do not stir up. Strain through a cloth, then add 1 pound of white sugar to every quart of wine. Stir well. Let stand 2 days then bottle and cork loosely.

GRAPE JUICE

Wash any amount of grapes and cook them, till they're soft, in half as much water as grapes. Strain through a coarse sieve; add half a cup of white sugar to each cup of juice; bring to a boil. To serve, add the syrup to ice water, ginger ale, or what you like, and make it as strong as you please.

GOOD DRINK

3 lemons	1¹/₂ quarts water
2 oranges	1 ounce tartaric acid
3 cups granulated sugar	

Dissolve sugar and boil to a syrup; add juices, rinds, and acid. Let stand for an hour or so, then bottle. Use about 2 tablespoons to a glass of water or ginger ale.

TOMATO JUICE

1 large basket of tomatoes (11 quarts)	1 cup sugar
4 onions	2 or 3 teaspoons of salt
¹/₂ bunch celery	2 bay leaves

Boil all together till tender; strain, heat again and bottle.

BEEF TEA

The only time this vitalizing drink appeared in Bevvy's house was when someone really needed coddling; Salome says it was almost worth while being sick to get it.

1 pound chopped lean beef	1 teaspoon salt
1 cup water	

Put the beef in a double boiler, add the water, and simmer over a very low flame for about 3¹/₂ hours. Add the salt, strain; keep the liquid in a cool place. If it is too strong for the invalid it may be diluted with boiling water.

UNCLE ELI'S EGG NOG

Mother used to give us this without the rum; I have discovered since that the rum greatly improves it.

1 fresh egg	¹/₂ tumbler of rich milk
1 large tablespoon sugar	¹/₂ glass of chopped ice
1 wineglass of rum	

Shake all together thoroughly (I do mine in a blender); serve in a large glass and grate a little nutmeg on top.

MINT COCKTAIL

I've known people who added rum to this fruity drink.

6 sprigs of fresh mint	1/2 cup strained orange juice
6 wedges of pineapple	1/2 cup pineapple juice
1 pint sweet cider (or apple juice)	1/2 cup grapefruit juice

Mix fruit juices with cider. Chill. Divide equally and place pineapple and sprig of mint in each glass, with ice cubes.

BLACK CURRANT CORDIAL

This is a heart-warmer on a cold winter's day.

It requires: any amount of black currents	an equal amount of white sugar
	more or less whisky

Take the stems off the currants; wash the fruit and spread it on paper to dry thoroughly, or it will become mouldy. Measure equal amounts of currants and white sugar into empty whisky bottles, filling as many whisky bottles as you like. Put the bottles on your porch or patio where they'll be in the sun and every day shake the bottles so the sugar and berries will be thoroughly mixed and the sugar becomes liquified. Except when you are shaking the bottles, don't cork them tightly. Black currants ripen late in July; you must keep the bottles on your patio and shake them every day until the weather becomes frosty; if you go away you must engage a bottle-sitter. When you think you need a bit of inner warmth, round about Christmas, fill the bottles with whisky and try to remember that this drink is purely medicinal.

APRICOT WINE

I haven't tried this, but I'm going to.

1 pound dried apricots	1 tablespoon ginger
4 quarts warm water	2 lemons, sliced thin
6 1/2 cups white sugar	2 oranges, sliced thin
2 1/4 cups brown sugar	1/2 yeast cake (or 1/2
1 1/2 cups seeded raisins	package)

Wash the apricots in several waters and then dry them and cut them in halves. Place the apricot halves in a large crock and pour over them the warm water, reserving half of it in which to dissolve the yeast. Stir in the sugars, fruit, raisins, and ginger. Add the dissolved yeast and mix well. Cover and let stand for 30 days, stirring the mixture every other day. After 30 days strain the mixture and bottle.

MULLED CIDER

A lovely, hot, Thanksgiving kind of drink to sip with fresh doughnuts.

¹/₂ gallon cider, sweet and fresh	1 cinnamon stick
	A few cloves
1 cup brown sugar	A little grated nutmeg

Simmer together for about 15 minutes, pour into mugs and sprinkle the nutmeg on top. It is also good cold, poured over ice cubes.

MULLED WINE

To sip in front of a fire on a cold winter evening.

1 bottle of red wine	1 cup brown sugar
3 or more cloves	Juice and finely pared rind
¹/₂ cup water	of 1 lemon
1 cinnamon stick	

Put all the ingredients, except the wine, into a pan and boil together until reduced to almost half. Strain, add the wine and heat until almost boiling. Serve hot.

RED WINE PUNCH

Simple and inexpensive, made with domestic wine.

1¹/₂ pints red wine	¹/₂ cup rum
1 pint medium-strong, freshly-made tea	¹/₂ to 1 cup sugar (optional)
	Finely shredded peel of
Strained juice of 2 lemons	¹/₂ lemon

Bring the wine, tea and rum almost to a boil with the sugar; add the peel and lemon juice just before serving, hot or cold.

RASPBERRY OR STRAWBERRY PUNCH

It's a beautiful colour.

1 pint sweet red wine	1/2 cup rum
1/2 cup lemon juice	1/2 to 1 cup sugar (optional)
1 pint medium-strong tea	1 cup fresh berries
1 cup raspberry or	(or 1 package frozen
strawberry syrup or juice	berries)

Bring all the liquids almost to the boil; add sugar. Before serving spoon a few whole berries into each glass.

RASPBERRY VINEGAR

Mother made this popular drink every summer.

Pick over as many raspberries as you like; almost cover them with white wine vinegar and let stand over night. Squeeze through a jelly bag. Add 1 pound of sugar to 1 pint of juice and boil half an hour. Bottle for use as either a cold or a hot drink, mixed with water or something fizzy.

Wouldn't you think a sweet white wine would be more palatable than vinegar?

LEMONADE

No lemonade has ever tasted as good to me as the kind Mother used to let us make by ourselves on a hot summer day.

3 lemons	5 or 6 glasses of water
1 cup sugar	Ice

We'd squeeze the juice out of 2 lemons, pour it over the sugar, add the water; then we'd stir and stir and stir till the sugar was dissolved. We'd slice the remaining lemon as thinly as we could, put the slices and ice into each glass and pour in the mixture. Then we'd drink and squeeze and suck and nibble on the lemon rind while we giggled at one another's screwed-up, sour faces.

LEMONADE-IN-A-HURRY

Mother usually made a syrup with lemons to keep in the fridge to use on demand.

Juice of 6 lemons	2 cups sugar
Sliced rind of 1 lemon	1 cup water

Make a syrup of water, sugar and lemon rind. Boil for 5 minutes. Cool. When cold, add lemon juice. For lemonade, pour 2 tablespoons of syrup into a glass and fill with ice water and ice.

Soups

The steaming soup bowl is passed around Bevvy Martin's table at suppertime and we ladle into our plates its clear, fragrant broth, thickened by tiny dumplings. Bevvy says, "Grossmommy Brubacher always told me drepsley (dripped batter) soup is especially nourishing for the sick."

"But I ain't sick," David's bright brown eyes are teasing. "I guess that's why I rather always would have bean soup."

"Ach, you like any thick soup where I sprinkle buttered browned bread crumbs on," Bevvy says with a smug little smile.

"Except rivel soup," Amsey reminds her. It is made from milk thickened with egg and flour rubbed into rivels (crumbs), Lyddy tells me.

"He eats that too if he has a slice of raw onion and summer sausage with it," Bevvy says.

"Ach, I eat anything if I like it real good or not, that's how we are taught not to waste," David holds his spoon like a sceptre.

"Have you never tried canned soup?" I ask him.

"We never bought a can of anything yet," Bevvy answers. "We always chust make our own."

"We got more different kinds yet than they got in the stores," Salome says. "We make soup from our vegetables, from our meat, from our leftovers, and we have all kinds of milk soups." She paused to sop up the remains of her drepsley soup with buttered bread to clean her plate for kochkase, summer sausage and pickled beets. "I think we make soup out of everything you could put in your mouth to eat."

"Ach, Salome, that ain't right." Amsey looks at his sister reproachfully. "You know we never yet had soup made from huckleberry pie."

21

DREPSLEY SUPP

This really old Mennonite favourite is easy and fun to make. "Drepsley" means little drops or dribbles. And the soup is delicious.

1 quart of beef or chicken broth	**For the drepsleys:**
Lots of cut-up parsley	**1/2 cup flour**
Salt to taste	**1 egg**
	1/4 cup milk

Beat the egg, blend in the flour, then the milk. The batter must be runny. When the meat broth is boiling rapidly put a collander over it and pour the batter through it into the broth, stirring to quicken the dribbling. Quickly put on the lid, turn the heat down to half, and cook slowly for four minutes in the covered kettle. Take off the lid, turn off the heat, add the parsley and serve the soup immediately so the dreps—like very tiny dumplings—don't absorb too much of the broth.

RIVEL SUPP

Though this may not be David's favourite, Bevvy says it is warm and comforting if your stomach is a little queezy or if you've just had all your teeth out; it is also good for the sick and the very young.

4 cups milk	**1 cup flour**
1 large egg	**1/2 teaspoon salt**

While you are heating the milk and salt over water in a double boiler, beat the egg, add the flour and mix them with two knives, then with your hands until the mixture forms lumps the size of cherry stones. Let these rivels fall lightly into the hot milk. Keep the milk over the boiling water for five minutes, until the rivels are blended with the milk. It will be thick and nourishing.

RIVELS can be used to give body to any number of soups made with vegetables, broth, or milk.

BEVVY'S BOHNA SUPP (Bean Soup)

This is David's favourite; Bevvy makes it often and after having it for supper with the Martins I know why.

1 pound dried soup beans	**Salt and pepper**
Water, about 2 quarts	**Butter the size of half a large egg**
2 cupfuls of milk	**3 slices of bread cut in cubes**

Soak the beans overnight in water to more than cover them. Pour off the water and cover the beans with salted fresh water—or ham broth—and boil them till they are tender. There should be some water left on the beans. Add the milk and simmer till it is hot. Meanwhile brown the butter carefully, add the bread cubes and stir them around till they all get the taste of the butter and are a bit brown. Put the bread into the soup, pour the soup into a bowl and serve it piping hot.

With the soup we ate summer sausage on slices of home-baked bread. When the soup was "all", and sopped up with the bread, we put canned raspberries and kochkase on our plates and ate them with Bevvy's molasses cookies, then her Quick Pudding, hot from the oven and rich with brown sugar sauce.

SOUPS WITH HAM BROTH

Don't ever throw away the liquid that ham was boiled in; after you've let it cool and have skimmed off the fat it can be the perfect base for delicious soups.

HAM AND VEGETABLE SOUP

The stock, bone and some leftover ham make this vegetable soup a complete meal.

1 pound dried navy or soup beans	2 cups canned or fresh tomatoes
4 cups ham broth	2 tablespoons cut-up parsley
Ham bone and leftover ham	1/2 cup celery leaves or stalks
2 sliced onions	

Soak the beans overnight, drain and cook in the ham broth until tender. Add the other vegetables and cook them till they are soft. Remove the bone, add the parsley and pieces of leftover ham. Simmer for a few minutes, then serve. It will be thick and delicious.

DRIED PEA SOUP

Here is another of Bevvy's tasty fillers.

2 cups dried peas	1 stalk of celery, cut up
2 quarts water—or ham broth	Salt and pepper
1 large onion, sliced	1 cup sliced potatoes
2 tablespoons butter	1/4 cup bread crumbs

Soak the peas overnight in plenty of water; drain, put them in the two quarts of water (or ham broth) and boil until tender. Add the onions—browned first in the butter, if you like—add the celery and potatoes and cook slowly until they too are tender. Brown the breadcrumbs in butter and sprinkle them over the soup when you serve it. If you have any mild leftover vegetables you may add them.

VARIATIONS: You might like to put the soup through a collander (or blender) and simmer for a moment after. Or you might add small pieces of cooked smoked pork sausage when you put in the celery, potatoes and onion.

CHICKEN AND CORN SOUP WITH RIVELS

This rich, thick, Mennonite soup is the most special there is. Bevvy says they always make it for company.

1 cut-up chicken; you can use pieces but old hens have the best flavour
4 quarts of cold water
1/2 cup cut-up celery stalk and leaves
1 medium onion, sliced
Corn cut from 6 or 8 cobs—(or a can or two of niblets for deprived city dwellers)   Rivels:
2 hard-boiled eggs, chopped   **1 cup flour**
Salt and pepper   **1 egg, beaten**
4 tablespoons cut-up celery   **A bit of milk if necessary**

Cook the chicken in the salted water until it is tender and can be easily removed from the bones. Cut it into bite-sized pieces and put it back into the broth without cooling it any more than you have to. Add everything else but the parsley and hard-boiled eggs; boil about 15 minutes while you make the rivels by rubbing the flour and egg into crumbs. Drop the rivels into the boiling soup, stirring to prevent them from becoming a single mass; cover and simmer for 7 minutes. Now add the chopped egg and the parsley. Serve from a soup tureen on the table and pass cream to be poured into the soup.

GRAESHT MEHL GRUMBARA SUPP

(Brown Flour Potato Soup)

Bevvy calls this "real Old Mennonite soup."

6 medium potatoes   **3 tablespoons flour**
3 cups water   **3 tablespoons butter**
3 cups milk   **Salt, pepper, and parsley**

Peel and cut the potatoes in slices. Boil them in salted water until tender. Add the milk and let simmer. Meanwhile brown the flour in the melted butter, stirring all the time at low heat; add it to the soup, keep stirring till the mixture thickens. Sprinkle with parsley and pepper and serve with buttered crumbs, or squares of fried bread, or pretzels on top. You might boil some sliced onion with the potatoes, if you like.

ONION SOUPS

Because Bevvy can keep onions in the cellar all winter, tzvivelle supp in various versions is a standby when the snow flies.

CREAMED ONION SOUP

Boil as many sliced onions as you like — say ¹/₂ a cupful per person.

While the onions are cooking make a cream sauce with

4 tablespoons butter
3 tablespoons flour
2 cups milk

Drain the onions; when they are soft add them to the cream sauce and put in as much milk as you need to thin the soup—or use the water in which the onions were boiled. Simmer for a few minutes, adding salt and pepper to taste. Serve with browned buttered bread cubes on top.

TZVIVELLE SUPP MITT KASE
(Onion Soup With Cheese on Toast)

I wonder if a Mennonite woman went out one night and had French onion soup which she interpreted this way for her family.

1¹/₂ cups chopped or sliced onions	**A large lump of butter**
	1 cup grated cheese
2 cups boiling water	**Salt and pepper to taste**
2 cups milk	**4 slices of buttered toast**

Cook the onions in salted water till tender, add the milk and simmer together about 10 minutes. Add butter and pepper. Put a slice of buttered toast in each flat-bottomed soup dish, heap grated cheese on the toast, pour the soup over it and you won't waste any time eating it.

TZVIVELLE RIVEL SUPP (Onion Rivel Soup)

Can you resist that name? It tasted good too at Bevvy's house.

4 medium onions, sliced (about 2 cups)	For rivels:
5 or 6 cups beef broth	1 beaten egg
Salt and pepper	Flour
4 tablespoons butter	

Melt the butter and cook the onions in it until lightly browned. Heat the broth, add the onions, bring to a boil, then simmer. For the rivels: add enough flour to the beaten egg to form crumbs. Let the rivels fall in flakes into the soup and simmer, covered, for about 10 minutes till the rivels are cooked, the soup thick.

MILK TOAST

I've never tried Bevvy's Rivel Soup for the Sick. When we weren't feeling well Mother used to give us a slice of buttered toast with white or brown sugar and cinnamon sprinkled over it, then enough hot milk to thoroughly soak it and party fill the soup dish. We liked it so well that we sometimes had it when we weren't sick.

SALSIFY OR MOCK OYSTER SOUP

Bevvy says the delicate flavour of salsify soup is just like oyster soup without the oysters.

1$^1/_2$ cups salsify (oyster plant)	Salt and pepper
1$^1/_2$ cups water	3 cups milk
3 tablespoons butter	Bread crumbs browned in butter

Cut salsify in small pieces and cook in salted water until tender. Add butter and milk and heat to a boil. Serve with bread cubes browned in butter.

CELERY SOUP PLUS

The leaves and coarse bits of celery make this soup tasty, economical and filling.

1 cup celery, cut up	3 cups milk
1 cup sliced potatoes	3 tablespoons butter
1 sliced onion	3 tablespoons flour
Salt and pepper	

Cook the celery, potatoes and onions in just enough water to cover them; when they are soft add the milk in which the flour has been blended and stir the mixture till it has thickened. Melt the butter on top. You can add chopped hard-boiled eggs to this too if you like a real chowder.

TOMATO SOUP

A pleasant change from the canned stuff.

4 tablespoons butter	Salt and pepper to taste
3 tablespoons flour	Parsley, cut-up
2 cups milk or tomato juice	
2 cups canned or raw	
tomatoes	

Melt the butter, blend in the flour; carefully add the milk and stir till the mixture thickens. Meantime simmer the tomatoes, then strain them into the milk sauce over low heat and simmer for about 5 minutes. Season, sprinkle with parsley and serve.

Soup in our family was the whole meal: it was always so rich, thick and delicious that one dishful was just a starter. We kept passing our plates back for more and more till the soup was all gone and our appetites too—except for dessert.

THE BEST VEGETABLE SOUP I'VE EVER TASTED

When Mother made this mild, thick soup with vegetables, rice and beef, we didn't need or want anything else. The amounts I give are approximate.

1 large, meaty beef bone (I think it comes from a cow's leg)
Water to cover the bone with at least 2 quarts left after the
   boiling

2 medium-sized sliced raw	1/2 cup raw rice
potatoes	1 small sliced onion
2 or 3 sliced carrots	(optional)
1/2 cupful sliced cabbage	1 cup cut-up green beans
1 cup celery, cut-up	1/2 cup green peas
Salt and pepper	Lots of parsley

Boil the beef till it falls off the bone. Add the rice and boil for 15 minutes, then add the vegetables and continue boiling until they are tender but not mushy—about 20 minutes. Cut the meat into more-or-less bite-sized pieces, keeping it hot in the soup. Add the cut-up parsley and serve into large, deep soup dishes—again and again.

BEEF NOODLE SOUP

On our birthdays Mother would cook whatever we especially wanted. I had a number of favourites but most often ordered beef noodle soup.

Fairly early in the morning, as soon as the butcher's boy delivered the meat—3 or 4 pounds of beef with a bone full of marrow —Mother would start it boiling in a kettle of salted water. Then she would make the noodles (see bottom of the page).

About fifteen minutes before she expected us to come running down the hill from school she'd let the long, thick, egg-yellow noodles slide through her fingers into the boiling broth and cook them till they were tender.

When our hands were washed clean, our pinneys tied under our chins, and we were sitting round the big square kitchen table, she'd fish the meat out of the kettle onto a platter, stir lots of cut-up parsley into the soup and ladle it into a tureen which she set in front of her place at the table. While we children watched and waited, Daddy cut the meat into chunks, then into bite-sized pieces on our large flat-bottomed soup plates; Mother ladled the soup on top and the birthday girl got the first serving. We blew on the hot spoonfuls, slurped up the long, lovely noodles—till Mother told us to eat like ladies—emptied our plates in no time and passed them back for more.

CHICKEN NOODLE SOUP

When Mother cooked a nice old fat hen for our Sunday dinner she'd make noodle soup the next day with the broth, her own home-made noodles and plenty of parsley.

NOODLES

Noodles are staples in our part of the world: Mother and Bevvy and I would no more think of being without noodles in the house than we would be without potatoes or salt. They are useful for casseroles, soups, luncheon and supper dishes; fried in butter with chicken, wiener schnitzel and ham; or just so. Bevvy makes hers and stores them in jars; I buy mine in packages at the store, though they're not nearly as good as the egg-yellow, thicker, slightly chewy, much more flavourful noodles that Mother makes fresh every time.

2 cups flour	**2 eggs, or several egg yolks**
Salt	

Mother never measured the ingredients for noodles. Whenever she had a supply of egg yolks she wanted to use up she'd put some flour into a bowl, slip the egg yolks into a well in the centre, and work them into the flour with a spoon till she had a smooth, stiff, yellow, pliable dough—like pie dough. Then she would divide the dough into several parts and shape each part into a ball the size of an apple. On a floured board, with a rolling pin, she would roll each ball as thin as she possibly could without tearing the dough.

The noodle dough then had to be dried. In winter she would put the rounds on a board on top of the kitchen radiator; in summer she would hang the dough over a broomstick supported by two chair backs in our sunny dining-room bay window. She would turn the pieces of dough several times during the drying. When they were dry, but not stiff, she'd put the rounds on top of each other on a board, roll them together like a jelly roll, then with a large, sharp knife slice across the roll to make fine strips. She'd unwind the strips by tossing them lightly with her fingers and let them keep drying on the board until she was ready to boil them in broth or salt water. If she made more than she wanted to use at the time, she'd let them dry thoroughly till they were stiff and store them away in a tightly covered jar.

NEW YEAR'S EVE OYSTER SOUP

Mother always gave us oyster soup for supper on New Year's eve; its delicacy was achieved by making a few oysters go a long way —the price of oysters being what it was even in those days.

1 cup oysters	**4 tablespoons butter**
1 quart milk	**4 or 5 soda biscuits**
Salt and pepper	

You may cut the oysters into pieces if you want a fairer distribution for your eaters. Heat the milk; melt the butter and pour the oysters with their liquor into it; stir the oysters in the butter just long enough to bring the mixture to a boil. You don't really cook the oysters at all or they'll toughen. Pour the milk over the oysters. Crumble the soda biscuits and stir them into the soup—using more if you like your soup thicker. Simmer the whole lot for about 2 minutes, flavour with salt and pepper, then ladle it into flat soup dishes and you're off to a Happy New Year.

Meats, Fowl and Fish

In a Kitchener butcher's shop I heard a customer complain: "One day I have beef, the next day I have pork, on Friday fish, on Sunday chicken and that's it. What else is there? Lamb in the spring and turkey for Christmas."

"Ach, Lady, we got lots more than that yet," the butcher told her. "There's schwadamahga sausage, braunschweiger, pigs' tails and ribs, liverwurst, kalbsbrust; I could easy name you seventy-five different kinds we got right here in this shop. You got only to take home and cook it."

There are no directions for cooking meat in either Mother's or Bevvy's black cookbooks; any woman in Waterloo County, where meat is eaten three times a day, just naturally knows how to prepare it.

Mother never uses anything but the best cuts her butcher can send her and, cooked in her own unorthodox way, they have a more wonderful flavour than I ever encounter elsewhere. Steaks, chops, veal cutlets, calves' liver, even hamburgers and bacon, she fries in butter. She never braises or broils anything, she never makes stews or casseroles. She doesn't like mixtures. She doesn't like leftover meat—she gives it away; beef dripping, chicken fat, gravy, she throws into the garbage. Mother is a city woman. She has no thrifty Mennonite ancestors.

But I have: one of my father's great grandfathers was a pioneering Mennonite, and now, almost one hundred and seventy years later, when I visit my Mennonite friends David and Bevvy Martin, they often say, "You still got a lot of Mennonite in you yet."

In Bevvy's and my house nothing is wasted. Leftover meats are jellied, pickled, warmed over, or combined with vegetables and noodles to make nourishing suppers. From Bevvy I have learned that hot gravy is delicious on bread; beef dripping makes the best-flavoured shortening for frying potatoes, onions, wieners, or steak;

31

chicken fat, pure and mild, gives cookies a delicate crispness; bacon dripping is the preferred base for warm sour-cream salads.

"And goose grease we use for rubbing on sore throats and chests when the children have colds," Bevvy tells me. "Or for waterproofing their boots. And whatever fat we have that we can't use any other way yet, we pour in a kettle with lye and make soap."

VEAL POTPIE

In Mexico a few years ago, I stayed at a gourmet's paradise, el Casa de Piedra in Cuernavaca. Every day wealthy Mexicans would drive seventy miles from Mexico City to have dinner there, Americans from neighbouring hotels came for a meal, movie stars and visiting celebrities dropped in to eat. For two weeks we dined on the kind of food I like to read about when I'm lonely: avocados stuffed with strawberry shrimp, crêpes flambées marquise, coq au vin, Milanesas with mushroom béchamel, bouillabaisse, artichoke mousse, soufflé pâté de foie gras. Every dish was a work of art produced by the owner of the Casa, a Spanish marquesa whose hobby was cooking.

After two weeks of savouring and delighting in her culinary surprises I suddenly couldn't face any more of them. I looked at my Lobster Costa Brava without any zest. I said to my companion, "I'd give anything right now for something really simple —like veal potpie the way Mother makes it at home."

Like this: She'd cut a pound or so of veal into pieces and slightly brown it in 3 tablespoons of butter, then pour enough boiling water over the veal to cover it entirely. When the veal was nice and tender she'd drop egg dumplings (see Index) into the pot, cover it tightly for 15 minutes till the dumplings were cooked, then thicken the broth and add lots of cut-up parsley.

Sometimes when I make veal potpie I cook potatoes, carrots, onions and peas along with the veal, but mostly I like the bland flavour of the unadulterated veal and dumplings best of all.

STUFFED VEAL HEART

Delicate and different, veal hearts are a rare treat; a beef heart can be baked the same way but it's tougher. An easy, one-dish oven dinner.

2 or 3 veal hearts (one heart
    should serve two people)
2 tablespoons beef dripping
Salt, pepper and flour for
    dredging
1 medium onion, sliced
A few leaves of celery, cut
    up
2 cups bread cubes
2 tablespoons parsley, cut up
1/2 teaspoon crumbled summer savory (or whatever is your
    favourite herb)
1 egg, blended with enough milk to moisten the bread cubes

To be added later:
Potatoes, sliced 1/2-inch
    thick
Carrots and onion, sliced
Peas and/or green beans
Celery and parsley
(Any of the above are
    optional)

Remove muscles and arteries from the hearts, dredge with salt, pepper and flour and brown all around in the beef dripping. Remove the hearts from the pan and in the same fat cook the onion till slightly tender; turn off the heat, add the dry ingredients for the stuffing, then moisten with blended egg and milk. Cram the stuffing into the hearts and pat it over the tops and hope it will stay there—no matter if it doesn't. Put the hearts in a casserole with a heavy lid, keeping the stuffing-side up. Pour an inch or two of water into the bottom of the dish and bake the hearts in a 325-degree oven for a couple of hours until quite tender— longer for the beef heart.

Half an hour before the end of the baking time add the cut-up vegetables, being sure there is some broth in the pot. Replace the lid till the vegetables are soft enough. Carry the hot dish to the table and enjoy it.

JELLIED VEAL LOAF

This decorative, mildly flavoured loaf usually accompanied a ham as a contrast in colour and taste—when Mother had a buffet supper.

3 pounds veal
    (or 1 pound lean veal and
    1 veal knuckle)
1 tablespoon gelatin
    (not needed if you use
    the veal knuckle)

1 large onion chopped fine
2 stalks chopped celery
1 tablespoon butter
Salt and pepper
2 hard-boiled eggs
1 tablespoon cut-up parsley

Cut the veal into pieces, add the onion, celery, butter and seasoning. Cover with water and let it cook slowly—about 2 1/2 hours—

or until the meat is tender and the liquid reduced to about 2 cups. If you don't have the veal knuckle, soak the gelatin in $^1/_2$ cup cold water for 5 minutes. Grind, chop or shred the veal. Strain the hot stock and dissolve the gelatin in it. Add the chopped veal and mix well. Place hard-boiled egg slices and chopped parsley in the bottom of a mould or loaf pan and pour the veal mixture carefully over it. Put it in a cool place for several hours to jell. Unmould it onto a serving dish and slice it with a sharp knife. If you'd rather you could make individual moulds and decorate them prettily on a plate.

VEAL TONGUE

To make a nice quick easy little dinner.

I simply cover the tongue with salt water in a pot, put in a couple of bay leaves, and boil till the tongue is tender—it takes about an hour and a half. Then I peel the tongue, put it back in the broth —from which I remove the bay leaves—add a couple of peeled potatoes cut in halves, some carrots and celery and onion. Cook till the vegetables are soft; pour it all into a bowl and that's it— except the enthusiastic eating.

WIENER SCHNITZEL

The first time I ordered this in a restaurant in Germany I was surprised when I didn't get wieners—Mother always called this BREADED VEAL CUTLET.

2 pounds veal steak, $^1/_2$ inch thick	$^1/_2$ cup milk
1 cup fine bread or cracker crumbs	Dripping or butter
	Salt and pepper
2 eggs, beaten	Chopped-up parsley
	$^1/_2$ lemon

Cut the veal steak into serving pieces. Sprinkle with salt and pepper, dip in milk, then in crumbs, then in egg, and again in crumbs. Heat the dripping or butter and brown the veal on both sides till it is golden—not too quickly. Turn down the heat and simmer, covered, for 10 minutes; uncover and brown again. Sprinkle with parsley and serve—letting your eaters sprinkle the veal with lemon juice if they care to.

TZVIVELLE SCHNITZEL

Onions and sour cream give this veal steak more flavour.

2 pounds veal steak, 1 or	**1 cup onions, sliced**
1¹/₂ inches thick	**³/₄ cup sour cream**
3 tablespoons dripping	**Flour**
Salt and pepper	

Cut the steak into serving pieces, sprinkle with salt and pepper and roll in flour. Melt dripping in a heavy frying pan, add the onions and cook gently for about 5 minutes. Push the onions aside, put in the meat and brown it lightly on both sides. Pour in ¹/₂ cup boiling water and cover tightly; simmer for ¹/₂ hour, turning meat once. Now add the sour cream, cover again and simmer another 15 minutes or until the meat is tender. The gravy this makes is divine.

MOTHER'S POT ROAST

All my cooking life I've been trying to make a pot roast like my mother's; though she has told me many times exactly how she does it, I've never achieved the wonderful flavour that she does.

Mother gets her butcher to send her "a nice piece of beef"—he knows the kind, she says, not too fat, no gristle or bone. Then, contrary to all the rules of meat cookery, she puts the meat in a heavy pot with *cold* water that comes about halfway up the sides of the roast. She lets it boil slowly, lifting the lid and looking at it, turning it over, adding more boiling water if she thinks it necessary, till the meat is tender. When the water has almost boiled away she keeps the lid off, drops in 2 or 3 bay leaves and a few parboiled onions. The meat by now should be browning. She watches it constantly, turning it carefully to brown it on all sides in the fat brown juices (while potatoes and vegetables are cooking separately). When all is ready, she puts the meat on a platter with the browned onions around it, pours off any excess fat from the pan and makes the most fabulous natural brown gravy that anyone has ever eaten. She blends smoothly 2 tablespoons of flour and 1 tablespoon of cornstarch with ¹/₂ to ³/₄ of a cup of cold water; pours boiling water—about 3 cupfuls—into the pot, lets it boil while she scrapes all the lovely brown bits from the sides and bottom of the pan; then she thickens it with the flour mixture.

POT ROAST WITH TOMATO GRAVY

This is another way to make a pot roast; it isn't as much trouble in the later stages as Mother's, and it's mighty good too—robust and flavourful.

3 to 4 pounds of beef— **rolled, rump, short rib—** **or whatever**	**2 tablespoons beef drippings**
6 medium onions	**1 quart canned tomatoes**
Salt, pepper and a bayleaf **or two**	

Fry the sliced onions in the dripping till golden, take them out and put aside. Salt and pepper the meat, brown it on all sides in the dripping, cover the pot tightly and let simmer for a couple of hours or until nearly tender, adding boiling water only if necessary. Add fried onions, tomatoes and bay leaf. Finish cooking in the oven at 325 degrees, without a lid, until the tomato gravy is thick and the meat is well browned.

SAUERBRATEN (Sour Beef Pot Roast)

In 1905 when Prince Louis von Battenburg, Vice-Admiral of the British Fleet, visited Ontario's Berlin (now Kitchener), the prince particularly relished the sauerbraten served to him at the Berlin Club. It is still a local specialty.

4 pounds beef—chuck, rump **or round**	**3 bay leaves**
Salt and pepper	**¹/₄ cup brown sugar**
3 cups vinegar	**2 tablespoons dripping**
(I prefer dry red wine)	**3 tablespoons flour**
3 cups water	**¹/₄ teaspoon ginger**
4 whole cloves	**¹/₄ teaspoon allspice**
5 sliced onions	**¹/₂ cup raisins**

Rub the beef with salt and pepper. Place it in a large earthen dish. Heat the vinegar (or wine), water, onions, bay leaf, pepper, sugar and cloves together—but do not boil. Pour the heated mixture over the beef to partially cover. Cool, then cover tightly and let stand in a cool place for 3 to 5 days, turning the meat over every day.

Then: melt the dripping in a heavy pot; dredge the beef with flour and sear it quickly in the hot fat, turning it to brown on all sides. Pour over the beef the mixture in which it had been standing, diluting a little with water if it seems too sour. Reduce heat, cover the pot, simmer for 2 or 3 hours until the meat is tender and the sour mixture fairly well reduced. Remove the beef and keep it warm. Strain the liquid, skim off the fat and return the liquid (about 3 or 4 cups) to the pot. Add the raisins, then the spices and flour blended in 1/2 cup of water; cook until thick and smooth and pour hot over the sliced meat. Serve with grumbara knepp (potato dumplings—see Index).

SWISS STEAK

The smell of this cooking when we came home from school gave us a thrill.

Sprinkle a one-and-a-half-inch-thick round steak with salt and pepper, dredge with flour on both sides, then pound it well with a wooden potato masher or the edge of a heavy old plate; keep dredging and pounding till the steak won't absorb any more flour. Melt two tablespoons of beef dripping in a large iron frying pan; when it is hot put the steak in and brown it on both sides. Now cover the steak with slices of onion and pour in enough boiling water to cover the steak—careful, it will spit. Cover tightly and simmer for one and a half hours. You may occasionally have to add more boiling water. Serve it with boiled or riced potatoes. The gravy is wonderful, and you won't need a steak knife to cut the meat, it can be cut easily with a dull fork.

BEVVY'S GESCHTUFFTE STEAK (Stuffed Steak)

Mother makes this too and calls it MOCK DUCK.

2 pounds flank steak	1 stem of celery, cut fine
1 tablespoon dripping or butter	Salt and pepper
	1/2 cup milk
1 medium onion, minced	2 more tablespoons dripping
2 cups bread cubes	2 sliced onions
A pinch of freshly crushed sage	Flour
	1 cup boiling water
2 teaspoons cut-up parsley	1 cup sour cream (optional)

Lay the steak on a board and pound it. Cook the minced onion in the one tablespoon of dripping, add bread crumbs, seasonings, celery, parsley and milk, then spread the mixture over the steak. Roll it up like a jelly roll and tie it with string so it looks like a little body. Dredge the body with flour, brown it all round in the two tablespoons of dripping. Cover it with the sliced onions, pour boiling water into the pan, cover tightly and simmer for two and a half to three hours. Or bake it in a tightly covered roaster at 350 degrees for two hours. When the body is tender and brown a cup of sour cream may be added to make marvellous gravy.

MEAT LOAF

I'm not fussy about the kind of beef I use for a meat loaf. I take advantage of the ground-beef specials (if they don't obviously have too much fat) and sometimes, for a change of taste, I put in half a pound of farmers' pork-sausage meat. With baked potatoes and vegetables it's a good easy meal.

1 package of ground beef
(1 1/2 pounds nicely fills
my 9 x 5 x 3 pyrex loaf
pan)
2 eggs
2 tablespoons cut-up parsley
Half a stalk of cut-up celery
1 finely sliced onion

1/2 cup fine bread or cracker
crumbs
2 tablespoons catsup
4 tablespoons milk
A squirt of Worcestershire
sauce
4 crumbled sage leaves
Salt and pepper

A few chunks of cheddar, other herbs, or a pinch of mustard
—if you like.

Mix everything, pack it into a loaf pan and bake it in a 325-degree oven for 1 1/2 hours. Sometimes I put about 1/4 inch of water on top of the loaf so it won't brown too quickly; or I put strips of bacon across the top for the last half hour.

VEAL LOAF

Mother called this "veal" loaf, though it has equal amounts of pork and beef. She preferred serving it cold—if she could save enough of it.

1/2 pound ground round
steak
1/2 pound ground veal
1/2 pound ground pork
1 green pepper, chopped
(optional)
Half a stalk of finely cut celery

2 eggs
2 tablespoons milk
1/2 cup bread or biscuit
crumbs
2 tablespoons cut-up parsley
4 crumbled sage leaves

Mix all together, pack into a loaf pan and bake at 300 degrees for at least 2 hours with 1/4 cup water on top to keep it from browning too quickly.

STUFFED MEAT LOAF

To stretch a meat loaf, you can stuff it.

Line the bottom and sides of a loaf pan with meat prepared for meat loaf, put in bread dressing made with three slices of bread and usual seasonings, cover with meat and bake in 325-degree oven for one and a half hours.

DUTCH BEEF PIE

Bevvy makes this with leftover meat or raw minced beef.

1 pound minced beef	**Salt and pepper**
1 cup chopped celery	**1/2 teaspoon mustard**
1 cup chopped onion	**2 tablespoons flour**
Pastry for double crust pie	**1 cup water**

Mix the meat, vegetables and seasonings and brown lightly in a frying pan. Lower heat and cook for about 10 minutes more. Sprinkle mixture with flour, mix well and add water, stir and cook a few minutes longer. Cool thoroughly and the mixture will be fairly thick. Then pour it into the pastry-lined pie plate, cover it with the top crust, make slits for steam and bake at 425 degrees for about 30 minutes. With it you need only a salad for a good supper.

HAMBURGERS WITH GRAVY

In winter when the charcoal grill on the patio has become a bird-feeding station, there's something to be said for the old-fashioned hamburgers Mother used to make for supper, with gravy, potatoes and a sour cream salad.

1 1/2 pounds ground beef	**1 onion, chopped very finely**
1 cup bread or cracker crumbs	**Salt and pepper**
1/2 cup whole milk	**1 egg, slightly beaten**

Soak half the bread crumbs in milk then mix all the ingredients and shape into round fat patties. Coat them with the remaining crumbs and fry in hot beef dripping or butter till browned. Then make gravy—you can't do that on the patio.

BEEF STEW

Why *stew* should be said with a disparaging inflection I can't understand; it's a perfect meal if you put enough into it.

2¹/₂ pounds of raw beef, cut into 1- to 2-inch cubes	4 potatoes cut in quarters
1 or 2 large onions	1 cup sliced carrots
4 tablespoons beef dripping or suet	1 cup green beans in 1-inch pieces
1 teaspoon salt	A few peas, and cut-up celery and parsley
¹/₄ teaspoon pepper	and 1 cup of tomatoes—
¹/₂ cup flour	or not

Dredge the meat with the flour, salt and pepper. Melt the dripping or suet, and when it is hot brown the meat on all its sides. Slightly brown the onion. Pour enough boiling water into the pot to completely cover the meat and boil it slowly till it is tender—at least 2 hours. Pour in all the vegetables—making sure there is plenty of water—but not enough to drown them, or all the flavour. Boil for another 20 minutes till the vegetables are done but not mushy. Remove all the solids from the broth with a draining spoon. Thicken the broth with 2 or 3 tablespoons of flour blended with water. If the stew doesn't look brown enough you may cheat as I sometimes do by adding a couple of bouillon cubes or beef-base powder. At the last minute add some fresh cut-up parsley and pour the broth over the vegetables and beef. If you want to make it even better you can drop dumplings (see Index) on the stew for the last fifteen minutes while the vegetables are boiling.

BEEF TONGUE WITH RAISIN SAUCE

Boil a beef tongue in salted water with a large onion, a stalk of celery and a couple of carrots until the tongue is tender—about three hours. Peel the tongue and keep it hot in the broth. To make the sauce: soak a cupful of raisins at the time the tongue is put on to boil. Before you peel the tongue melt 2 tablespoons of butter, blend in 2 tablespoons of flour and gradually add 1 cup of tongue broth, 1 tablespoon of wine or vinegar, ¹/₄ teaspoon mustard, 1 tablespoon ketchup, pepper, salt and raisins. Simmer for about 20 minutes—while you peel the tongue. Serve the tongue hot with the sauce or cold without it.

PICKLED BEEF TONGUE

Mother always made this between Christmas and New Year's as an antidote to all the sweet things we ate too many of.

She boiled a beef tongue in salted water till it was tender, peeled it and removed all the ugly little valves and fatty bits on the bottom side. She cut it in thin, even slices which she put neatly with alternating layers of raw, thinly sliced onion into an earthenware dish. Over the meat, and enough to cover, she poured a mixture of vinegar, sugar and tongue broth that suited her taste —fairly sour. The slices of tongue were served cold on a plate and any left over were returned to the dish where they could be kept for a week.

A cured tongue, which stays red after cooking, looks nicer and will keep longer.

LIVER AND BACON

A few strips of crisply fried bacon, and calves' liver fried in the bacon fat just long enough to be not quite pink, is a rare treat at present astronomical prices. Mother dredges the liver in flour, salt and pepper; I don't bother.

LIVER IN SOUR CREAM

If you want to buy liver a bit more mature than calves' liver— and less expensive—here is a way that's delicious. The sour cream tenderizes the meat and gives it a thick, clinging sauce.

6 slices of bacon	**Salt and pepper**
1 pound of sliced baby beef liver	**2 cups sour cream**
1/2 cup flour	

Fry the bacon until it is crisp. Take it from the pan and break it into small pieces. Dredge the liver slices with a mixture of the flour, salt and pepper. Brown the liver in the bacon fat, then put it into a baking dish with the bacon bits spread over the liver slices. Pour in the sour cream. Cover and bake at 325 degrees for an hour—till the liver is tender. Uncover and bake another 20 minutes or till it looks brown and irresistible.

ROAST PORK

You won't have fresh roast pork that is stringy and dry if you cook it the way that Mother does hers.

Sprinkle a 5- or 6-pound roast with salt and pepper (and a bit of ginger); put it in a roasting pan that has a tight lid. Pour about 1 cupful of water into the pan with the meat and bake in a 300-degree oven for most of the afternoon—4 or 5 hours. Look in now and then to make sure there is still some liquid in the pan, until the last hour. The meat will become brown with the lid on; if for some reason yours doesn't, turn up the oven to 350 degrees. During the last hour of roasting you might put some onions into the pot to cook along with the meat and to flavour that delicious brown gravy. On a cold winter's day you might add a can of sauerkraut. And don't forget the baked potatoes.

Sometimes Mother would have the butcher cut a slit in the roast and she'd fill it with savoury bread dressing.

SCHWEINE SCHWANTZ (Pigs' Tails)

Sticky, browned, succulent pigs' tails are a superlative local specialty; no stag party or office picnic in Kitchener-Waterloo is a success without pigs' tails and rolls of barbecued spareribs prepared by local caterers. But you can make them at home and you will be blessed. Pigs' tails really are the greatest treat of all.

Suppose you have 24 or more pigs' tails (never underestimate —they're good warmed over): lay them on a rack in a covered roasting pan and let them roast in a 300-degree oven for 3 or 4 hours till most of the fat has baked out of them. Pour off and remove all the fat and coat the tails all around or dip them in the following sauce:

1 cup of tomato sauce (1 tin)	Salt and pepper
¹/₂ cup of tomato paste (1 tin)	A shot or two of Worcester sauce
1 cup of brown sugar	A teaspoon of dry mustard

Add also whatever you like: a few spoonfuls of prepared barbecue sauce, or soy sauce, or ketchup, hickory smoke salt, et cetera: keep tasting until you think your mixture is marvellous. Put the coated tails, covered, back into the oven at 300 degrees for another hour or so (if you're impatient try them uncovered at 350 degrees for half an hour) until they are bubbly and a deep, reddish brown.

Provide your guests with big serviettes—or wet washcloths—because they must hold the tails with their fingers to get all the sweet, sticky skin and meat off the bones. The local caterers always have scalloped potatoes and coleslaw to go with the pigs' tails—and of course plenty of beer. I like baked potatoes, rolls and bean salad with mine.

BREADED PORK TENDERLOIN

In the good old days when pork was a bargain, Mother often bought pieces of tenderloin. She'd lay it on a board and pound it with her wooden potato masher till it was stretched and quite flat; then she'd cut it into serving pieces and dip them on both sides into slightly beaten egg, and bread crumbs. She'd sprinkle the pieces with salt and pepper, then gently fry them in butter till they were golden brown on both sides and thoroughly cooked throughout.

STUFFED PORK TENDERLOIN

This was a company dish; and knowing how much I enjoyed it, Mother used to send some to me in a box with other goodies when I was away at college—for those midnight chats with the girls.

Mother would flatten the pork tenderloin to stretch it as far as she could then she'd spread a bread dressing over it—the same as she used for stuffed steak (see Index). She held the edges of the tenderloin together and sewed them with string to enclose the dressing and make a neat, firm little roll. In a covered roasting pan with very little water she'd bake it in a 300-degree oven until it was tender and delicately brown. When she served it at home she made gravy; in our school residence we were happy to have it in neat, cold little slices.

SPARERIBS

We always rejoiced when Mother came home from the market with a long meaty piece of spareribs. She would sprinkle the ribs generously with salt and pepper, stretch them out in a roasting pan, pour in a cup and a half of boiling water, put on the lid and roast in a 350-degree oven for an hour and a half, longer if the meat was thick. She'd remove the lid and let the ribs brown on both sides. Sometimes she'd spread bread stuffing (see Index) between two layers of ribs.

Spareribs being skimpy and almost meatless nowadays, I usually paint mine with a barbecue sauce for the browning at the end of the roasting.

PORK CHOPS

Of course you know there are two kinds of pork chops: rib chops with the bone along the side of the solid meaty part, and loin chops which are larger, boneless, with bits of fat marbling the slightly darker meat. I prefer loin chops to bake in the oven.

1. SMOKED PORK CHOPS are a gourmet's delight and the quickest and easiest of all chops to do because they are pre-processed. Buy them from a German butcher. While your guests are having their last drink put the chops under the broiler till they are brown round the edges on both sides—about 20 minutes. Your husband will bless you too because they're so easy to serve.

2. FRIED PORK CHOPS: if you want to cook ordinary, raw pork chops in a hurry you can simply fry them or broil them till they are thoroughly cooked. Mother always fries hers in butter and I've never had any better.

3. WITH TOMATO SOUP: Norm usually puts her pork chops into an oven dish with tomato soup poured over them and bakes them for a couple of hours in a 300-degree oven, with baked potatoes on the side. Halfway through the baking she sometimes adds enough green beans, celery or carrots to complete her meal; or near the end she dumps in a can of corn or drained peas.

4. WITH SCALLOPED POTATOES: loin chops baked on top of scalloped potatoes till they are very, very tender—one of my favourite ways; covered till the last half-hour in a 300-degree oven. I always put a pan under the baking dish to catch any milk that might bubble over.

5. WITH ONIONS AND CONSOMMÉ: Coat loin chops with a mixture of flour, salt and pepper, put them into a greased casserole on a layer of thinly sliced onions and over all pour 2 cups boiling consommé or bouillon. Bake in a 300-degree oven for two hours with potatoes baking alongside. During the last hour you might toss in a few other vegetables.

6. WITH SOUR CREAM: This is super. Season 4 loin chops cut half an inch thick with salt and pepper, dredge them with flour and brown them in a small amount of fat. Put them into a casserole, blend and add:

1/2 cup water	1 tablespoon brown sugar
1 bay leaf	1/2 cup sour cream
2 tablespoons wine or vinegar	

Cover and bake in a 350-degree oven for 1 1/2 hours or until the chops are done and the baked potatoes, squash, or other vegetables you've naturally put into the oven at the same time are tender.

KRAUT WICKEL (Cabbage Rolls)

This is an old German dish that can be made with variations.

10 or 12 outer cabbage leaves	1 stem of celery, cut fine
1 pound of ground beef (raw or cooked)	1 onion, chopped fine
1 cup of rice	Seasonings
	Bouillon cubes or consommé or beef broth

Cook the cup of rice in bouillon, consommé or beef broth until half-done. Remove the heavy part of the stems from the cabbage leaves, pour boiling water over the leaves and let stand while mixing the meat, parboiled rice, celery, onion, and seasonings. (If you're using leftover meat you might want to add your favourite herbs as well.) Place 2 tablespoons of the mixture into each cabbage leaf (drained and dried); roll or fold the cabbage leaf round the meat mixture—securing with toothpicks if you like. Melt a generous piece of butter in an oven dish or roasting pan, place the cabbage rolls close together, but not on top of each other in the pan, and sprinkle with salt and pepper. Pour about 1 cupful of bouillon or consommé or broth or tomato juice into bottom of pan, cover and bake at 300 degrees for about $3/4$ of an hour, adding more liquid; remove cover and continue baking and basting for another $1/2$-hour. Remove the rolls carefully, brown the juice in the pan (I add a bit of soy sauce), thicken with flour mixed with sweet or sour cream and pour over the cabbage rolls.

SAUER SOSSE

Because I didn't like onions or vinegar I'd turn up my nose when Mother made pickled pigs' feet; the rest of the family thought it was a treat.

4 or 5 pigs' feet	1 teaspoon whole cloves (optional)
$1^1/_2$ cups vinegar	4 sliced onions
3 cups meat stock	1 bay leaf
2 tablespoons salt	

Put the feet in a kettle with enough salted water to cover them; simmer them for about 2 or 3 hours—or until the meat falls from the bones. Skim off the fat. To the meat stock add the vinegar, spices and onions (the spices tied in a bag); simmer about half an hour longer. Take out the spices, put the meat in a crockery bowl and pour the sour liquid and onions over it. Serve hot, or chill until completely cold and the liquid jells; then slice and serve. As I said—this is fine for anyone who likes onions and pigs' feet.

GALLRICH

Jellied pigs' hocks are a Mennonite favourite—not mine.

Cover a couple of pig's feet or a pig's knuckle with salted water and boil till the meat falls from the bones. Chop up the meat fairly finely, removing the fat and any bits you don't like the look of. Return the meat to the broth which should by now be reduced to about two or three cupfuls. Put in a couple of bay leaves, pepper and any other flavouring you like; simmer the mixture for about fifteen minutes. Pour it into a loaf pan and set it away to cool and become firm.

PIGS' KNUCKLES WITH SAUERKRAUT

A pig's knuckle or knee, cut through the joint so it will go into a normal-sized kettle, has 12 inches of bone, well scraped skin, and tasty dark meat. My neighbour, another sauerkraut-loving friend and I can easily polish off two knuckles and a quart (28-ounce can) of sauerkraut at a joyous sitting.

Wash the pigs' knuckles thoroughly. Cover them with boiling water and boil them slowly on top of the stove till the meat is quite tender.

Put the sauerkraut into a baking dish; stir a small handful of brown sugar into it (if you must be precise, 2 tablespoons should do). Put the pigs' knuckles on top of the sauerkraut and pour in enough of the broth to cover the kraut. Cover the pot, put it into a 325-degree oven for about half an hour before you take off the lid to brown the meat.

My neighbour cooks her pigs' knuckles and sauerkraut on top of the stove and 20 minutes before serving time she cooks potato dumplings (see Index) on top of the kraut. In my house I prefer the oven method because of the smell. But when I've got used to that lovely, tasty aroma I take the lid off the pot in the oven so the part of the knuckles that emerges can brown and I turn them so the skin all around becomes golden. When the meat is very tender and you can't wait any longer, serve the knuckles and sauerkraut with boiled or baked potatoes.

If you have any guests or relatives who won't eat sauerkraut, open a can of peas for the miserable deprived creatures and take a moment from your own gloating delight to pity them.

PORK SAUSAGE, PLAIN OR SMOKED

Nothing could be more Waterloo County than this: tons of it are sold every Saturday morning at the Kitchener Market. Buy as much as you think you can eat, then double it. It does shrink a little and also it is good to eat cold—especially the smoked kind.

Coil the sausage in your iron frying pan, cover with boiling water, put a lid on it and let it boil for about half an hour—or longer, or shorter—till the water boils away. If you want, then, you can brown it by frying it on top of the stove, pricking the skin to let out the fat or, best of all, put it into your oven at 400 degrees or under the broiler to become a perfect, even, rich brown. Serve it with brunch or with mashed potatoes and a sour-cream salad.

LITTLE PORK SAUSAGES

These can be cooked in the same way as the large piece of pork sausage—boiling first in water, then frying, broiling, or browning in a hot oven.

BROTEVASCHT MIT EPPEL (Sausages with Apples)

An old German way that is always welcomed.

6 large cooking apples	**1 wineglass of red wine**
¼ cup currants	**2 or 3 tablespoons sugar**
1 or 2 pounds of sausages,	**Cinnamon**
or pork sausage	

Cook the sausages in water, then in the oven until nicely browned. Cover the sausages with pieces of apple, peeled, quartered and sprinkled with sugar, cinnamon and currants. Put a lid on the pan and cook gently in a 350-degree oven. When the apples are tender lift them and the sausages from the pan into a serving dish, pour the wine into the pan, stir it carefully into the juices, boil for a second then pour over the sausages and apples. Serve with mashed potatoes, a vegetable and a green salad.

HOT HEADCHEESE

Sometimes Mother would buy a piece of headcheese at the Kitchener market, put it in a pot with ¼ cup of water and let it heat till it melted and bubbled; then she'd serve it to us poured over boiled hot potatoes. With an endive, lettuce or dandelion salad it was a real treat.

SAUSAGES IN BEER

Another good old German way.

1¹/₂ **pounds pork sausage or**	1 **cup brown ale**
small sausages	1 **tablespoon flour**
1 **finely minced onion**	

Boil and brown the sausage, putting the onion with the sausage while it is browning. Take the sausage from the pan, remove excess fat, stir the flour into the pan-juices and onion, add the ale and cook to a smooth sauce. Arrange the sausage on a mound of mashed potatoes with a border of cooked carrots; pour the beer sauce over the carrots.

SAUSAGE PUDDING

Like a Yorkshire pudding with sausages as a dividend.

1 **pound sausages**	**Salt and pepper**
or wieners, or Smokies	1 **egg, beaten**
1 **cup flour**	1 **cup milk**

Beat the egg, add the milk, flour and seasonings; let stand while you boil and brown the sausages then pour the batter over the sausages in the hot pan and bake in a 400-degree oven till the pudding is puffy and brown.

GRUMBARA GLEESS (Potato Sausage Dumplings)

Merle Witmer, who keeps my house shining, says her kids are crazy for this old German dish inherited by generations of Witmers.

4 **good-sized raw potatoes**	**Maybe a tablespoon of flour**
2 **cups small potatoes**	**A chunk of butter**
cooked in their skins	**About a tablespoon of**
1 **pound—or more—sausage**	**brown sugar**
meat	**Almost a tablespoon of**
Salt to taste	**vinegar**

Grate the raw potatoes; put them and their juice into a cotton bag or cloth, and *squeeze* as much juice as you can out of them; let the juice stand. Grate the cooked potatoes; chop up or slice the raw sausage, taking it out of the skin. Mix the squeezed raw potatoes, the grated cooked potatoes, the sausage meat, salt and flour and shape into long sausage-like rolls or into round patties.

Drop carefully into boiling, slightly salted water. Boil for 20 to 30 minutes, depending on how thick you've made the rolls. While they are boiling pour the potato water off the top of the potato juice you have saved (save the potato water); mix the starch remaining in the bottom of the bowl with the vinegar, sugar and butter, then add the potato water. Remove the cooked dumplings from the boiling water and pour in the potato juice mixture; the potato starch will thicken the gravy which is then poured over the dumplings. Merle says you need only a salad to make this a wonderful meal—and cheap too.

WIENERS AND BUTTONS

Mother considered this a nice easy dish to make on a busy day.

Wieners—as many as you
   need
Onions—as many as you
   like—try 3
Potatoes—2 or 3

$^1/_4$ cup cut-up parsley
$^1/_4$ to $^1/_2$ cup butter
Batter for egg dumplings
   (see Index)

Peel and cut the potatoes into inch-thick pieces. Peel and slice the onions. Stir up the egg-dumpling batter and drop bits from a spoon into boiling salted water to cook while the potatoes are boiling, the onions are gently browning in the butter, and the wieners are being heated in hot water. When all is done put the buttons (dumplings) in the centre of a platter, arrange the wieners and potatoes nicely round the outside and pour the onions and browned butter over all of them; then sprinkle on the parsley to make it pretty.

WIENER-KRAUT

Another quickie that Bevvy likes to make on wash-day.

$^1/_4$ cup butter
4 cups shredded green or
   red cabbage
2 cups chopped apple
2 tablespoons vinegar
5 or 6 wieners cut in
   $^1/_4$-inch slices

$1^1/_2$ teaspoons salt
$^1/_2$ teaspoon allspice
$^1/_4$ teaspoon ground cloves
$^1/_2$ cup sour cream

Melt the butter in a frying pan; add the other ingredients except the sour cream and cook over low heat for about 10 minutes until the cabbage is tender but not mushy. Add the cream and as soon as it too is heated the dish is ready to be eaten.

GESCHTUFFTE WIENERS (Stuffed Wieners)

With a green salad this makes a good lunch.
Split wieners and mould a bread dressing on top, put on a flat pan in a 350-degree oven till hot and nicely browned.

HAMS

The only kinds of hams I've seen in Canadian cities for years have been pink, pre-cooked, delicate, and fool-proof to prepare. They are completely unlike the smoked, dark-red ham my mother used to cook for hours and in several waters to make it less salty; as we ate it someone was sure to say, "This is a good ham, not too strong."

I recently had dark red smoked ham in an Old Amish-Mennonite farmhouse in North Waterloo County and in Colmar, a charming, mouldy little thirteenth-century city in southern Alsace, where there is still a Mennonite meeting house and the ham was served cold, paper-thin, with crusty French bread, tender leaf-lettuce, and bleached asparagus dipped in melted butter.

GEBROTENE SCHUNKA (Fried Ham)

If somewhere in this world you can find a ³/₄-inch slice of old-fashioned red ham, plop it into an inch of boiling water in your iron frying-pan, cover it and cook it gently till the water has boiled away; uncover it, watch it, turn it and let it fry till it browns a bit on both sides. Serve it with potatoes and a sour-cream salad of beans, cabbage, dandelion or endive, and you'll never forget it.

SCHUNKA IN MILLICH (Ham Baked in Milk)

Put this in the oven, go to church, come home and have it for brunch with scrambled eggs and hot biscuits.

1 round slice of ham, 1¹/₄ to 1¹/₂ inches thick	2 tablespoons brown sugar
³/₄ teaspoon mustard	Milk to cover

Put the ham in a large iron frying pan, rub it with dry mustard and sprinkle sugar over it. Pour in enough milk to barely cover the ham. Bake at 325 degrees and hope that the preacher doesn't keep you longer than 1¹/₂ hours. By then the milk should be absorbed and crusty over the ham.

SEIFLAISCH UND BOHNA (Ham with Green Beans)

Bevvy makes this when she's having a crowd.

She covers a ham with water and cooks it slowly for three hours —or until it is tender, adding boiling water from time to time to have at least one quart of broth at all times—more if she has a lot of people to feed. Then into the pot with the ham she puts as many potatoes, peeled and cut in quarters, and as many green string beans, whole or broken into one-inch pieces, as she thinks she needs. She cooks all together till tender, serves the meat on a platter, the vegetables in a bowl. With a salad, thick apple sauce and a couple of sours, her meal is a feast.

SCHNITZ UND KNEPP (Apple Segments and Dumplings)

My gourmet friends from Toronto were enthusiastic about this Mennonite specialty.

2 cupfuls of dried schnitz (or peeled, raw apple segments if you can't get dried ones)	¹/₂ cup raisins (optional) 2 tablespoons brown sugar Egg dumplings (see Index)
A smoked ham (butt or picnic)	

Soak the dried schnitz over night. Boil the ham for two or three hours, covered with water. Add the dried apples with the water in which they were soaked, or the raw apples, the raisins and the sugar. Boil together for fifteen minutes then drop the stiff dumpling batter by spoonfuls into the boiling broth with the apples and ham. Cover tightly for fifteen minutes without lifting the lid.

Ready to eat? Put the ham in the centre of a deep platter, surround it with the apples and a circle of knepp sprinkled with browned buttered crumbs. Buttered cauliflower, green beans, and red cabbage and beet salad go well with schnitz und knepp.

BAKED HAM

I must concede that if I want to serve a lot of people there's nothing simpler than a big, modern, tenderized, easily-carved ham, placed fat-side up in the oven at 325 degrees, allowing 16 minutes per pound if it's over 12 pounds, and 20 minutes if it's less. About 45 minutes before the end comes, make a paste of:

1 cup brown sugar	1 teaspoon dry mustard
¹/₄ cup flour	¹/₄ cup maple syrup

Remove the rind and some of the fat from the ham, cut the remaining fat to form diamonds, rub the paste over the ham, stud it with cloves and return it to the oven to brown, basting it occasionally with dribbles of cider or sherry.

HAM LOAF

Mother was very proud of this when she had people for Sunday night supper.

3 pounds ham, chopped	1 teaspoon vinegar
2 slices of bread, cut in cubes	1 teaspoon prepared mustard
2 eggs	1 can pineapple rings
³/₄ cup milk	¹/₄ cup brown sugar
1 tablespoon butter	Maraschino cherries
1 teaspoon pepper	

Line a loaf pan with waxed paper, place pineapple rings and cherries in a pattern around sides and bottom; sprinkle them with brown sugar. Mix up all the rest and press into the loaf pan—being careful not to disturb the fruit. Bake 1 hour.

FRESH HAM LOAF

For flavour, this ham loaf was even better.

1¹/₂ pounds of fresh pork	1 cup tomato juice
1¹/₂ pounds of cured pork	3 eggs—large ones
3 cups bread crumbs	Salt and pepper to taste

Mix all together and bake 1¹/₂ hours at 350 to 400 degrees.

SALLY'S MEAT BALLS

Mother thought Sally Moogk was a wonderful cook.

³/₄ pound pork, ground	1 cup breadcrumbs
³/₄ pound beef, ground	1 cup ketchup or tomato sauce
1 onion, chopped finely	
Salt and pepper	
³/₄ cup rice, soaked in water	
2 eggs	

Mix all but the ketchup and form into balls; brown balls in a pan, put in an oven dish and cover with blended ketchup and one quart of boiling water. Let simmer in oven for 3 to 4 hours, making sure the balls haven't gone dry.

RABBIT

I've always liked cotton-tail bunnies hopping around in the grass, and the bold one who comes to my patio to eat sunflower seeds with the cardinals. But right now, after seeing how all winter the rabbits have been nibbling the bark off my new little trees, I wouldn't mind trying a few rabbit recipes.

HASE KUCHA

A Mennonite woman at the Kitchener market gave me this recipe when she sold me a rabbit.

Cut up a rabbit and cook until tender; take the meat from the bones and cut it into unidentifiable pieces.

While the rabbit is cooking make the potato filling:

2 cups hot mashed potatoes	1/2 teaspoon summer savory
1 tablespoon minced parsley	or sage
1 egg, well beaten	4 cups fresh bread cut in
2 tablespoons butter, melted	cubes
1 onion, minced	1/2 cup celery, cut up
1 teaspoon salt	Pepper

Mix all the ingredients well. Butter a casserole and put a layer of the filling in the bottom, then a layer of the meat and rabbit broth, thickened with the flour; put in another layer of the filling, and rabbit and broth, the filling on top. Bake in a 350-degree oven about half an hour until nicely browned.

FRIED RABBIT

If you have a hunter in your family here is a way to please him with very little effort—he might even try it himself.

After the rabbit has been skinned and cleaned and cut in pieces (let him do it), soak it in salt water over night. Remove it from the water, drain it and roll it in flour. In a hot frying pan melt about 1/4 cup of lard and butter; put the rabbit pieces in, cover, and fry slowly to a golden brown, turning often. Season with salt and pepper, add 1 cup of boiling water, cover and simmer till the rabbit is tender. Take the rabbit from the pan and make rabbit gravy.

HASENPFEFFER

This is the de luxe way to cook rabbit.

1 or 2 cut-up rabbits	1/2 teaspoon ginger
3 cups vinegar or dry wine	1 teaspoon whole cloves
3 cups water	4 bay leaves
1 large onion	2 slices of lemon
Salt and pepper	1 cup thick sour cream

Skin the rabbits, clean them and cut up in pieces. Put pieces in a large bowl or crock and cover with wine and water. Add the sliced onion, and seasonings. Let the meat soak in this solution for two days, on the third day put the rabbit in a kettle, cover it with water, add the lemon slices to keep the flesh white. Boil until the meat is tender—about an hour—and remove from the kettle. Dip the pieces of rabbit lightly in flour and fry in hot fat in a frying pan, browning quickly, turning often. Gradually add some of the mixture in which the meat was pickled. Let simmer until the broth is brown—about 30 minutes. Just before serving, stir 1 cup of thick sour cream into the sauce.

RABBIT PIE

This is wonderful on a cold winter's night—while the other rabbits are out there on the lawn nibbling the bark off your trees.

1 rabbit—though a dozen would be better	1¹/₂ tablespoons flour for each cup of liquid
3 tablespoons butter	Rabbit broth
2 tablespoons sliced onion	Salt and pepper
2 tablespoons parsley	Pastry crust

Cut the rabbit into pieces, place in a saucepan and barely cover with water. Cover the pan and simmer until the meat is tender. Add salt half-way through the cooking. Drain and measure the broth. Remove the meat from the bones, keeping it in large pieces. Heat the butter in a frying pan, add onion and cook about 5 minutes, stirring constantly. Pour the broth into the pan and thicken with the flour. Add pepper and parsley. Put the rabbit meat into the sauce, then pour the whole mixture into a greased baking dish. Cover with a pastry top and bake in a 350-degree oven for 35 minutes—till the crust is golden. No one will know this isn't chicken.

CHICKENS

Chickens just aren't what they used to be: they're pale, flabby, immature, and the little ones—to my way of thinking—are almost tasteless unless they're zoomed up with wine, herbs, honey, orange juice, and goodness-knows-what. I remember nostalgically the good old days when chickens had flavour, when Mother used to go to the Kitchener Market and pick out a *bird*. She'd feel the lower end of the breast bone to make sure it was flexible—that meant the chicken was less than a year old and would be just right for roasting. If she wanted to make chicken stew, soup or potpie, she'd choose a plump little hen with a yellowish skin and a breast-bone that was a bit firmer. No wily farmer ever sold Mother a stringy old rooster.

Nowadays all chickens are young: they are force-fed and butchered before their breastbones are set; I suppose it would be impossible to get a tough bird. The best buy is a capon: big, meaty, raised to be tender and flavourful. Remember that chickens have bones, and the thinner and smaller the chicken the greater the proportion of waste.

ROAST CHICKEN

In my family this was the most special way to cook a chicken; this was the ultimate, the best meal there was. Mother wouldn't cook chicken any other way for company.

Rinse the bird under the tap, dry it, sprinkle salt in the body cavity, then stuff it—I'll tell you how later. Rub the skin with soft butter, sprinkle it with salt, then with flour. Put the critter on its back in a roasting pan and pop it into a 325-degree oven till it's done. I allow plenty of time, 30 minutes per pound, and more for a really big capon. If it seems to be browning too fast I lightly place a crumpled piece of foil over the breast. After the first half-hour or so of roasting I pour half a cupful of water in the bottom of the pan and with it I baste the bird now and then.

The giblets were always a treat in our family: Mother liked the liver, my little sister the heart; Daddie and I took turns with the gizzard. I put them in the pan with the bird, the heart and liver for just the last hour.

To test if the capon is done, jiggle the drumstick; if it moves readily, the roasting is probably finished; to be doubly sure, insert a sharp, two-pronged fork into the thickest part of the breast or thigh, but not till the leg-moving test has been made and confirmed—you don't want your chick to lose his juices.

When the supreme moment has finally come, lift the bird to a hot platter, make the brown gravy, remove the skewers or string used for holding in the dressing and then carry that golden-brown, gorgeous cock to the slavering hoard at your table. You'll never know a prouder moment.

STUFFING FOR ROAST FOWL

In some of the best dining rooms, public and private, I've tasted dressings that seemed mouldy or flavoured with soap; I don't like highly seasoned, dark stuffings that destroy the delicate flavour of the bird; I can't eat dressings that are seasoned with stale, prepared, powdered herbs. The way my mother makes her stuffing is the way I try to make mine.

For a 4 or 5 pound bird use half a loaf—or a bit more—of not-too-fresh bread cut into cubes or torn into pieces (using the crusts).

A half-inch slice of butter	**Salt and pepper**
1 medium onion, sliced fine	**1/2 teaspoon dried sage,**
2 large stems of celery with	**freshly crushed**
leaves	**2 eggs, slightly beaten**
3 tablespoons cut-up parsley	**1/2 cup milk**

Melt the butter slowly in a large frying pan; add the onion and cook slowly till it is soft. Add the celery, cut up fine, and mix it with the onion. Turn off the heat but keep the pan on the warm burner. Now add the bread; sprinkle over it the parsley, seasonings and herbs; mix thoroughly with the onion, celery and butter. Beat the eggs and the milk together and pour them over the bread mixture—it should be moistened but not soggy.

You can make the dressing ahead of time and refrigerate it but don't put it into the bird till you're ready to roast it. Stuff the bird lightly, in the body cavity and around the neck. To keep in the stuffing truss the body opening with skewers, or sew it with a darning needle and string.

VARIATIONS:

With mushrooms: Sometimes I fry tiny or sliced mushrooms— fresh or canned—and add them to the onions and celery. If I use canned mushrooms I use the liquid as part of the moistening, instead of all milk.

With apples: Sometimes I add one or two finely sliced apples. If I have non-onion-eating guests I substitute apples for onions.

With *Roast Turkey* I sometimes use fewer eggs in the dressing and slightly less liquid. For a very large bird I double or triple my recipe.

With *Roast Duck* and *Goose* I sometimes use orange or apple juice as my moistener, instead of milk, and I throw in a few raisins.

A few onions or apples, peeled and cut in half, then thrust into the cavity of a small chicken or duck, make roasting a bird quite effortless.

Sauerkraut stuffed into a goose or a duck as dressing is something that quite a number of Kitchener-Waterloo old-timers rave about. I've never tried it but people who use it tell me they think it's the best.

BROWN GRAVY FOR FOWL

Don't bother reading this if you make good brown gravy; I add nothing new. Blend 4 tablespoons of flour or 2 of flour and 2 of cornstarch with cold water in a cup. Pour all the fat you can from the roasting pan into a dish in which you can keep it for later use. Put the pan on the hottest burner of your stove and brown the drippings. Pour in 2$^1/_2$ cups boiling water; dissolve, stir and scrape all the brown from the bottom and sides of the pan. Slowly, and stirring the broth as you do it, pour the flour-water mixture into the pan and keep stirring till it thickens. Taste to make sure there is enough salt. Sometimes I find there is not enough flavour and I add some prepared chicken concentrate powder.

BUTTER-FRIED CHICKEN WITH MILK GRAVY

This is the way Mother cooked chicken most often and the way I like it best—even better than roast chicken—though that was supposed to be the most special. The milk gravy with this could be digested by a ninety-five year old grandmother with a stomach ulcer, I'm sure, or a three-month-old baby.

Mother would cut up a nice yellow little hen into pieces—drumsticks, thighs, wings, back, breast, neck and giblets; she put the pieces skin-side-up in a kettle, covered them with boiling salted water and cooked them slowly until they were tender. Then she'd lift out the pieces, drain them, and drop them into melted butter in her big iron frying pan, turning them carefully until all the skin was crisply, delicately browned.

Meanwhile the broth in the kettle would have boiled down to about 3 cupfuls. She'd skim off the pure yellow fat that was floating on top (to be saved for making cookies). Into the broth she'd pour a cupful of whole milk (if there was less broth left she'd pour in more milk), bring the mixture almost to a boil, then add a smoothly blended mixture of 4 tablespoons of flour with another ¾ cup of milk, stirring it as it thickened. Just before serving she'd sprinkle in lots of cut-up fresh parsley—at least ¼ cupful. This gravy—or sauce—poured generously over plain boiled or riced potatoes with the butter-fried chicken and fresh vegetables is my favourite of all meals—as I think of it at this moment.

And if there's any milk gravy left over it's wonderful warmed up the next day and poured over buttered bread in a soup plate.

CHICKEN WITH DUMPLINGS

If anything could be better than butter-fried chicken with milk gravy it is butter-fried chicken with dumplings and milk gravy. Also it is an easy and wonderful way to stretch a chicken dinner if you find you suddenly have to.

Dumplings:

2 cups flour	**½ teaspoon pepper**
1 teaspoon salt	**1 egg, well beaten**
4 teaspoons baking powder	**3 tablespoons melted butter**
Milk	

Sift the dry ingredients, work in the melted butter, the egg and enough milk to make a moist, stiff batter. While the chicken is slowly frying, drop the batter from a spoon into the boiling broth. Cover tightly, turn down the heat to medium, and cook for 18 minutes without looking or the dumplings will be heavy. With a draining spoon remove the dumplings to a serving dish; add the milk and thickening to the chicken broth, then the parsley. Pour the milk sauce over the dumplings, and purr as they and the fried chicken disappear into your happy family.

CHICKEN STEW WITH DUMPLINGS

If you'd like a chicken stew you might add vegetables—carrots, peas, celery, green beans, to the chicken while it's boiling; cook the dumplings on top then thicken the broth. The chicken can be served just plain boiled, or fried in butter.

HINGLE POTPIE (Chicken Potpie)

Both Bevvy and Belle gave me this really old Mennonite recipe; they say it is a special treat for early summer when the carrots and peas are young and fresh from the garden—but I think it's good any time. They call the noodle squares dumplings.

Cut up a plump chicken—or use chicken pieces—and cook till tender with enough salted water to cover well throughout the cooking.

While the chicken is boiling prepare the noodle-dumplings:

2 tablespoons butter	**2 well-beaten eggs**
2 cups flour	**Milk**
1/2 teaspoon salt	

Blend the butter with the flour, add the salt and the eggs and just enough tablespoons of milk to make a very stiff dough, like pie paste. Roll out as thinly as possible on a floured board and let stand for at least half an hour. Cut the sheet of dough into 1¹/₂-inch squares with a knife. Then:

Peel 2 potatoes and slice them 1/4-inch thick	**Remove enough peas from their pods to make**
Scrub a dozen—more or less —tiny new carrots	**2 cupfuls**
	Cut up 2 tablespoons of parsley

When the chicken is tender put a layer of the potatoes into the bottom of a large kettle, then a layer of the noodle-dumplings, then one of the carrots and peas; sprinkle with salt, pepper and parsley; put in a layer of chicken, then repeat until all the vegetables and chicken have been put in—the top layer to be noodles. Pour the boiling chicken broth over all. Cover tightly and don't uncover for 20 minutes while the potpie simmers.

Pour it all into a beautiful bowl and it will be fit for serving a queen—but what queen would ever be lucky enough to get this humble Old Mennonite dish?

CRUSTY CHICKEN POTPIE

A delicious meal-in-one company dish that will stretch as far as you like and is no trouble at the last minute. It could be made with a pastry crust too.

1 cut-up chicken	**1 or 2 cups of peas—**
2 or 4 medium-sized	**preferably fresh**
potatoes, sliced ¼ inch	**2 or 3 tablespoons parsley**
thick	**½ or 1 cup of diced celery,**
2 or 4 carrots, sliced in	**or beans, or any other**
rounds	**vegetable you like that**
1 or 2 onions, sliced	**won't overpower the**
	others

Simmer the chicken in enough salted water to cover it well. Add boiling water if needed to be sure of having plenty of broth. Simmer for about 2 hours. When the meat is very tender remove it from the bones—keeping the chicken hot in the broth from which you have skimmed off the precious fat.

Now make the biscuit crust—mixed in the order given:

2 cups flour	**½ teaspoon salt**
3 tablespoons baking	**3 tablespoons shortening**
powder	**½ cup milk**

Roll out lightly and thin on a floured board. Line a deep, greased casserole with the dough—leaving enough for a top crust. Fill the dish with alternate layers of chicken and vegetables. Pour in the broth to 1½ inches from the top; cover with the biscuit crust, pinching it to the bottom crust and cutting vents in the top so the broth won't boil out—but don't trust it. Bake about an hour in a 350-degree oven, pouring more broth through the vent at half time. Thicken the remaining broth with flour blended with milk; add parsley to it and serve it as a gravy with the potpie.

"CHELLIED" CHICKEN

Of this cold chicken loaf Bevvy says, "I generally make it with the parts of the chicken that aren't so nice to put on the table to eat so, but it's even nicer yet if you use the whole chicken."

1 small chicken—or pieces	**¼ teaspoon pepper**
1½ teaspoon salt	**2 tablespoons gelatine**
Water to cover	

Cook the chicken in the salted water until it is tender enough to fall off the bones. Take it out of the broth and drain it. Remove the bones. Cut the meat into pieces and put it in a loaf pan or a mould or individual dishes. You might want to put a few green peas, pimento bits, pepper rings, or slices of hard-boiled egg in the bottom "for nice," Bevvy says.

Remove the fat from the broth. Dissolve the gelatine in ¹/₂ cup of cold water, then in 5 cups, more or less, of the hot chicken broth. Pour the mixture over the meat, mix well together and pour or spoon it into the moulds. Put it in a cool place till you want to use it. Unmould on a serving plate and garnish as fancily as you please.

ROAST TURKEY

Every Christmas newspapers and magazines publish directions for roasting The Turkey. I have always followed these directions faithfully and with good results. But this year when I was having fourteen members of my family for Christmas dinner I decided to cook the bird the way Mother used to do it.

I rinsed it, dried it, and sprinkled the cavity with salt; then I stuffed it with the same kind of dressing that I use for Roast Chicken (see Index), except that I doubled the amount and fried a half-pound of cut-up mushrooms along with the onions. I rubbed soft butter over the skin of the bird—a 16-pounder— sprinkled it lightly with salt and put it on the rack of my large roaster that has a heavy bottom into which I poured about 2 inches of water. I laid the neck and giblets alongside, covered the pan tightly and put it on the large burner on top of my stove where I let it boil and steam gently for 4¹/₂ to 5 hours—the same length of time it would have taken to roast the bird. I looked into the pan occasionally during the steaming to be sure the water hadn't disappeared; it hadn't, and I didn't have to add any either.

When the drumsticks were loose and the meat thermometer I'd jabbed into the cavity dressing indicated that the bird was about done, I dribbled soft butter over the skin, sprinkled it with a bit of white sugar and flour and put it into a 350-degree oven where it was perfectly browned while the vegetables were cooking on top of the stove.

The drippings in the bottom of the roasting pan were a rich dark brown; I removed the fat and made thick brown gravy.

Everyone in the family agreed it was the best bird they had eaten since Mother used to cook all our Christmas dinners; the meat was deliciously tender and moist. We're going to cook our Christmas turkey the same way next year.

Mother always used to cook her geese, ducks and chickens that way too.

ROAST GOOSE WITH GOOSEBERRY STUFFING

When we locals want to celebrate an occasion or give an outsider a treat, we go to Kitchener's well-preserved Walper Hotel (built in 1895) where the combination of haute cuisine and German cookery is the most varied and delicious in southwestern Ontario. Joe Zuber, the third of the family owners, gave me this recipe for one of the hotel's favourites.

Stuffing:

> 1/4 cup butter
> 1/2 cup diced celery with
>   leaves
> 1 1/2 cups gooseberries
> 1 eight-ounce package
>   prepared bread stuffing
>
> 1/2 pound ground roast veal
>   or roast pork
> 1/2 teaspoon poultry
>   seasoning
> 3 cups cooked rice
> 1/2 cup stock or water

Melt the butter in a pan, add the celery and cook over medium heat about 10 minutes. Combine the gooseberries, bread, ground cooked meat, seasoning, rice and stock. Add the cooked celery and butter and mix together lightly with a fork.

Stuff and truss the goose, place it, breast up, on a rack in a shallow open pan and roast in a moderate oven at 325 degrees until the leg joints move readily or twist out. Toward the end of the cooking time, test by moving the drumstick up and down. During the roasting, spoon or siphon off the fat as it gathers in the pan. Save the fat for use in other cooking.

An 8-pound goose (ready-to-cook weight) will take 4 hours to roast; a 10-pound goose will take 4 1/4 hours; a 12-pound goose will take 5 hours, and a 14-pound goose 6 hours.

MEAT ACCOMPANIMENTS

Besides relishes, ketchup, pickles, celery, shallots and carrot sticks Mother always has other special accompaniments for different meats on her table at dinner: cranberries with turkey, spiced gooseberries with goose, raisin sauce with ham, apple halves with chicken and pork, hot or cold horseradish sauce with beef, and sliced Spanish onions in vinegar with sausages.

CRANBERRY SAUCE

4 cups cranberries 2 cups water
2 cups sugar

Boil all together without stirring until all the skins of the cranberries pop (about 5 minutes). Cool and serve. It will keep for ages in your fridge.

SPICED GOOSEBERRIES

6 cups gooseberries 1 tablespoon cinnamon
3 cups brown sugar 1 teaspoon ground cloves
1 cup vinegar

Bring the vinegar and brown sugar to a boil then put in the berries and spices. Cook for about 20 minutes and serve hot or cold. This sauce can also be kept in sterilized jars.

RAISIN SAUCE

2 tablespoons butter 1$^1/_2$ cups cider or fruit juice,
2 tablespoons flour or water
1/2 cup raisins

Blend the butter and flour, add the juice and raisins and cook until mixture boils, stirring constantly. Simmer for about 10 minutes until thickened. Serve hot with ham. Sometimes I'll add a bit of sherry; if my ham hasn't a fancy glaze I'll also put in 3/4 teaspoon mustard.

STUFFED APPLES WITH PORK

An old German treat, easy and simple, to bake along with a roast of pork or spare ribs.

6 apples 1/4 cup raisins, soaked and
1 cup breadcrumbs chopped
1 onion 2 crumbled sage leaves
Salt and pepper

Chop the onion and cook it in some dripping from the roast (or in butter), add sage, raisins, salt, pepper and crumbs and 2 or 3 tablespoons of drippings; brown all slightly. Core the apples and stuff them with the mixture. Put the apples around the roast, about three-quarters of an hour before the meat is ready to come out. Without a lid, keep on roasting at 350 degrees till the apples are soft but not mushy. These are good with sausages too.

APPLE HALVES

Mother prefers to use Northern Spies but any firm cooking apples will do. She peels the apples, cuts them in half, removes the core and places the apples flat side down in a flat-bottomed cooking pot. She pours in about 1/4 to 1/2 a cup of water and turns on the heat, watching the apples while they cook, turning them when they are soft on the bottom but making sure they do not cook too fast or too long, and lose their firmness and shape. She then sprinkles them with white sugar and a bit of cinnamon, carefully lifts them, one at a time, onto a flat serving dish to be eaten hot or cold with chicken or fresh pork. Much better than apple sauce.

HORSERADISH

I don't know whether bottled horseradish wasn't sold in the olden days when I was young or whether my parents were masochistic. Anyway Mother bought the fresh, tough, knobbly roots at the market and peeled them with tears streaming down her face while Daddy, also streaming, put them through the food chopper. Mother added vinegar and sugar to taste and they almost gasped as they ate it.

HOT HORSERADISH SAUCE

They loved this with roast or boiled beef.

2 tablespoons butter	1 small egg
2 tablespoons flour	1 cup milk
Pinch of salt	2 tablespoons grated
1 tablespoon white sugar	horseradish

Mix all but the horseradish and stir over medium heat until thick, then add the horseradish. Serve hot, hot, hot.

FEATHERLIGHT DUMPLINGS

White fluffy dumplings, supposed to be foolproof.

2 cups flour	4 teaspoons baking powder
1/2 teaspoon salt	Milk to make a stiff dough

Sift the dry ingredients and add only enough milk to make a stiff dough—not at all runny. Drop tablespoonfuls of the thick batter into boiling broth, cover tightly, cook gently, and don't lift the lid for 10 minutes. Then lift the lid and sigh with relief. The dumplings will be snowy white puffs.

OIYA KNEPP (Egg Dumplings)

These dumplings are slightly heavier but have more flavour.

2 cups flour	**1 egg, well beaten**
1 teaspoon salt	**3 tablespoons shortening**
4 teaspoons baking powder	**Milk to make a stiff batter**
¹/₄ teaspoon pepper	

Sift dry ingredients, add melted shortening, egg, and just enough milk to make a moist, stiff batter that you can plop by tablespoonfuls into boiling liquid; reduce heat and cook gently, with the dumplings tightly covered, for 15 minutes. Don't peek or your dumplings will be tough and heavy—though sometimes I rather like them that way.

BEVVY'S GRUMBARA KNEPP (Potato Dumplings)

These potato dumplings are heavier, but delicious with stew or beef and gravy.

4 potatoes, boiled and peeled	**2 teaspoons grated onion (optional)**
¹/₂ cup bread crumbs	**1 tablespoon flour**
1 egg, slightly beaten	**Salt and pepper**
2 tablespoons milk	**2 teaspoons cup-up parsley**

Grate the potatoes, moisten breadcrumbs with egg and milk; add potatoes, salt and pepper, flour, onion and parsley. Form into walnut-sized balls dusted lightly with flour. Drop carefully into boiling salted water or stew; cover tightly and cook gently for 15 minutes without lifting the lid.

POTATO DUMPLINGS

Belle pours browned butter and browned buttered breadcrumbs over her dumplings to be eaten with gravyless meat or with sauerkraut (or stew, or a roast *with* gravy).

1 pound or 3 or 4 medium potatoes	**³/₄ teaspoon salt**
1 egg, slightly beaten	**¹/₂ teaspoon baking powder**
¹/₂ cup flour	**Dash of nutmeg and pepper**

Peel and boil the potatoes until tender; drain and rice or mash them until there are no lumps. Cool slightly and beat the egg into them. Sift the flour, nutmeg, salt and pepper and baking powder and beat thoroughly into the potato mixture. Shape into a roll on a floured board about 1 inch in diameter and cut into 1-inch lengths. Drop into boiling, salted water—or broth—stirring very gently for a minute to keep them from sinking. Dumplings will rise to the top in the boiling water. Cook uncovered for 8 to 10 minutes. Lift out carefully with a draining spoon; let drain. Immediately pour plain or browned butter over them to prevent sticking together.

FISH

Until I started living in my cottage on Sunfish Lake I was annoyed that my pioneering ancestors had settled in a completely land-locked county that had only little lakes and rivers. I longed for ships and great seas. My father was brought up on part of his great-grandfather's land which ran for two miles along the Conestoga River where as a boy little Johnny went fishing every chance he got.

When we were very young Daddy used to take us fishing along the Conestoga's low, safe banks. If we were exceptionally lucky we caught enough chubs and shiners to give everyone in the family a taste. Daddy cleaned the tiny fishes; Mother dipped them in flour or in egg and breadcrumbs, and fried them in butter till they were crisp and golden. No fish has ever tasted so good—not even the brook trout, black-bass and lake trout that Daddy caught and brought home from fishing trips in faraway places with The Men.

Bevvy and David live on the land along the Conestoga where her great-great-grandparents settled, and while I visited them for a week in the spring, Salome, Lyddy and Amsey went fishing and Bevvy fried the chubs and shiners in the same way that Mother used to fry them for us.

Mother has never cooked any fish any other way—except tinned salmon and smoked finnan haddie.

SALMON LOAF

Mother usually baked potatoes when she made this loaf, and served it with a green salad.

1¹/₂ cups milk	2 tablespoons lemon juice
³/₄ cup breadcrumbs	Rind of ¹/₂ lemon
3 eggs, separated	1 stick of cut-up celery
2 cups flaked salmon	(optional)
Salt and pepper to taste	

Scald the milk, add the breadcrumbs; cook for 5 minutes, stirring constantly over boiling water in double boiler; add 3 beaten egg yolks and cook five minutes longer, stirring. Cool slightly. Add salmon, salt and pepper, lemon juice and rind. Fold in 3 egg whites stiffly beaten then turn everything into a greased loaf pan. Set dish in pan of hot water and bake ³/₄ hour at 350 or 375 degrees.

SALMON PATTIES

When she wanted a quick meal, Mother often made these; we liked them with mashed potatoes and a lettuce salad.

1 cup-size tin of salmon	**1 stem of celery (optional)**
2 eggs, beaten slightly	**Cut-up parsley**
Pepper	**Breadcrumbs**

Mother removed the skin and bones from the salmon (I don't, I squash them with a fork and mash them in the rest—they probably do you some good). Then she put in the eggs, pepper, parsley, celery and just enough crumbs to make the mixture dry enough to make patties. Dropping tablespoonfuls of salmon into a dish of breadcrumbs she would roll them around, shape them into patties and fry them slowly in butter till they were golden brown and firm. I like mine with lemon butter sauce.

LEMON BUTTER SAUCE

Wonderful with any fish—bland or strong. Put it into a sauce dish on the table and help yourself; I always pour it all over my fish, others seem to like little dabs.

Juice of 1 large lemon	**1¹/₂ tablespoons flour**
¹/₂ cup water	**1 tablespoon sugar**
¹/₄ cup butter	

Melt the butter, stir in the flour and sugar, then the water and lemon; stir till it thickens, taste it, if it seems too sour add a bit more sugar.

FINNAN HADDIE

I don't know why finnan haddie is supposed to be humble: I think it's a treat.

Buy a thick, fresh-looking, golden piece of fish and simmer it in water until it is just tender. Make a medium thick cream sauce, lots of it, and into it cut up gobs of parsley and as many hot hard-boiled eggs as you like. Now you can pour the sauce over the whole piece of fish, or flake the fish into the sauce as I do. Serve it with mild vegetables, a salad, or on buttered toast, or with hot biscuits or buns.

CODFISH

I remember when people used to spurn codfish as an inferior, coarse kind of fish that only starving natives would eat. Since the price of cod has gone up it has become more respectable and there are many fine ways of preparing it.

Of course the best way is done in Neil's Harbour where Henry would catch it, split it, and carry it home from the shore by the tail and within fifteen minutes of its demise in the sea Clara May would cook it in butter.

COD CRISP

Here is my favourite inland method: Lay slices of cod in a well-buttered baking dish, salt it lightly, and over it spread a bread dressing made with cubes of soft bread or fine soft crumbs, onion juice, melted butter, summer savory and enough milk to moisten it when it's all mixed together. Now cover the dressing generously with finely cut-up bacon, fat and lean. Bake it in a 450-degree oven for about 10 minutes; by then the fish should be done and the bacon crisp. Serve it with mashed potatoes and vegetables or just with a crisp green salad.

Vegetables

There isn't a Mennonite farm that hasn't a garden near its sprawling farmhouse. As soon as the well-manured ground in Bevvy's garden has been cultivated in spring, she plants seeds in long neat rows; then she looks out of her kitchen window to watch the vegetables grow. "Quick, Salome," she'll call on a sunny June morning, "I think the beans came up last night." And out they'll both run to rejoice at the promise of coming abundance. Every day they keep watching, comparing growth progress with neighbours and friends. "My beets are slow this year," one will say; or "I don't think my cauliflower will amount to much," or "There's going to be a bumper crop of peas."

All Waterloo County benefits from the Mennonites' love of their land and what it produces. Nowhere else in the world that I've seen can vegetables be purchased in such variety, profusion and excellence. The Kitchener market on Saturday (and on Wednesday in summer and fall) is crowded with people buying baskets and baskets of vegetables that a few hours earlier were sparkling with dew.

Yet one day my sister Norm said to me, "Vegetables are a necessary nuisance, aren't they? Ever notice when you go out for dinner you remember the meat, the dessert, and maybe the soup or the salad? You never remember the vegetables."

And even Bevvy has said, "Vegetables are always extra good in summer when I can fetch them from the garden and put them right in the boiling water, fresh and sweet, but in winter they have to be kind of doctored up a little to give them some schmeck—except, of course, sauerkraut."

Must vegetables be the also-ran part of a meal? Trying to remember the vegetables in my life that were outstanding, I recall those I've been thrilled with in France where they were served with subtle mysterious sauces; those in good Chinese restaurants

69

where they were cooked very little; some at Kitchener's Walper Hotel; only at Mother's and Bevvy's houses where the vegetables were flavoured with meat broths, sprinkled with butter-browned crumbs, or stirred into a sour cream dressing, have I heaped up second helpings—or thirds.

SCHNITZEL BEANS UND SCHPECK (Cut-up Beans and Bacon)

The Mennonite woman who sold me green beans at the Kitchener market told me how to cook them with bacon.

1 quart of beans	**1¹/₂ cups boiling water**
4 slices of bacon	**1 teaspoon salt**

Wash the beans, cut off the stems and snap the beans into one-inch lengths. Cut bacon into ¹/₂-inch pieces and fry them in the bottom of a saucepan till the bits are crisp. Remove the bacon bits, add boiling water to the bacon fat in the saucepan, put in the beans and cook until they are just tender. Pour off the water and serve the beans with the bacon as a garnish.

BEAN SALAD

Can be used as a vegetable (see Index).

BAKED BEANS

Wonderful if you want to feed a lot of young people who are going skating or skiing—or the older folks who are just going out for a walk.

4 cups little white beans	**2 teaspoons mustard**
¹/₂ pound salt pork	**¹/₂ cup molasses**
¹/₂ teaspoon pepper	**¹/₂ cup catsup**
2¹/₂ quarts water, or liquid in which ham was boiled	

Soak the beans overnight. Drain the beans and add fresh water; cook them slowly till the skins burst. Drain and save the liquid. Mix molasses, seasoning, catsup and 2 cups of liquid from the beans—or ham broth. Put a piece of pork in the bottom of a bean pot or baking dish, add the beans and put the rest of the pork on top. Pour molasses mixture over beans and enough more bean liquid or ham liquid to cover. Bake, covered, for 5 hours at 300 degrees, adding more liquid during the baking as the beans become dry. Take off the lid for the last half-hour of baking. The beans should be brown and rich, moist and abundant. Remember beans swell, but don't be afraid to cook plenty of them, they're just as good heated over.

ANAEMIC CANNED BEANS

Can be made flavourful if you doctor them up with one tablespoon of brown sugar, one or two tablespoons of molasses and a tablespoon or two of ketchup. Let them simmer for a few minutes. Of course they can't be compared with the real home-baked beans, but the doctoring does make them edible—and it's fast.

LIMA BEANS

Fresh limas are best, but if you can't get them you might soak dried limas overnight in cold water, drain them and proceed:

3 cups limas—fresh or
    soaked
3 cups water
6 slices of bacon
Salt and pepper

$^1/_4$ cup cream or $^1/_2$ cup
    whole milk
$1^1/_2$ cups water in which
    limas cooked

Cook the beans in salted water till they are tender. Drain and save $1^1/_2$ cups of the water. Cut the bacon into $^1/_2$-inch bits and fry till crisp; remove from the pan, pour out all but 2 tablespoons of the fat. Blend the flour with the bacon fat in the pan and slowly add the hot water from the limas, stirring until it thickens, then pour in cream or milk. Add the limas and bacon bits, and simmer a few minutes before serving.

ASPARAGUS

You probably know more about preparing asparagus than I do. I boil mine in salted water and I like it so well simply with butter melted over it that I never try anything fancy except a cream or mild cheese sauce. But I do want to tell you: never throw away the water your asparagus was cooked in. Keep it in your fridge to use in soups or with a bouillon cube melted in it and served hot in a mug, or mix it with tomato juice or V8 for a cold or hot drink. It's full of vitamins and flavour.

FRESH GREEN PEAS

The most delicate, rare and delicious vegetable of all. Peas need to be boiled only a few minutes in salted water and served with melted butter. I like to put fresh mint in the water as they're cooking. If the peas are rather mature (or frozen) I also add a tablespoon of sugar to the cooking water.

BEETS

If you are lucky enough to have little beets fresh from a garden, boil them quickly till they are tender, skin them and drop them into hot melted butter, sprinkle them with salt and pepper and be happy.

To prepare beets—cut off the leaves (cook them like spinach if they are fresh) leaving a 1-inch stem and the tail root to preserve the color. Young beets will cook in 1 hour, old, larger beets from 3 to 4 hours unless you use a pressure cooker. When beets are tender drain off the water, blanch them with cold water but don't let them stand in it; slip the skins from the beets before they are cold. Old beets are best when finely chopped, sprinkled with sugar, salt, pepper and plenty of butter.

SUESS UND SAUER ROTE RIEVE (Sweet and Sour Beets)

This Pennsylvania Dutch recipe went to Harvard.

3 cups beets, cooked, sliced or diced	2 tablespoons butter
1/2 cup sugar	1 tablespoon cornstarch
1 teaspoon salt	1/4 cup vinegar or red wine
	1/2 cup water

Mix the sugar, salt, cornstarch, and stir as you add the vinegar and water. Cook the mixture 5 minutes, or till it thickens a bit; add the beets and let stand half an hour. Before serving heat to boiling point and stir in the butter.

GESCHPEISTE ROTE RIEVE (Spiced Beets)

An old German way—and especially good, I've been told.

4 cups small beets, boiled till tender and peeled	3 or 4 tablespoons thick sour cream
1/4 cup butter	1/2 small onion chopped fine
1 tablespoon flour	1 tablespoon sugar (or more)
Pinch of ground cloves	Salt and pepper
1/4 cup wine vinegar	2 tablespoons horseradish
1/4 cup meat stock	(optional)

Slice beets thinly. Heat the butter, stir in the flour, add the spices, onion, and boiling stock. Cook and stir to a smooth sauce then stir in the vinegar, sugar and salt to taste. Simmer 5 minutes, stir in the sour cream, horseradish and beets.

BROCCOLI

I hate to say this but it is safer to soak broccoli in salted water for a while so worms may come out and float on top. Remove any discoloured parts and part of the stem. Cook whole, or broken into flowerets. Boil for 15 to 20 minutes—don't let it get too soft or it's horrid. Serve with melted butter or white, cheese or brown sauce and buttered crumbs.

BRUSSELS SPROUTS

Remove discoloured parts and boil in salted water for 10 to 15 minutes—they should stay a bit crisp. Serve with melted butter, a sauce and buttered crumbs.

CAULIFLOWER

Remove outer leaves and stalks; leave whole, cutting out centre core, or break it into flowerets. Boil the whole 15 minutes, flowerets 10 minutes, in salted water. Don't overcook—nothing is worse than the soggy, grey, water-logged cauliflower they serve in most restaurants. Drain it the moment it's tender and serve it immediately with melted butter or sauce. Don't put a sauce over it till you're ready to take it to the table or it will become watery. Buttered crumbs sprinkled over it make it pretty special.

CHINESE CABBAGE

Shred; boil or sauté 4 or 5 minutes. No longer. It's good with a cheese sauce.

JERUSALEM ARTICHOKES

Bevvy loves these knubbly, dark roots, pares them thin, leaves them whole or slices them. She boils them for about half an hour and covers them with a sauce.

KOHLRABI

Peel, cut into slices and boil for over half an hour. Serve with a sauce and crumbs.

SALSIFY

Clean this long spindly root which tastes like oysters; slice it and cook it in salted water till tender. Serve it with a cream sauce or dip the pieces in a light pancake batter and fry to a golden brown.

CELERY

Cut celery into pieces, boil till tender and serve with a sauce.

CARROTS

No vegetable is used so often as the commonplace, colourful carrot, from the time it is tender and sweet and fresh from the garden till it is limp and tired after spending the winter packed in leaves in a cool-cellar. Young carrots need no embellishment: the sweet, delicate flavour of the vegetable eaten raw or cooked for a few minutes in salted water is all that is necessary—with a bit of butter added before serving. But as time goes on and the carrot grows older it may need some ingenuity to make it delectable. Never, never cut carrots into chunks, they look as if nobody cared.

GLAZED CARROTS

Scrape carrots lightly—let a bit of skin stay on if wants to, it will do you good if it's clean. Cut the carrots into long slivers—or leave them whole if they're skinny ones. Boil them in a small amount of water till they're tender but firm. Pour off the water, if it hasn't all boiled away. To every 8 or 10 carrots add 2 or 3 tablespoons butter and 2 or 3 tablespoons of honey or brown sugar. Turn the carrots carefully till they're coated and simmer slowly till they are glazed.

BRAISED CARROTS

Scrape and slice carrots paper thin. Cook them over a very low flame in a heavy pan, tightly covered, with 1/4-cup of water, a pinch of salt, 1 teaspoon of sugar and a good lump of butter. In about 20 minutes the water should be completely evaporated and the carrots cooked and beginning to glaze. Sprinkle them with chopped parsley before serving.

If you're having an oven meal you can put the whole lot into a covered casserole and cook them in the oven for about half an hour or slightly longer. The taste is a new experience.

TIRED CARROTS

Towards the end of the winter when carrots are limp—and I am too—I sometimes give them a shot by sprinkling them with any of a variety of things in my herb cupboard: a tiny bit of sage, summer savory, a dash of any of the savoury salts. Sometimes I'll cut up an onion or two or a couple of sprigs or leaves of celery or parsley. A cream or brown sauce over carrots is good with some meats. Best of all I'll sprinkle a tablespoon or two of sherry or lemon juice over the carrots before serving. And always I use plenty of butter and pepper.

Nothing depresses me more than the constant sight of carrots-and-peas on every main dish in restaurants, hotel dining rooms and at banquets. There they inevitably are, a dull, dry pile of flavourless orange and green. I won't have the combination in my house.

BAKED CARROTS

This has a nutty, tangy flavour that amazes me.
Shred enough raw carrots to make 3 cups—about 6 large carrots; the shredder should have holes about 1/4-inch in diameter. Put the carrots in a well-greased baking dish that can be used for serving. Sprinkle 1/2 a teaspoon of salt, 1/4-teaspoon of ginger and 1/4-teaspoon of pepper over them; then pour on 1/2 a cup of water and mix well. Bake uncovered in a moderate oven for 45 minutes.

To make an easy, economical meal broil a pound of sausages or frankfurters and arrange them on top of the carrots when they have finished cooking. Bake potatoes in the oven at the same time, and that's it.

CORN PUDDING

Very good, with a custardy bottom. A salad would make it a complete lunch or supper. It's nice too with maple syrup poured over it.

2 cups corn—fresh or canned	1 tablespoon sugar
1 teaspoon salt	1 tablespoon flour or cornstarch
2 eggs, beaten	1 cup milk
2 tablespoons butter, melted	Pepper to taste

To the corn add salt, sugar, flour and melted butter, then eggs, and milk beaten together. Pour into a greased baking dish and bake at 350 degrees for 35 minutes.

WELSHKAHN OYSTER PUFFA (Oyster Corn Fritters)

You won't regret trying these with canned or fresh corn.

2 cups corn	$1/2$ teaspoon salt
2 tablespoons flour	$1/4$ teaspoon pepper
2 eggs, separated	

To the corn add the beaten egg yolks, flour and seasonings. Add the stiffly beaten egg whites and blend. Drop by spoonfuls the size of an oyster on a hot, buttered frying pan and brown gently all around.

FRIED CORN

This has a nutty, delicate flavour and is easy to make.
You can use corn cut from the cobs after boiling for 5 minutes, or a can of drained whole-kernel corn. Melt 2 or 3 tablespoons of butter in a frying pan, add the corn, sprinkle it with salt and pepper and a teaspoon of sugar and let it fry slowly. Watch it as it browns, it sticks easily.

BOILED CORN

You don't know how delicious corn can be until you taste it fresh off the stalk. I phone the farmer's wife down the lake to pick me some corn, put a big kettle of water on the stove, paddle down the lake in my canoe to get the corn, husk it, and pop it into the boiling salted water for 5 minutes. Then I eat it, 8 or 10 cobs of Golden Bantam slathered with butter; and that's all I want for supper, thank you.

DRIED CORN

In Lancaster County, Pennsylvania, you can buy dried corn in packages; in Ontario you must make it yourself.
Cut the kernels from the cobs and spread them flat and thin on pans to dry in a 250-degree oven; stir often to prevent them from burning or browning, and to dry them evenly. When the kernels are hard as chicken feed, with no moisture left in them (or they'll become mouldy), put them in jars and store them in a dry place. They'll keep a long time but not forever. (I kept some I brought back from Lancaster, it became wormy and the winter birds on my patio loved it.)

COOKED DRIED CORN

This has a rich, nut-like flavour.

2 cups dried corn, with
    water to partially cover
1 teaspoon salt
2 teaspoons sugar

Pepper
$^1/_2$ cup cream or whole milk
2 tablespoons butter

Soak the corn overnight in warm water. Cook slowly until it is tender and most of the water is absorbed. Add salt, sugar, butter and cream, and heat to just under a boil. Sprinkle with pepper and serve as a vegetable with meat and potatoes.

ONIONS WITH CHEESE

Easy to do and delicious—especially with beef.
Skin some large onions and cut them into thick slices. Lay them on a buttered oven dish, spread them with soft butter and put them into a 350-degree oven till soft. Mix grated cheese with salt, pepper and a little mustard; add enough red wine to make a thick paste. Spread the paste on the hot onions and put under the grill to brown the cheese.

BOILED ONIONS

With a cream or cheese sauce, boiled onions are mighty tasty.

BAKED ONIONS

Parboil peeled onions or put them in a covered oven dish with about an inch of water before you put them to brown in the pan with the roast.

TZVIVELLE PIE (Onion Pie)

Generations of Mennonites have served this, smothered with gravy, when they had a roast beef dinner. (Compare this with Quiche Lorraine—see Index.)

Rich pastry to line a deep
    pie plate
2 cups sliced onions
3 tablespoons butter

6 eggs, beaten
1 cup milk
Salt and pepper

Gently fry the sliced onions in the butter till they are almost soft, then spread them over the pastry in the pie plate. Combine the beaten eggs, milk and seasonings and pour the mixture over the onions. Bake the pie on the floor of the oven for 40 to 50 minutes at 350 degrees.

STEWED TOMATOES

A nice accompaniment for chops or fish.

3 cups tomatoes—fresh or canned	**¹/₂ cup bread or biscuit crumbs**
A small sliced or minced onion	**1 tablespoon sugar**
2 tablespoons butter	**Salt and pepper**

Cook onions slowly in the tomatoes till they are tender—about 20 minutes, stirring occasionally. Add butter, breadcrumbs, and seasonings; cook a few minutes longer. Serve hot. Add cooked lima beans if you like.

FRIED OR GRILLED TOMATOES

Firm slices of red or green tomato dipped in flour or fine breadcrumbs and fried in butter, or grilled, are easy to do and add colour and flavour to a plate. I like them with bacon and eggs for breakfast as I had them in England.

STUFFED BAKED TOMATOES

Easy to do in the oven along with something else.

6 large tomatoes	**2 tablespoons melted butter**
1 cup breadcrumbs	**1 teaspoon minced parsley**
¹/₂ teaspoon salt	**Pepper and a snippet of sage or savory**
1 tablespoon minced onion	
1 egg, well beaten	

Cut out the centres of the tomatoes and stuff them with a combination of the rest of the ingredients listed. Put in a baking dish and bake in a 350-degree oven for about 30 minutes. Don't let the tomatoes get mushy.

FRIED EGGPLANT

One time at Trader Vic's exotic restaurant in Vancouver I had eggplant served in a slurpy sauce; it wasn't half as good as this.

1 eggplant	**1 tablespoon milk**
Salt and pepper	**Fine breadcrumbs**
1 egg, beaten	**Fat for frying**

Peel off the beautiful purple skin of the eggplant and cut the remaining, denuded, now homely vegetable into slices less than 1/4 of an inch thin. Sprinkle salt on each slice and pile slices in a bowl. Cover with a plate to weight the slices and let stand about 30 minutes to draw out the juices. If you like you can now simply dip each slice in flour mixed with pepper and fry it, but if you want it crisp, golden and divine, dip each slice in egg mixed with milk and pepper, coat with breadcrumbs and fry slowly in a little fat till the eggplant is tender inside the crisp crust.

FRIED OR GRILLED CUCUMBERS

Even people who can't digest raw cucumbers seem to have no trouble with these. Peel—or don't peel—the cucumbers and cut them into 1/4-inch slices. Proceed exactly as for fried eggplant. If you'd rather grill the breaded slices put them side by side on a pan with a dot of butter on each slice and grill till golden, turn each slice over, dot again with butter and grill till crisp.

BAKED CUCUMBERS

Delicate and delicious.

Peel cucumbers and cut in quarters lengthwise. Scoop out the seeds if they are large, sprinkle with salt and pepper. Put into a baking dish with dots of butter and bake at 350 degrees till the cucumbers are more or less transparent and soft. It doesn't take long. If you want to be a bit fancier, cut the cucumbers in half, scoop out the seeds, sprinkle with salt and fill the cavities with a mixture of breadcrumbs and grated cheese, dot with bits of butter and bake until clear.

BAKED SUMMER SQUASH AND ZUCCHINI

These can be done in the same way as cucumbers, or slices can be boiled in a little water.

BAKED SQUASH

There are so many kinds of squashes—hubbard, acorn, pepper, summer—you name them. I prefer the acorn squash: it is mealy, meaty, a rich orange colour, is never stringy, has a wonderful flavour and is so easy to prepare.

I simply wash the squash, put it on a foil plate that can be squashed into a corner of the oven when I'm doing a roast and baked potatoes. While it's baking I have the serene feeling that

all's well and on its way. When the squash is soft all I have to
do is cut it in half, scoop out the seeds, slice it into as many pieces
as I have people to feed, put seasonings and dabs of butter in the
hollows and that's that. If I want to be fancier I scoop the squash
out of the shell into an oven dish, mash it, beat lots of butter into
it and enough cream to make it smooth like mashed potatoes. I
sometimes sprinkle it with brown sugar and buttered crumbs, then
put it back in the oven to wait till I'm ready to serve it.

BAKED STUFFED PEPPER SQUASH

You can make a complete meal of this with a light salad.
Wash the squash, cut it in half, scoop out the seeds and place the
halves cut-side down in a pan. Pour 1/4-inch of boiling water
around the squash and bake at 400 degrees for half an hour. Now
turn the squash cut-side up and fill the hollows with partially
cooked sausage meat. (You can form the sausage into patties and
put them in the oven when you first put the squash in.) Bake
until tender—about half an hour.
Or you can stuff the squash with a rich bread dressing and serve
your meat separately.
Or you can combine a bread dressing with ground beef or sausage
meat and bake in the squash.

PARSNIPS

This sweet-tasting, inexpensive vegetable is delicious with sausage
or pork. Bevvy says she peels hers, cuts it in slices and cooks it
with a ham bone or in ham broth.

Sometimes she'll boil it in salted water and serve it with a cream
sauce and buttered crumbs.

I like mine browned in the oven. I cut the parsnips into long
slivers, boil them till they're almost tender; then I melt beef
dripping or butter in a pan, stir the parsnips around in it and put
them into the oven till they're nicely browned, turning them
occasionally. They come out slightly chewy and people who have
never liked parsnips ask me how it was done.

SAUERKRAUT

I don't know why so many "superior" Anglo-Saxon types raise
disparaging eyebrows at the mention of sauerkraut. They have
probably never let themselves taste this easily digested, easily
prepared delicacy that is a favourite in northern Europe and

Waterloo County. It is simple and pure: nothing but shredded cabbage, salt, and boiling water. I've never made it: I think the sauerkraut that comes in cans is just dandy.

There seem to be several ways to prepare it, but all agree that the fresh cabbage should be shredded very finely and packed into glass jars or a stone crock. One recipe says: "Mix salt, enough to taste good, through the cabbage until it forms its own juice before you pack it tightly into quart jars." Bevvy says: "Stomp the cabbage down hard in a stone crock, keep adding and stomping till the crock is filled, sprinkling salt through the crock as you fill it, then add enough hot water to cover the cabbage." "My friend Magdaline says: "Don't pack the cabbage tightly in the jars, just add a teaspoon of salt and fill the jar with boiling water." All agree that the jars should not be sealed tightly and should be put in a pan, as some of the juice will run out while the cabbage is fermenting—as it will do for several days. When the cabbage is no longer fermenting, remove the lid of the jar or crock, add enough cold water to fill the jar and seal it tightly.

COOKING SAUERKRAUT

There are several ways: I've eaten it in Paris boiled in white wine, in Germany cooked to a mush with onions and caraway seeds; I prefer it the Waterloo County way which is "chenerally chust plain."

Most people boil it with a piece of fresh pork till the pork is tender. Often they put in some dumplings and boil the lot for 15 minutes more.

I bake my sauerkraut in a covered earthenware dish in the oven. I roast a piece of pork separately, then during the last hour of its roasting I put the dish of sauerkraut into the oven, adding 2 tablespoons of brown sugar and enough water to almost cover the kraut. When the meat is brown I take it out of the pan, pour off most of the fat, turn the sauerkraut into the brown meat drippings and stir it around till the brown dripping bits are all dissolved and absorbed. I pour the kraut back into the baking dish and carry it to the table where its wonderful warm aroma has lured everyone to wait with eager impatience as if they hadn't been fed for a month.

THAT SAUERKRAUT SMELL

I don't know any way that you can prevent the smell of cooking sauerkraut from permeating the house. Because it can be rather overpowering I open the draft of my fireplace, light a bayberry-scented candle and occasionally open a door to let in a breeze. After a while I get used to the sauerkraut smell and let it take over, assuring myself that on a cold winter's day no aroma could be more warmly inviting.

TURNIPS IN BREE (Broth)

This is how Mother and Bevvy cook turnips.
They peel the turnip and slice it thin on a cutter, then boil it in broth with boiling beef and serve it with lots of pepper, butter, and some of the broth.

MASHED TURNIPS

Turnip with turkey is a local tradition; the two flavours seem to complement each other. (Yellow turnips are stronger in flavour than white ones; to make them milder, combine with equal amounts of mashed potatoes.)
Peel and slice the turnip and boil it till tender in salted water. Drain, then mash or whip the turnip, add about 1/4 of a pound of butter, cream and plenty of pepper. Keep it hot in the oven till the bird is ready to be served. A garnish of buttered crumbs and bits of parsley could do it no harm.

GREENS: SPINACH, BEET GREENS, SWISS CHARD, KALE

These are so good for you. Any of the greens can be used in the spinach recipes that follow. Wash greens in several waters—luke-warm at first, lifting the greens from each water so sand sinks to the bottom. Remove imperfect leaves, root ends. Boil in the water that clings to the leaves—10 to 15 minutes—but don't let them get mushy. Drain. Season with butter, salt and pepper, or serve with lemon or vinegar, garnished with hard-boiled egg slices or bacon bits (or both), or buttered crumbs.

SPINAT MIT BREE (Spinach with Broth)

You don't have that grim feeling about getting your vitamins when you eat spinach like this.

2 pounds spinach	2 tablespoons breadcrumbs
2 tablespoons butter	1 cup soup stock
1 teaspoon grated onion (optional)	Salt and pepper

Cook washed spinach until tender and press out excess water. Heat the butter, add the onion, then the bread crumbs and gradually the soup stock; let it thicken. Add the hot drained spinach. Garnish with hot, sliced hard-boiled eggs and bacon bits or, if you want a whole supper, serve with a poached egg on top and toast underneath.

SPINACH IN A CHEESE SAUCE

Put cooked spinach into a cheese sauce and garnish with buttered crumbs. You won't know you're taking in iron.

SPINACH WITH SOUR CREAM

A friend's German cleaning woman does it this way. I like it, too.

1 package of spinach	**1 tablespoon bacon fat**
4 slices of bacon	**1 tablespoon flour**
Salt and pepper	**¹/₂ cup sour cream**

Cook spinach till tender; drain and press out most of the water. While the spinach is cooking cut the bacon into bits and fry till crisp. Fish the bits out of the pan and pour off all but 1 tablespoon of the fat. Over low heat blend in the flour, then the thick sour cream, stirring until it is hot. (You may put in a teaspoon of vinegar and one of sugar too, if you like.) Mix the sauce with the spinach, put it into a serving dish and sprinkle the bacon bits over it. Serve it with meat and potatoes or fish.

HERBS WITH VEGETABLES

A slight sprinkling of dried herbs cooked with winter vegetables gives them a lift. Use with:

Green or wax beans—basil, marjoram, thyme
Limas—savory
Beets—basil, savory, coriander
Carrots—basil, savory, thyme or mint
Squash—marjoram
Tomatoes—basil, sage, tarragon or marjoram
Cabbage—mint
Kohlrabi—marjoram
Peas—mint, basil, savory, thyme or tarragon

POTATOES

There seems to have been a conspiracy lately against potatoes. I've heard women say, "They're so fattening," and they've served rice instead, though one medium baked potato has ninety-five calories; one cup of boiled rice has two hundred. For me no dinner is complete without potatoes; Bevvy cooks them three times a day.

BAKED POTATOES

Best of all—but *not* wrapped in foil. Last year on a ride around Lake Superior every hotel dining room or restaurant gave us the usual choice of baked, mashed, or French fried potatoes. I always chose baked and invariably it came wrapped in foil: the peeling was soft, scarred and unappetizing, the potato itself was heavy, soggy, grey. Not till we reached the very special Flame Restaurant in Duluth were we given a treat: a baked potato that came to the table without foil. It had a crisp skin and a creamy, flaky interior; a dab of butter, salt and freshly milled pepper made it a potato I'll never forget. I wish I could bake one as well.

I scrub my potatoes—preferably potatoes with a light, almost transparent skin; while the potato is wet I sprinkle it with salt which sticks throughout the baking. To get the heat into the centre of the potato and to let the steam out I usually pierce the potato with an aluminum nail—to be pulled out after the potato is baked. I put the potatoes on a foil plate that can be shoved and squashed into a corner of the oven to make room for the roast—or whatever. I bake potatoes for an hour at 400 degrees or 1½ hours at 350 degrees, depending on the size and age—the young ones take longer. The more quickly they're done the better they'll be. Remove them from the oven, remove the nails, cut the skin on top to let the steam out and serve immediately.

If you forget to put your potatoes into the oven soon enough to be ready on time—or if you're cooking something that doesn't take as long as it does to bake a potato—you can parboil them for a while first, then finish them in the oven—but don't expect that superb Duluth Flame texture and flavour.

FRIED POTATOES

Bevvy serves fried potatoes at least once a day: always for breakfast with summer sausage, and often for supper with slices of leftover roast, an old-fashioned sausage, relish, pickled beets and a sour-cream salad of cucumbers, endive or leafy green lettuce. "What could you have better?" she says. She'd be surprised to know there are people in the world who won't or don't know how to fry potatoes: "I never know what to do with leftover potatoes," they mutter as they throw the good vegeable into the garbage—while my thrifty soul cringes.

Beef dripping gives fried potatoes the best flavour, but you can use lard or vegetable shortening or butter—though butter burns quickly. Let the shortening melt and get hot in the frying pan before you put in your thinly sliced boiled or baked and peeled potatoes. Turn the heat down and let the potatoes brown slowly, turning them occasionally but not enough to make them mushy. Sprinkle them with salt and pepper—the seasoned variety if you like. Some people fry onions with potatoes; they should be fried till soft before putting the potatoes into the pan. If you use vegetable shortening as your fat, a bit of butter added before serving gives a better flavour. Parsley, chives or herbs can be added as well.

If you don't have quite enough potatoes to go round tear up slices of buttered bread to make up the amount you need and fry it along with the potatoes—it's almost an improvement.

RAW FRIED POTATOES

Quick, easy, and very very good Pennsylvania Dutch fare.
Use as many potatoes per person as you think will be eaten, remembering that they shrink in the frying. If your potatoes are thin-skinned, it is only necessary to scrub them. Slice them thin on a slicer then spread them in a frying pan where the fat is almost sizzling. Turn down the heat, cover the pan and let the potatoes fry till they're golden brown and crisp on the bottom and the mass of potatoes is soft when you prick it; with an egg turner flip them over and brown on the other side without the lid. If you have summer sausage to eat with these so much the better.

CREAMED POTATOES

I used to laboriously make a cream sauce and pour it over sliced boiled potatoes; with parsley cut into them, they were very good; but Bevvy has an easier way. She slices raw potatoes into boiling, salted water—about 4 medium potatoes into 1 cup of water—in a saucepan with a tight lid. When the potatoes are soft—but not mushy—she adds 1/2 a cup of cream with a tablespoon of flour stirred into it, or she pours off half the water and adds a cup of whole milk with a tablespoon of flour stirred into it. It takes only a few seconds to thicken. She adds a good dollop of butter, then parsley or chives.

POTATOES WITH A CHEESE SAUCE

Often when I have company from out of town where they can't get Kitchener's specialties, I like to serve smoked pork chops and with them potatoes that can be put in the oven and left there indefinitely till whatever hour my guests arrive, settle down, and have a drink or two.

I peel and boil in salted water as many medium-sized or cut to medium-size potatoes as I'll need—usually two per person because they really make a hit. While the potatoes are boiling I make a medium thick, fairly rich, cream sauce (allow about a 1/2-cup for each potato if you're the careful measuring type). To it I add chunks of cheddar cheese—about 1 cupful for 6 potatoes. I put the hot, firm, boiled potatoes into a buttered casserole, pour the sauce over them and pop them into the oven to keep warm at 200 degrees till my guests arrive. The top of the dish should be golden with streaks of brown.

I leave my potatoes on the bottom layer of the oven while I'm grilling my smoked pork chops above them.

Warning: At no time during this process let the potatoes get cold.

NOTES ON POTATOES

Mealy potatoes are best for baking, boiling and frying—waxy ones for salads, scalloping and creaming.
Boil new potatoes in their skins.
Shake potatoes over heat after they are drained to keep them dry.
Don't let potatoes stand in water—they lose minerals and vitamins.

MASHED POTATOES

Need I tell you how? But some are so much better than others.
Peel your potatoes, cut them up into boiling, salted water and as soon as they're soft pour off the water, mash the potatoes and add warmed milk and butter; I can't tell you how much because

I don't know how many potatoes you're using, but don't make the mixture too thin (if you heat too much milk give it to the cat). Keep beating till the potatoes are creamy; lumps are unforgivable. To keep them fluffy, add a bit of baking powder.
Serve at once. Parsley looks and tastes good whipped along with them.

SCALLOPED POTATOES

Peel and slice the potatoes fairly thin. Butter a baking dish, or a cake pan if you want to expose more surface so everyone at your table can hope to get some of the crusty brown top when Pappa is serving. Arrange some of the potato slices in the bottom of the baking dish, sprinkle them lightly with flour, salt and pepper, and any other flavours or herbs you might like; dab on a few bits of butter and continue putting in layers of potatoes, et cetera, till you've used all the potatoes you've sliced. Now pour in enough milk to come not closer than an inch and a half from the top of your pan or it will boil over and be horribly smelly and messy. Put the potatoes into the oven at 300 degrees and leave them there for an hour and a half, or till they are soft with a golden crust.

POTATOES BOILED IN THEIR JACKETS

When we were children we had a lazy maid at our house who, when our parents were out, used to boil potatoes in their jackets, peel them quickly and give them to us hot, hot, in a soup dish with warmed milk and lots of salt and pepper. That's all she'd give us for our meal but we loved it; the potatoes had a really special flavour.

POTATO PATTIES

If you have leftover mashed potatoes you can find all sorts of recipes to use them up, but the easiest way is to make potato patties. You can add a slightly beaten egg to the potatoes if you like or just take a good-sized heaping tablespoon of potatoes and with your hands shape it into a patty about 3/4 of an inch thick. Coat it with flour or fine breadcrumbs and place carefully into a frying pan where you have melted and heated dripping or butter. Lower the heat and let the patties brown on one side, turn them over and brown on the other side. Very good.

POTATO SCONES

This is the best thing to do with leftover mashed potatoes.
Combine half as much flour as you have leftover mashed potatoes—for example:

1 cupful potatoes	**1 teaspoon baking powder**
¹/₂ cupful flour	**1 egg**

Mix all together, bake on a griddle or in a frying pan in a bit of
melted butter till they're golden and puffy; turn them over and
brown the other side. They're delicious with meat or with butter
and jam or syrup.

WHOLE FRIED POTATOES

A rare treat one can have only in early summer when the first
new potatoes come on the market. I always buy a basketful when
I see them, marble-sized, less expensive than the larger ones,
and with a flavour all their own. I boil them in their pale, clean,
thin little jackets, turn them into a frying pan in which I have
melted butter; I brown them, constantly stirring them around,
sprinkle them with salt and pepper and, just before I serve them,
I sprinkle a lot of cut parsley over them. Divine! Could anything be better? Yes—if you peel all the dear little potatoes after
you've boiled them, as my patient, painstaking mother does.

OVEN-GRILLED FRENCH FRIES

Because one can hardly avoid French fries when one eats out in
a restaurant or a drive-in (and they are very well done), I never
fry potatoes in deep fat. But I do occasionaly make their equiva-
lent in my oven.

After peeling and cutting the potatoes so they vaguely resemble
French fries, I melt beef dripping on a large cookie sheet under
my broiler. I pour the potatoes into the hot fat and turn them
with an egg turner till they're all coated, then I put them under
the broiler till they're golden brown, turn them over and brown
them all round. By that time they should be soft in the middle
and ready to eat—not saturated or soggy or impregnated with fat.

KARTOFFELKRAPFEN (Potato Meat Cakes)

Another wonderful way of using up leftover potatoes and leftover meat as well.

4 cups mashed potatoes	Meat Mixture:
1 cup flour	3 cups chopped leftover
2 teaspoons baking powder	meat
3 eggs	3 tablespoons ketchup,
1/4 cup butter	mushroom sauce,
	or gravy
	Cut-up chives and parsley
	Salt and pepper
	Fine breadcrumbs

Blend the potatoes, flour sifted with baking powder, 2 beaten eggs. Roll to almost 1/2-inch thickness on a well-floured board. Cut into rounds about 5 inches across. Put a large dollop of the meat mixed with the ketchup and seasonings in the centre of each. Fold and press the edges firmly together. Brush with the third beaten egg, dip in breadcrumbs and bake to a golden brown in a 350-degree oven. A fish filling, made with a thick cream sauce, may be used instead of meat.

SAUCES FOR VEGETABLES

WHITE SAUCE

In case you need reminding how to make this:

2 tablespoons butter	1 cup milk
2 tablespoons flour	Salt and pepper

Melt the butter, add the flour and stir until blended. Slowly add the milk and cook until the mixture thickens, stirring constantly. Add seasonings.

CHEESE SAUCE

Make a white sauce and in it melt 1/4 to 1/2 a cupful of cut-up or grated cheese. Stir till smooth.

BROWN SAUCE

Has more flavour than plain white sauce.

2 tablespoons butter or beef dripping
2 tablespoons flour

Salt and pepper
1 cup meat or vegetable stock

Melt the butter or dripping (and, if you like, add a small chopped onion). Carefully let the butter brown, add the flour, and stir till it too is brown. Add the liquid gradually, stirring constantly. Cook until thickened.

This should be timed so you can use the water in which your vegetable has been cooking. Or you might use a combination of vegetable stocks. Or you might add a teaspoon of meat broth base, or a bouillon cube. Or use meat stock instead of vegetable stock. Taste it, then pour it over your vegetables.

You can use this same sauce over hot meats, dumplings, noodles, et cetera. It's especially nice over vegetables when you're having steak or chops, or meat that hasn't any gravy of its own.

BUTTERED CRUMBS

Mother and Bevvy and I sprinkle them over all vegetables with a sauce and over some that are merely buttered.

Melt and brown 2 tablespoons of butter in a pan; add ¼-cup of fine breadcrumbs and brown them in the butter—stirring all the time.

Salads

Bevvy has never bought oil for a salad and Mother has despised it as something fit only for axles. Sour cream with a bit of sugar and vinegar is the favoured dressing for most local Pennsylvania Dutch salads. It is poured over lettuce or spinach leaves, cucumbers, dandelion, boiled "schnippled" string beans, cabbage, endive, onions, and potatoes; sometimes it is thickened and warm, sometimes it is chilled; always it is rich and surprisingly zestful.

A sour-cream salad is never a basic meal —as it might be for a modern luncheon; it is never a separate course; it is something delightfully leafy and fresh, or a vegetable, to be eaten as part of a dinner.

Bevvy has no recipes for salads in her little hand-written cookbook and in Mother's there are recipes only for those she makes when she entertains friends, or her bridge club. They never measure exactly what they put into a salad, they make experienced guesses about the amounts of vegetables and greens they might need for the number of people they're feeding, and they keep schlecking (tasting) the sour-cream dressing till it seems to be just about right.

The amounts I've specified in the recipes here are as accurate as I can make them after frequent and impatient measuring with teaspoons and cups. A sour-cream salad should be rich, buttery; and subtle—not sour; I use red wine vinegar which I think is less strident—and very little of that; Mother would use even less, and Bevvy puts in more sugar.

Since flavouring the dressing is a personal thing I'm afraid you'll just have to consider my recipes as a guide from which to develop a formula that tastes right to you, that will give you and yours the same lip-smacking pleasure that sour-cream salads have been giving to the natives of Waterloo County since the first cow was led up here through forest and swampland from far-away Pennsylvania in 1798.

LETTUCE SALAD

When Waterloo County gardens are flourishing a lettuce salad appears on dinner tables every day. Tender, soft, yellow butter lettuce, red speckled, oak leaf, and vivid green leaf-lettuce are the favourite varieties; the solid, crisp head lettuce that is imported and sold in the supermarkets is seldom used with this sour-cream dressing.

Enough lettuce leaves for 4 people	About 1/2 cup sour cream
1 teaspoon sugar	Fresh chives, cut fine—or finely sliced onions
1 teaspoon vinegar	Salt and pepper

Wash and drain the lettuce. Stir the other ingredients together and pour over the lettuce, mix lightly. A sliced hard-boiled egg may be used as a garnish if you want to be fancy or give it more body. This salad won't keep long—it should be served immediately or the lettuce will wilt and be miserable.

SCHNIPPLED BEAN SALAD (Frenched Bean Salad)

This most popular Waterloo County specialty serves as both salad and vegetable. How many beans to use is a problem: people always eat more than they think they can; one summer Sunday I had ten guests for dinner, I used six quarts of fresh yellow beans for the salad and there was just a nappieful left.

1 quart of green or yellow string beans	Dressing:
1 smallish onion	1 teaspoon sugar
Salt and pepper	1 teaspoon vinegar
	3/4 cup sour cream

Cut the stems off the beans, wash them, then schnippel them—that means cutting the beans on a slant in very thin slices, one bean being cut into 3 or 4 long slices. (Or you could use frozen Frenched beans.) Put the beans into boiling salted water and cook them just long enough to be barely soft. Drain and cool them. Meantime, peel and slice the onion and sprinkle it liberally with salt and stir it around; let it stand at least 15 minutes, giving it a stir now and then. In a bowl large enough to contain the beans, put the sugar, vinegar, ½ teaspoon of salt, a good sprinkling of pepper and sour cream. Stir all together. Now take the salted onion into your hand and with the other hand squeeze as much of the juice out of the onion as you can. Put the squeezed onion into the dressing, pour the drained beans into the bowl and mix with the dressing till all the beans are generously coated—you might need more cream.

Some people like the beans to be slightly warm or hot—but then the dressing becomes thin and runny and doesn't properly coat the beans. Some like the squeezed juice of the onion in the dressing as well as the onions. Some like more onions. If by some strange miscalculation the bean salad isn't all eaten, you can put it in your fridge and keep it for a day or two.

CUCUMBER SALAD

Cool, fresh and delicious on a hot summer day with cold meat left over from Sunday and tiny new boiled potatoes browned in butter and sprinkled with parsley. But just as good in winter with a piping hot dinner. Cucumber salad gives a piquant touch to any meal.

2 large cucumbers	Dressing:
1 small onion (or chives)	¾ cup sour cream
Salt	1 teaspoon sugar
	1 teaspoon vinegar (or less)
	Pepper

Peel the cucumber and slice it thinly. Sprinkle it with salt and slosh it around a bit so the salt is well distributed amongst all the slices. Now peel the onion and slice it finely too, sprinkle it with salt. Let both cucumber and onion stand in their separate dishes for about 15 minutes, giving each a swish whenever you happen to pass. Squeeze the onion between your fingers, using both hands and leaving the slices quite limp. In the same way squeeze the juice from the cucumbers—only don't squeeze quite so hard.

Combine the onion and cucumber and over them pour and stir a dressing made of the blended sour cream, sugar, vinegar and pepper.

And that's it. If there's any left it will keep in the fridge to be eaten next day; Mother loves to finish it up with her breakfast.

TZVIVELLE SALAT

A lot of people around here are crazy about this.

2 large Spanish onions or
3 Italian onions
Salt

Dressing:
³/₄ cup thick sour cream
1 teaspoon sugar
1 teaspoon wine vinegar
Pepper

Slice the onions very thin, separate the rings and sprinkle all lightly with salt; let stand about 15 minutes; then over them pour and stir a dressing made of the sour cream, vinegar, sugar and pepper.

WALPER HOTEL SPINAT SALAT (Spinach Salad)

I have heard dozens of eaters at the Walper House try to figure out exactly how this super salad is made. Joe Zuber, the owner, has generously given me the recipe.

1 pound raw spinach
¹/₄ cup crumbled crisply
fried bacon
Dressing:
1 cup table cream
¹/₆ cup white vinegar

1 teaspoon grated onion
1 teaspoon prepared
mustard
Salt, pepper, and sugar
to taste

Wash the spinach well in several changes of clear cold water. Cut away the tough stems and discard them. Drain the spinach leaves and chill in a damp cloth. Roll a handful of leaves and slice with a very sharp knife into quarter-inch strips. Toss the spinach with the dressing and serve on a bed of leaf lettuce; sprinkle the crumbled fried bacon on top.

GEMIXDE GREEN SALAT (Mixed or Tossed Green Salad)

This gets raves whenever it appears—with any meat-and-vege-table or casserole meal. I give you Bevvy's own words:

"The salad we like the best, and easy to make, is from spinach, endive, lettuce or whatever crisp greens you have—all the same kind or mixed. For each person that's going to be eating you fry a slice of bacon till it crackles, take it out, and to the fat in the pan put 1 teaspoon of brown sugar, 1 teaspoon of vinegar and some salt and pepper; it will sizzle and spit, so have care for yourself, the sugar might get kind of lumpy; let it melt, then cool it all a little before you mix in 2 tablespoons of sour cream. Now pour it over the greens, break the bacon in with it, mix it up, and on top slice eggs or radish rings, or anything nice looking you got that goes good."

I might add: As you keep multiplying the amount of the ingredients by the number of people you are going to be serving, you might want to pour off some of the bacon fat and reduce the amounts of sugar and vinegar.

DANDELION SALAD

Any old timer in Waterloo County will tell you that dandelion greens will purify your blood, grown sluggish and thick through the winter. As soon as spring comes I have a compulsive hunger for dandelion salad. I could—and should—dig the dandelion out of my lawn the moment it appears, young and tender, but I lazily buy the long, bleached stems with yellow-green leaves that some Mennonite farmers cultivate under sawdust or straw and sell at the Kitchener market—though they say the natural green dandelion that is slightly bitter is much better for you.

1 quart of dandelion greens	**2 teaspoons vinegar**
4 bacon slices	**2 teaspoons flour**
1 or 3/4 cup sour cream	**Salt and pepper**
2 teaspoons sugar	**2 hard boiled eggs**

Keep the dandelion crisp. Pick it over and wash it, then drain it. Cut the bacon into bits and fry it till crisp. Remove it from the pan and drain it on paper. Pour all the bacon dripping from the pan but 2 tablespoons; then add a well-blended mixture of the sugar, flour, salt and pepper, vinegar and sour cream. Stir over very low heat till it thickens slightly. Don't let it boil. Just before you are ready to eat, and while the dressing is warm, pour it over the dandelion greens and mix well. The greens should be well coated—you might need more cream. Add the bacon bits and the sliced eggs, saving some for the garnish. Serve immediately with baked or mashed potatoes, farmer's pork sausage, fried ham, smoked pork chops—any kind of pork—and as soon as you taste this wonderful salad your sap will start flowing.

ENDIVE SALAD

Curly, crisp, bleached yellow endive with a warm sour-cream dressing and bacon is a wonderful change from the eternal tossed lettuce salad, served with a dinner or buffet supper.

1 (medium-size) head of endive (since heads vary in size you'll have to figure out how much you need and increase or decrease the amount of dressing—but don't skimp it).

3 or 4 slices of bacon	**1 cup sour cream**
2 teaspoons sugar	**Salt and pepper**
2 teaspoons flour	**2 hard-boiled eggs**
2 teaspoons vinegar	

Wash the endive and let it drain; break it into pieces to make eating easier. Cut the bacon into bits and fry until crisp; remove the bits from the drippings and drain on paper. Mix salt, sugar, flour, vinegar and cream; stir till blended then pour into 2 table-spoons of the bacon drippings left in the pan. Over very slow heat stir the mixture till it thickens a bit—don't let it boil. When the sauce has cooled to lukewarm pour it over the endive and mix it lightly. Garnish it with sliced eggs and bacon bits and serve at once with meat, potatoes, vegetables, or a casserole. It won't last long.

WARM POTATO SALAD

If you have ever tasted the warm, creamy, butter-yellow potato salad made in Waterloo County you'll never again be satisfied with the stiff white blobs they call potato salad everywhere else.

6 potatoes, medium size	**Dressing:**
1 medium onion or fresh chives	**2 beaten eggs**
2 hard-boiled eggs	**¼ cup butter**
Parsley	**1 cup sour cream**
	1 tablespoon vinegar
	1 tablespoon sugar
	Salt and pepper

Boil the potatoes in their jackets. Slice the onion finely and sprinkle it with salt, being sure all the onion is salted. Melt the butter and stir the sour cream, eggs, vinegar, sugar and seasonings into it; cook long enough in a double boiler or heavy saucepan to make a sauce that is thick but not stiff. Taste it. If you have used large potatoes you might need more cream. Don't be afraid to be lavish: my mother always put in extra butter; my Aunt Rickie, who made the best potato salad I've ever tasted, used the yolks of 6 eggs instead of 2 whole eggs so her salad would look yellower.

Keep the sauce warm over hot, but not boiling, water while

you peel the boiled hot potatoes and slice them finely. Squeeze the onion slices between your fingers and add them to the dressing—in summer it's prettier to use finely snipped chives. Pour the dressing over the potato slices—still warm—and mix them gently so they won't be mushy. (My mother, when she was making potato salad for a picnic or company, used small round potatoes so all her slices would be the same size.) Put the salad into your prettiest bowl, slice the hard-boiled eggs and decorate the top of the potatoes with them and the parsley or chives. Serve warm with cold meats and lettuce and tomatoes.

If you prefer, you might fry four slices of bacon cut into bits, pouring off all the fat but 1/4 cupful to be used instead of the butter in the dressing—the bacon bits to be used in the garnishing.

COLESLAW

Not at all like the wretched sour stuff you get in most Canadian restaurants.

4 cups cabbage (after putting it through the food chopper)
1 small onion, chopped   **1/2 cup thick sour cream**
2 teaspoons sugar   **Salt and pepper**
1 teaspoon vinegar

Put the cabbage and onion through the food chopper, using a medium blade that won't extract the juice. Mix the other ingredients together, pour the mixture over the cabbage and onion and combine them. Sprinkle with pepper. If you want more nip add a pinch of mustard or a teaspoon of horse-radish.

This salad goes quite a long way and is best eaten with a dinner.

HOT SLAW

Mother called this HOT COLESLAW. It's simple and wonderful served with mashed potatoes and farmer's sausage, pork chops, or fried ham.

Half a medium-sized cabbage (4 or 5 cups after shredding,
it shrinks a lot)
1/2 tablespoon vinegar   **Plenty of pepper**
3 or 4 tablespoons butter   **1/2 cup sour cream**
1 teaspoon salt

Slice the cabbage about 1/4 inch wide, then chop it a bit—but not fine, just so you don't have long strings to cope with. Put butter in a heavy pan, melt it, add the cabbage, salt and pepper; stir the cabbage over low heat until it is softened and hot but not really cooked—certainly not soft and mushy—the spines should remain almost crisp. Blend the sour cream and vinegar, and pour over the cabbage, stirring till well coated. Remove from the stove and serve.

DAMPFEKRAUT

Another old-timer—and very good tasting, Bevvy says.

1 medium cabbage (about 2 quarts, finely sliced)	
4 tablespoons butter, or lard or bacon fat	**2 tablespoons vinegar**
	2 tablespoons flour
1 teaspoon salt	**1 egg, well beaten**
Pepper	**3 cups milk**
1 teaspoon dry mustard	**2 cups grated cheese**

Melt the butter in a saucepan, pour in the cabbage and cook slightly, stirring constantly to coat it with the butter. Add the vinegar. In another saucepan or double boiler mix the pepper, salt, mustard, and flour; add the well-beaten egg blended with the milk; cook till thick. Sprinkle the cabbage with the grated cheese and pour the hot sauce over it. Serve hot.

RED CABBAGE AND APPLE SALAD

This unusual salad looks pretty on a plate and has a pleasant taste.

1 quart shredded red cabbage	**2 tablespoons vinegar**
1 cup apples, quartered and sliced thin	**3 tablespoons butter**
	1/2 teaspoon mustard
1 teaspoon salt	**1/2 cup sour cream**
2 tablespoons brown sugar	**Pepper**

Melt the butter in a saucepan, add the cabbage and apple and stir until the butter coats the mixture and there are signs of softening, but the mixture is not really cooked. Add the vinegar, sugar, seasonings and mustard; simmer another 2 minutes then stir in the sour cream. Serve hot.

CANNED TOMATO SALAD

For supper one night at Bevvy's, I found this surprisingly good and refreshing—with fried potatoes and summer sausage and kochkase.

2 cups drained, canned
    tomatoes cut in quarters
2 or 3 hard-boiled eggs,
    sliced or chopped
    coarsely

2 teaspoons mayonnaise
Salt and pepper to taste

Stir all together and it's ready to serve.

DADDY'S TOMATOES

My father liked his tomatoes sliced into a nappy with brown sugar, salt, pepper and vinegar sprinkled over them. Mother was scornful but one day consented to taste the concoction: she became a convert—using white sugar instead of brown.

MISS SNIDER'S SALAD

Sarah Snider, a one-time Mennonite and superb cook, used to help when Mother had a party.
Celery, apples, grapes, walnuts and well-drained canned pineapple; cut up as much as you think you need for the occasion. Mix generously with whipped cream salad dressing (see Index) and pile lightly in a lettuce-lined bowl.

FRUIT SALAD

This one was for Mother's bridge club.
Oranges, grapefruits and raw or canned pineapple—as much as you need, cut in pieces. Mix with whipped cream salad dressing and put some red cherries on top for looks.

CABBAGE-PINEAPPLE SALAD

This is my mother's favourite company salad—with ham, chicken, cold cuts, or roast pork.

1 small head of cabbage (or enough to make 6 cupfuls when
    finely shredded)
1 cup cut-up celery
1 cup drained pineapple
    chunks, cut in half
20 marshmallows, each cut
    into 4 pieces
1/2 cup milk

1 cupful of cream, whipped
3 or 4 tablespoons of
    whipped cream salad
    dressing concentrate
    (See Index)

Slice or shred the cabbage about 1/8 inch wide. Cut up the marshmallows and let them soak in the milk for about 15 minutes.

Drain the pineapple chunks and cut them in half. Just before serving, whip the cream and blend the concentrate with it. Mix the cabbage, pineapple and marshmallows and stir in the dressing so all the ingredients are generously covered. Mother serves hers in a hand-painted bowl with bits of parsley and pimento or maraschino cherries to pretty it.

DILL PICKLE SALAD

This was a company salad that Mother thought was wonderful.

3 large dill pickles ("sometimes I use only 2," Mother writes in her book)
3 hard boiled eggs, cut not too fine
3 good-sized pimentos

A finely sliced little onion
2 tablespoons catsup

Mix with whipped cream salad dressing and serve from a bowl.

PERFECTION SALAD

This is Mother's old stand-by.

1 tablespoon plain gelatine
1/4 cup cold water
1 cup boiling water
1/4 cup sugar
1/4 cup mild vinegar
1 tablespoon lemon juice

1/2 teaspoon salt
1/2 cup finely shredded cabbage
1 cup celery, cut up fine
1 pimento, cut in small pieces

Soften gelatine in cold water. Add sugar, salt and hot water; stir until dissolved. Add vinegar and lemon juice. Cool and, when mixture begins to stiffen, add chopped vegetables. Turn into individual moulds, chill until firm; serve on lettuce, with mayonnaise.

CRANBERRY SALAD

Another company one. Pretty and very good too.

4 cups cranberries
Juice of 1 can of pineapple and enough hot water to make 3 1/2 cups
2 tablespoons plain gelatine (or a little more)

1/2 cup cold water
2 cups sugar
1/2 cup walnuts, chopped
1 cup grapes, cut in half and seeded
1 can pineapple, diced

Cook the cranberries in the pineapple juice and hot water. Soak the gelatine in the cold water; add the hot cranberries and the sugar, and stir till sugar is dissolved; cool. When cold add nuts, grapes, diced pineapple, and stir well. Cool until firm, in individual moulds. Turn out and serve with mayonnaise on shredded lettuce.

RED TOMATO MOULD

For company too.

4 cups tomato juice	2 tablespoons brown sugar
1/3 cup chopped onion	1 teaspoon salt
1/4 cup chopped celery leaves	2 small bay leaves
2 tablespoons plain gelatine	4 whole cloves
3 tablespoons lemon juice	

Combine 2 cups of the tomato juice, onion, celery leaves, sugar, salt, bay leaves and cloves. Simmer uncovered for 5 minutes. Strain. Meanwhile, soften gelatine in 1 cup of remaining cold tomato juice; dissolve in hot tomato mixture. Add lemon juice and remaining cup of tomato juice. Pour into a 5-cup ring mould, or individual moulds; chill till firm.

WHIPPED CREAM SALAD DRESSING CONCENTRATE

A little of this thick, nippy dressing goes a long way when blended with whipped cream. Mother uses it with her cabbage and pineapple salad, fruit and jellied salads.

1 egg, well beaten	1/2 cup water
1/4 cup vinegar	A little handful of brown
1 teaspoon dry mustard	sugar
Pinch of salt	A sprinkle of cayenne
1 teaspoon flour	pepper

Mix the flour, salt and mustard with the water, add to the beaten egg and brown sugar. Carefully, slowly, stir in the vinegar and sprinkle in the cayenne. Thicken the mixture over hot water, in a double boiler, stirring all the while. Chill it before you blend it with whipped cream. How much whipped cream you use depends on what size your salad will be, and the amount of the mayonnaise added depends on how strong you like it. There's no other way but to taste it. The basic dressing keeps well if tightly covered and refrigerated.

MOTHER-IN-LAW'S SALAD DRESSING

Have you ever noticed how many men want the kind of salad dressing their mothers used to make? You might as well humour them—it's easy to make this.

7 tablespoons granulated sugar	1 tablespoon mustard
2 heaping tablespoons flour	$^1/_2$ cup water
1 tablespoon salt	$^1/_2$ cup vinegar
	1 egg, beaten

Put everything but the egg into a double boiler, mix well and cook until the mixture is very thick. While hot pour it over the beaten egg in a bowl and beat again. To make sure the egg is cooked, I pour the whole bit back into the double boiler and stir it for 2 minutes. It keeps well in the fridge and middle-aged men, especially, think it is wonderful.

Sweets and Sours

Towards the end of summer, wherever you go in Waterloo County there is a pungent aroma of vinegar and spices as thousands of housewives stir long-boiling relishes and prepare crocks of pickles and jars of fruit to last through the seasons till canning time comes again. No Mennonite meal is served without some kind of sour and sweet on the table—and when company comes there are traditionally seven of each.

SOURS

In our old house in Kitchener Mother always kept bottles of sours in the sliding dumb waiter to be eaten every day with our dinner. Though she is now eighty-seven, lives alone, and no longer feeds multitudes, she still pickles beets and pimentos, fills jars with her favourite relishes and lines them up on the shelves in her basement.

Bevvy's little note book has more recipes in it for sours than for anything else but cookies. With a garden that keeps growing all summer she has to work hard to keep using and preserving the vegetables and fruits it produces. The abundance and variety give scope for invention. Bevvy says, "Some of the recipes are almost alike but each one is a little bit different yet because we have to use up what we got."

I hate to admit it but I make and like only a few of these sour things. I haven't tasted most of the recipes I'm giving you here but they come well recommended by my mother and Bevvy and my sister in Peterborough, who make them year after year. Some you might halve or quarter—unless you have fifteen children or want to supply the sours for all your church socials.

The homely aroma of vinegar and pickling spice might be a way of anti-polluting the air; you'll need only a coverall apron, a big, big preserving kettle, a long spoon, a tall stool, and a good book to read while you stir, stir and stir.

BEET AND RED CABBAGE SALAD

A zippy and colourful accompaniment for almost any dinner. It's foolish to make just enough for one meal: while you're at it you might as well fill several jars and put them away in your basement or fridge where the salad will keep for a year—though I'm sure you won't let it.

3 or 4 quarts of beets (Mother says it must taste like beets, not cabbage, so don't skimp.)	Water
	2 or 3 teaspoons grated horse radish
	1/2 cup sugar
1 small head of red cabbage	1 tablespoon salt
1 pint of white vinegar	1/4 teaspoon pepper

Boil the beets till they're tender; pour off the water, cover the beets with cold water and slip off their skins. Chop the beets, not too fine but not in big lumps either. Shred or slice the cabbage as thin as you can, chop it a bit too. In a large bowl mix the beets, cabbage, and enough horseradish to give it a nip. Bring the vinegar, sugar and salt to a boil. (Mother says if the vinegar is too strong she adds water—perhaps a half to 1/3 cup to 1 cup of vinegar; she says you have to taste it to know when it's right— not too sour.) Pour the vinegar solution over the beet mixture, stir it all up. Now pack it into sterilized jars, being sure the liquid covers the beets and cabbage—if you haven't enough you can easily mix up a bit more. When you serve it don't put too much of the liquid into your serving dish—it makes the plates messy. Whatever isn't used can be put back into the jars and kept for the next time you want a ready-made salad. Mother serves this as a sour with almost every company meal.

FRUIT RELISH

Every fall for years and years I have made this local specialty to please my visiting friends and relations who can't seem to get through a meal without it.

20 ripe tomatoes	4 cups white sugar
8 pears	1 quart vinegar
8 peaches	2 tablespoons salt
6 large onions	2 tablespoons whole spices tied in a bag
2 red sweet peppers	

Peel the tomatoes, pears, peaches, onions. Cut the tomatoes in pieces, slice the fruit about 1/4-inch thick, the onions more finely.

Put everything into a large kettle; boil and stir the mixture till it's thick enough not to have any watery liquid—about 2 hours. Ladle the relish into sterilized jars and it will keep for years if you don't put it on your table every day as most Kitchener-Waterloo natives do.

GREEN TOMATO RELISH

I wouldn't want to be without this relish; I like it very much. It is a rather dark greenish brown, not too sour, delicious with cold meat and fried potatoes.

A 6-quart basket of green tomatoes (You don't have to peel them—the skins are so thin—but do cut out the stem bit)
1 quart vinegar, white or cider

$2^{1}/_{2}$ pounds brown sugar
3 teaspoons ground cloves
4 or 5 onions, sliced
3 teaspoons cinnamon
1 tablespoon salt

Into a large preserving kettle put the tomatoes, cut into quarters or eighths. Pour in the vinegar and add all the rest. Boil till the relish is thick enough to plop off the spoon. Don't boil too quickly —pull up a stool, sit there and stir fairly often—almost continuously towards the end when it becomes really thick and a bit spitty. Remember while you're doing it that you'll enjoy it all winter. Ladle into sterilized jars; it keeps for years.

RED PEPPER SANDWICH SPREAD

After school Mother used to give us this, spread on bread; it was a treat—and a change from eternal peanut butter.

12 large tomatoes
4 medium-sized onions
1 cup white sugar
1 cup flour

2 tablespoons salt
1 cup vinegar
6 or 7 sweet pimentos

Peel the tomatoes and onions. Slice the onions fine. Boil together for about 20 to 25 minutes then strain through a sieve. Put the pimentos through a food chopper—there should be about 1 heaping cupful—drain the juice off the peppers and add them to the tomato mixture and boil 3 minutes longer. Mix the flour, sugar, vinegar and salt and add to the mixture, boiling for 10 minutes, stirring till it thickens. Pour into sterilized jars. It won't keep forever.

TOMATO BUTTER

Dark red and rather sweet.

A 6-quart basket of ripe tomatoes	**1 ounce powdered cloves**
4 pounds white sugar	**1 ounce cinnamon**
1 pint vinegar	**1 ounce salt**

Peel the tomatoes; cut them in quarters, into a kettle, and drain off the juice. Add the other ingredients and boil and stir the mixture till it's thick. Ladle into sterilized jars.

MUSTARD PICKLES

6 large cucumbers	**2 cups brown sugar**
1 quart onions	**1/2 teaspoon turmeric**
1 ounce mustard seed	**1 heaping tablespoon flour**
1/2 teaspoon curry powder	**2 cups vinegar**

Cut cucumbers into small or sliced pieces, peel and chop the onions. Let onions and cucumbers stand overnight with 2 table-spoons of salt sprinkled over them. Drain and add the rest of the ingredients. Boil about 20 minutes and bottle.

CHILI SAUCE

Bevvy's cookbook calls this "chilly" sauce; no Waterloo County housewife would be without it.

9 ripe peeled tomatoes	**1 tablespoon ginger**
1 onion chopped fine	**1 tablespoon cinnamon**
1 cup brown sugar	**1 tablespoon allspice**
1 tablespoon salt	**1 cup vinegar**

Mix in the order given and boil till thick. Pour into sterilized jars.

MUSTARD BEANS

Daddy especially liked this; his mother used to make it.
A 6-quart basket of beans, cut or broken into inch-long pieces and boiled in salted water until barely soft.

Sauce:	
3 cups vinegar	**1 teaspoon celery seed**
1/2 cup water	**1/2 cup dry mustard**
1 teaspoon turmeric powder	**3/8 cup flour**
	2 1/2 cups brown sugar
	1 cup white sugar

Blend 1/2 cup of the vinegar with the dry stuff. Bring the rest of the vinegar to a boil and gradually, as you stir it, add the mixture.

Boil for 5 minutes, stirring all the time as it thickens. Drain the beans and put them in the hot sauce. Let the combination come to a boil—no longer. Bottle in sterilized jars.

PICKLED BEETS

Mother and Bevvy and I always have jars of pickled beets on our shelves to be eaten with cold meats and potatoes, or any meal that needs a bit of colour, or sour, or vegetable. Fresh, young beets about 1 inch in diameter are the best kind—but hard to get. Bevvy uses any size and cuts them after they're cooked.
Boil the beets till they're tender—but not too soft; plunge them in cold water and slip off their skins. Mix the following and boil a few minutes:

1^1/$_2$ **cups vinegar**	**^{1}/$_2$ cup water**
2 cups sugar	**^{1}/$_2$ teaspoon salt**

Immerse beets in the boiled syrup on the stove till the beets are warm—but don't boil them. Drop the beets into sterilized jars, pour the syrup over them, cover tightly, store them away.

After you've fished all the beets out of the jars and used them, keep the syrup to make:

PICKLED EGGS

Drop whole, hard-cooked, shelled eggs into the beet liquid and let pickle for 2 days before using. A small piece of cinnamon stick and 3 or 4 cloves might be slipped in along with them. They are pretty and piquant with cold meats or salads, and very Pennsylvania Dutch.

PICKLED BABY CORN

These crisp, delicate little cobs of corn are constantly sought by visitors to Waterloo County. We locals serve them on a tray with radishes, celery, pickles, olives, etcetera.

2 quarts of immature field corn ears, picked when only 2 or 3 inches long	
1 cup water	**2 teaspoons salt**
2 cups sugar	**1 tablespoon pickling spice**
2 cups white vinegar	**tied in a bag**

Husk and boil the corn for 4 minutes—no longer. Pack it into hot sterilized jars and cover with a syrup made by boiling the other ingredients for 5 minutes. Seal, store in your basement and bring them out when you want to impress and intrigue your most interesting guests.

CANNED PIMENTOS

Mother always has these brilliant red, rather sweet, pimentos for use as garnishes and for eating "just so."
A 6-quart basket makes 3 small quarts and 2 pints; for that number you need to make 3 amounts of syrup—done separately. Stem and seed the pimentos and cook them until barely tender in salt water. (Mother says the trick is not to boil them too long— they are done almost before they have started to boil). Drain and pack the pimentos in sterilized jars and cover with syrup:

1 pint vinegar   **2 pounds white sugar**

Bring vinegar and sugar to 2-minute boil, then pour over the pimentos in jars.

PICKLED CRAB APPLES OR PICKLING PEARS

Mother never seemed to make enough of these—so pretty, meaty, and good eating.

1 peck of crabapples—or   **3 pounds of white sugar**
**   pickling pears**   **Cinnamon stick and cloves**
4 cups vinegar   **   tied in a bag**
4 cups water

Bring liquid and sugar to a boil for 10 minutes or a little longer, add cinnamon stick and cloves tied in a muslin bag; when the syrup gets syrupy put in the apples and simmer them until done, but not too soft.

Mother's note to my sister in Peterborough: "Don't use too-small crabapples; Norma made them one time and she bought too small an apple—when they were done they were only skin and core. I wouldn't try to do too many. Try half the recipe and then taste them and if you like them you can make more. If not sweet enough you can add more sugar. Hope you'll have good luck."

MOTHER'S NINE DAY PICKLES

Mother hasn't made these for many years and can't remember much about them except that people who ate them always asked for her recipe.

4 quarts of pickles (about 4 inches long)
**4 tablespoons salt dissolved in enough hot water to cover
  the pickles**

1/2 gallon white wine vinegar	**4 cups white sugar**
4 tablespoons mustard	**1/2 cup mixed spice**
3 tablespoons salt	**1 ginger root**
	5 more cups of white sugar

Scrub the pickles, put them into a crock, sprinkle salt over them
and pour in hot water to cover the pickles; let stand for 24 hours
—stirring occasionally. Next day—you'll love this—wipe each
pickle dry and put it back into the dry crock.

Now mix up all the other ingredients except the 5 cups of sugar
and pour the mixture cold over the pickles; if there isn't enough
to cover them you'd better mix up some more. Every day for nine
days after that you add some of the 5 cups of sugar you have
measured out; stir it in. When you've completed this process,
cover the crock, wait a few weeks, then start enjoying the pickles.

My sister in Peterborough has a garden and is a great one for canning. I copied these recipes from her hand-written book.

RED PICKLE

6 quarts tomatoes	**12 large onions**
4 red peppers (not hot)	

Put all through the food chopper.

Add:

8 cups white sugar	**2 teaspoons salt**
2 cups vinegar	

Boil until jellyish, then bottle in sterilized jars.

RUMMAGE PICKLE

2 quarts green tomatoes	**6 red sweet peppers**
3 small bunches celery	**6 green peppers**
1 quart red tomatoes	**1 large ripe cucumber**
3 onions	**1/2 cup salt**

Chop the vegetables, cover with salt, let stand a few hours. Drain
well.

Add:

3 cups vinegar	**1 teaspoon mustard**
2 pounds brown sugar	**1 teaspoon pepper**

Cook until thick—almost 1 hour—then bottle in sterilized jars.

DOROTHY'S RELISH

7 large cucumbers peeled	2 sweet red peppers—
5 onions, peeled	for colour
2 large cucumbers, not peeled	

Put through chopper, add 3 teaspoons salt. Let stand a few hours then press out juice.

Mix:

3 cups white sugar	Pinch of cayenne pepper
1/2 cup flour	1 1/2 tablespoons mustard
1/2 teaspoon turmeric powder	2 1/2 cups vinegar
1/2 teaspoon curry powder	1 cup water

Bring to a boil then add cucumbers, onion and peppers; boil 10 minutes and seal.

WATERMELON PICKLE

Crisp, semi-sweet and clovey. Nice to serve in a tray of hors d'ouvres.

2 quarts watermelon rind	1/2 teaspoon powdered alum
1/2 cup salt dissolved in	
2 quarts water	

Peel the rind, cutting off all the pink part and the hard, green outer skin. Cut into squares or oblongs, put into a kettle and cover with brine; let stand overnight. Drain and rinse with clear water. Cover with cold water to which you have added 1/2 teaspoon of powdered alum. Cook until tender. Drain again.

Mix:

1 quart white wine vinegar	1 ounce whole cinnamon
1 quart water	1 tablespoon whole cloves
6 pounds white sugar	

Cook mixture several minutes before adding rind. Cook slowly until rind is transparent. Just before the end you might add a few drops of red or green colouring. Pack into sterilized pint jars, pour the syrup over the rind and seal.

MARG V's SLICED PICKLES

50 cucumbers, not peeled	1 quart vinegar
15 or 20 onions	2 1/2 pounds sugar
1/2 cup salt dissolved	1/4 cup mustard seed
in water	2 tablespoons celery seed

Slice the cucumbers and the onions $1/8$-inch thick. Soak in weak salt brine for 3 hours or overnight. Drain well, rinse and drain again. Boil vinegar, sugar and seeds for a few minutes then add cucumbers and onions. Heat in the vinegar solution but do not boil. Pack in sterilized jars and seal.

DILL PICKLES

Put a small bunch of dill in the bottom of sterilized pint jars. Wash gherkins and pack them in the jars. Put 2 tablespoons of white sugar and $1/2$ teaspoon salt on top of each jar—also 1 teaspoon mixed pickle spice. Cover with hot vinegar and seal.

These are some of Bevvy's favourites.

MAGDALINE'S CORN RELISH

18 ears of corn	2 green peppers
6 large cucumbers	5 cups white sugar
10 onions	4 tablespoons salt
3 sweet peppers	$1^1/2$ pints vinegar

Strip the corn from the cobs, chop up the cucumbers, onions and peppers; cook all with the vinegar, sugar and salt for 30 minutes. With a little vinegar blend:

2 tablespoons flour	1 large tablespoon mustard
2 large tablespoons celery seed	

Cook with corn mixture slowly for 5 minutes, stirring all the time. Bottle and seal.

GROSSMOMMY MARTIN'S KUDDLEFLECK

12 ears corn	2 green peppers
1 quart cucumbers	2 red peppers
2 bunches celery	1 quart vinegar
1 quart tomatoes	$2^1/2$ cups brown sugar
1 large onion	1 tablespoon salt
1 teaspoon turmeric	1 tablespoon mustard

Chop the cucumbers, celery, onion and peppers; cut the corn from the cobs and boil all together for 50 minutes. Bottle and seal.

INDIAN RELISH

12 ripe tomatoes	4 cups vinegar
9 onions	1/4 cup salt
12 sour apples	1 teaspoon each of pepper,
4 cups brown sugar	mustard, ginger, cloves

Blanch, peel and cut tomatoes; peel, core and cut apples and onions. Combine with remaining ingredients and simmer for 3 or 4 hours, then bottle and seal.

ANNIE'S HOT DOG RELISH

8 cucumbers, not peeled	1 1/2 dozen green tomatoes
6 large onions	1 handful of salt
1 small cabbage	

Put through food chopper, sprinkle with salt and let stand overnight. Drain next morning and add:

1 bunch of celery, chopped with a knife	1 hot pepper, put through food chopper
4 green peppers, put through food chopper	1 sweet red pepper, put through food chopper

Barely cover with vinegar; boil for 15 minutes.

Add:

7 cups white sugar	1/2 cup flour
1 teaspoon celery seed	A little vinegar to blend dry
1 teaspoon mustard	ingredients
1 teaspoon turmeric	

Boil 5 to 10 minutes longer, stirring constantly. Bottle and seal.

LILLY PICKLE

12 large cucumbers	1 head cauliflower
3 quarts onions	2 stalks celery
1 head cabbage	

Chop all fine, sprinkle with salt and let stand overnight. Drain in the morning and add:

3 quarts vinegar	2 tablespoons turmeric
5 cups brown sugar	powder
	1 dessertspoon curry powder

Cook until tender. Mix:

6 tablespoons mustard	**6 tablespoons flour with a little cold vinegar**

Stir into the pickle and boil for 10 minutes. Bottle and seal.

GOOSEBERRY RELISH

4 pounds gooseberries	**1 tablespoon cinnamon stick**
4 cups sugar	**and**
1 cup vinegar	**1 tablespoon whole cloves**
1 teaspoon salt	**tied in a bag**

Wash and stem gooseberries. Combine sugar, salt, spices and vinegar and bring to a boil. Add the gooseberries and cook until thick—about 20 to 30 minutes. Pack in sterilized jars and seal.

SPICED PEACHES

7 pounds peaches	**1 teaspoon whole cloves**
4 pounds brown sugar	**1 tablespoon cinnamon stick**
1 quart vinegar	**1 teaspoon allspice, whole**

Tie the spices in a bag and add to the vinegar. Bring to a boil and stir in the sugar. Scald and peel the peaches leaving them whole. Drop peaches, a few at a time, into spiced liquid; cook until tender—but not too soft. Fill sterilized jars and seal.

GROSSMOMMY MARTIN'S CANTALOUPE PICKLE

6 cups cantaloupe, peeled and cut into pieces 1½ inches long and ½ inch thick	**2 quarts water**
	3 cups sugar
	2 cups vinegar
	2 sticks cinnamon
1½ teaspoons alum	**2 teaspoons whole cloves**

Dissolve the alum in the water and bring to a boil; add the fruit and boil for 15 minutes. Drain. Combine the sugar, vinegar and spices; add the drained cantaloupe and simmer slowly until it is clear—about 20 minutes. Bottle in sterilized jars.

SWEETS

"It wouldn't be healthy if we didn't have fruit with every meal," Bevvy tells me as I marvel at the bags of dried fruit and hundreds of jars of jams, jellies and fruits she has preserved and stored on shelves in her basement. "A lot of it we make into pies in the winter," she says, "some we eat just so, and for breakfast we need schnitz und gwetcha (dried apples and prunes boiled together)."

My mother, too, used to can dozens of jars of fruit every summer and for years I did the same thing till one day I decided I'd never bother again. As I walked round the bountiful Kitchener market and didn't buy baskets and baskets of fruit to preserve I felt guilty, as if there would surely be a famine as there had been in biblical Egypt and I wouldn't have laid in my supply.

The year passed; we didn't starve and my guilt has worn off.

I won't give you any fruit-preserving recipes here, just a few favourite jams and jellies that Bevvy makes, or that I make because I can't buy them in a store.

ELDERBERRY JELLY

Because elderberries grow wild almost anyone can go for a car ride and gather them along the roadsides.

2 quarts elderberries	**about 6 cups sugar**
1 quart apples	**Lemon juice**
2 quarts water	

Clean and stem the elderberries then measure 2 quarts. Remove the stems and blossom ends from the apples but don't peel them; Slice or chop the apples and measure 1 quart. Put the fruit into a preserving kettle with the water, cover and simmer for 15 minutes, stirring occasionally. Pour the cooked fruit into a jelly bag and let it drip over night. Measure the juice, adding 1 cup of sugar and 1 tablespoon of lemon juice for every cup of elderberry juice. Bring to a boil and boil vigorously until the jelly stage has been reached (a drop will congeal when dripped on a cold plate). Remove from fire, skim and pour into hot sterilized jars. Seal with paraffin.

CARROT MARMALADE

Bevvy says carrots are more plentiful than oranges and make a good substitute.

2 quarts of carrots	**Juice and grated rind of**
3 oranges, unpeeled	**1 large lemon**
	1 cup sugar

Peel the carrots and boil them till tender; strain, reserving the carrot water. Put the carrots and oranges, cut in quarters, through the food chopper. Add lemon juice and rind. Mix well, add carrot water and sugar. Boil for half an hour, stirring often. When the mixture has thickened, pour it into sterilized jars and seal. (I've copied this from Bevvy's book; I haven't tried it.)

JEWEL JAM

Fresh from Bevvy's garden, this is wonderful.
1 quart pitted cherries put into a kettle with 2 cups sugar: boil 2 minutes.
Add 1 quart gooseberries and 2 cups sugar: boil 5 minutes.
Add 1 quart red currants, 1 quart raspberries and 4 cups sugar and boil for 5 minutes. Put in sterilized jars and seal when cool.

GRAPE CONSERVE

This is rich and special.

5 pounds of blue grapes	**1 pound raisins**
4 pounds sugar	**1 pound walnuts, chopped**

Slip the insides out of the grapes and heat them till the seeds come free; strain out the seeds and discard them. To the remaining grape juice add the grape skins and the sugar; boil 10 minutes. Add raisins and walnuts and boil 10 minutes more. Pour into hot sterilized jars and seal with wax.

PLUM CONSERVE

This is wonderful with hot biscuits.

6 pounds plums—I use prune plums that pit easily.	**Juice of 2 lemons**
	1 pound walnuts
5 pounds sugar	**1 pound seeded raisins**
4 oranges put through chopper	

Pit plums and cut into pieces; add sugar and boil for 10 minutes, stirring constantly. Add the chopped oranges, the juice of the lemons, the raisins and walnuts; cook 10 minutes longer and keep stirring. Put into hot sterilized jars and seal with wax.

AUNT MATTIE'S BLACK CURRANT JAM

Nice and tart.

1 quart of black currants; clean but don't take off the blossom end. Boil 10 minutes with an equal quantity of water. Add twice

as much sugar as the amount of fruit you have left after boiling, then boil 5 to 10 minutes longer. (I use 1 cup less sugar because I don't like mine too strong.)

LOTVARRICK (Apple Butter)

I'm sure there isn't a Mennonite household that doesn't have crocks of apple butter in the cellar to be spread on fresh "butter-bread", on muffins, hot biscuits, and pancakes, or to be used in pies and cakes. Apple butter can be bought at the Kitchener Farmers' Market but if you don't live near enough you might make your own.

2 quarts apple cider	2 cups corn syrup or
2 quarts apples	cooked pumpkin
2 cups sugar	1 teaspoon cinnamon

Boil the cider until it is reduced to 1 quart. Peel the apples, core and cut into thin slices, add to the cider and cook slowly until the mixture begins to thicken, stirring most of the time. Add the sugar, syrup and cinnamon and keep on cooking until a little when cooled on a plate is of a good spreading consistency. This should make 5 or 6 pints. The Mennonites always make gallons.

MOCK MAPLE SYRUP

Sometimes on Sunday mornings at Sunfish Lake we'd have our neighbours for breakfast; I'd mix up a great bash of buttermilk pancake batter, my brother-in-law, Ralph, would bake the pancakes over an open fire on the lawn and twenty people would sit at our picnic tables and eat them smothered with maple syrup (they thought). Actually I had made the syrup the day before and no one knew the difference.

6 cups brown sugar	1/2 teaspoon vinegar
4 cups boiling water	1 pint real maple syrup

Put the sugar into the boiling water, let the mixture boil for 5 minutes, when it has cooled add the vinegar and real maple syrup and stir till well blended. You don't have to put in the real maple syrup but it does add flavour. When Mother made this she used water in which very clean potatoes in their jackets had been boiled.

Brunches, Lunches, Suppers and Leftovers

Often at the market I meet friends who say, "Isn't this eating a problem? I never know what to have." I blithely agree, because there is so much wonderful food in our bountiful world that it's hard to decide what to try next. And hard to find time and space for it.

Breakfasts are fairly conventional. Dinners are usually prescribed—meat, potatoes and vegetables. But lunches and suppers are flexible. That's when one can be truly inventive, eat up the leftovers, create concoctions and casseroles and make special favourites that wouldn't fit into—or that one couldn't get enough of—at any other meal. That is when, at Mother's house, we gorged on potato pancakes, fetschpatze, fritters or dumplings. Of course our meal was not always well balanced, but what matter? Our family all had what were called "cast-iron stomachs" because of, or in spite of, the wonderful things that we ate.

At Bevvy's house the table is always laden for supper. First she serves soup, and when it's been sopped up with bread, we help ourselves to the platefuls of cold sliced meat and sausage, fried potatoes, kochkase, pickled beets or eggs, lettuce salad, several sours, canned fruit, doughnuts, cookies, cake, pie, or pudding. Bevvy says, "Supper is always mostly made from just what we've got that needs eating."

QUICHE LORRAINE

Sounds too sophisticated to be a Mennonite dish but it did originate in the Vosges Mountains where many of the Mennonites lived in the days of their religious persecution.

117

Pastry for a deep pie plate
1 cup shredded Swiss cheese (I've often done it with mild
    cheddar)

6 eggs	**1 tablespoon Kirsch**
6 slices of bacon	**1/2 cup milk**
1 teaspoon pepper	**1/2 cup cream**
A slight sprinkle of nutmeg	

Line a deep pie pan with rich pastry. Sprinkle 1/2 a cup of shredded
cheese evenly on the bottom. Cut bacon into bits and fry until it
has lost about half its fat. Distribute the bacon bits on top of the
cheese and sprinkle 2 tablespoons of the bacon fat on top. Into
a bowl break the eggs; beat them, add salt, pepper and nutmeg,
then the Kirsch, milk, cream, and the rest of the bacon and
shredded cheese. Blend; then carefully pour this mixture over the
bacon and cheese in the pie. Bake it on the floor of your oven at
350 degrees for 40 to 50 minutes.

Your guests won't want more than one glass of sherry when
they catch a whiff of the quiche in the oven. Serve immediately
when you take it out, puffed-up and golden; it will flatten if you
keep it waiting—but it will still taste good.

VARIATION: One day when I was having the girls in for lunch
I decided I'd better have two quiches, one for seconds. I had 2
cobs of fresh corn left from dinner the night before: I cut off the
kernels, fried them for a few minutes in bacon fat, then spread
them (instead of bacon) over the cheese in the pie shell before I
poured in the egg and milk mixture. The girls were just as enthusiastic about their seconds as they had been about their firsts.

MARJE MOYER'S CHICKEN CASSEROLE

This makes enough for a lot of people—a real Sunday company
supper.

2 boiled chickens	**1 green pepper fried with**
6 cups noodles, boiled	**mushrooms**
2 pounds mushrooms, fried	**1 can mushroom soup**
1 cup breadcrumbs, for	**2 cups chicken broth**
topping	**1 can evaporated milk**
	3 tablespoons corn starch

Cut up the chicken into bite-sized pieces; combine all the rest
in a saucepan on top of the stove, but don't put in the mushrooms

and peppers until you are ready to put the whole thing into a casserole to heat—or they'll turn the whole mixture grey. About 45 minutes before you're ready to serve it, put the casserole into the oven to heat through and brown the breadcrumbs on top. Serve with a salad, hot rolls, a vegetable and sours. Apple halves sprinkled with sugar and cinnamon are nice with it too.

BEEF CASSEROLE

Mardi Robinson, next door, thinks this is the best there is.

³/₄ package large noodles	1 or 2 tins of mushrooms
1¹/₂ pounds of beef (or 2 pounds)	1 large tin of tomatoes
3 or 4 tablespoons chopped green pepper	1 pound grated cheese (some on top)
2 or 3 large onions	Breadcrumbs for topping

Fry the meat till it's brown; fry the onions; add everything to the cooked noodles and mix, but don't stir too much or you will break up the noodles and the dish will be mushy. Put the mixture into a big casserole, cover it with a topping of cheese and breadcrumbs and heat it in the oven for about 45 minutes. You can add a few other things to this if you like—I always put in some soy sauce.

BELLE'S BEEF AND PORK-SAUSAGE CASSEROLE

This is slightly sophisticated and very flavourful.

¹/₂ pound uncooked spaghetti (or 1 package of noodles)	2 tablespoons almonds
	1 teaspoon salt
	Pepper
³/₄ pound ground beef	1 package French's Spaghetti Sauce
³/₄ pound pork sausage meat	
1 clove of garlic, cut very fine	¹/₄ cup fresh lemon juice
¹/₂ cup mushrooms (or more)	2 cups stewed or canned tomatoes
4 tablespoons crumbled blue cheese	

Cook noodles or spaghetti (we use noodles). Brown meat with garlic, salt and pepper, then drain off fat. To meat add mushrooms, tomatoes and lemon juice; blend in spaghetti sauce and simmer for 20 minutes. Add blue cheese. Mix with noodles—being careful not to overdo it. Bake at 375 degrees for 25 minutes. Sprinkle slivered almonds over the top and brown slightly.

NORM'S CHICKEN-POTATO CHIP CASSEROLE

This is easy to prepare and makes a big hit at a supper party.

**1 or 2 chickens, cut into big
chunks after boiling till
tender
Potato chips—several
cupfuls, crumbled
1 pound mushrooms, fried
in butter**

**1 tin mushroom soup and
equal quantity of milk
2 or 3 long stems celery,
cut up
1/2 pound almonds, blanched
and slivered and
browned in butter**

Mix the celery, mushrooms, mushroom soup blended with milk. Into a greased casserole put a layer of the cooked chicken pieces, cover them with a layer of crumbled potato chips, sprinkle on some of the almonds, then add some of the mushroom mixture. Repeat until you've filled up the dish and used up all the ingredients, with chips and almonds on top. Bake at 350 degrees for about 40 minutes. Serve with a hot vegetable, jellied or green salad, cranberry sauce or apple halves and hot rolls.

SALLY'S LADIES' CASSEROLE

Though the men like it just as well, it's really one of the very best.

**1 pound ground beef
1/2 pound ground pork
2 onions, finely cut
20-ounce tin tomato soup
3-ounce package cream
cheese
Butter
1/4 pound chopped almonds**

**2 tablespoons white sugar
1 1/2 tablespoons Worcester
Sauce
2 teaspoons salt
1/4 teaspoon pepper
1/2 pound wide noodles
1/4 pound mushrooms
1/2 cup crushed cornflakes**

Cook beef and pork and onions in 2 tablespoons butter until golden brown. Add tomato soup, crumbled cream cheese, sugar, Worcester Sauce, salt and pepper; simmer 5 to 10 minutes, until thick.

Have noodles ready, cooked, and in a large greased casserole; pour meat mixture over noodles. Brown the mushrooms in 1 tablespoon butter and spread on top. Sprinkle crushed cornflakes on top and bake at 350 degrees for 1/2 an hour. Five or 10 minutes before serving sprinkle chopped almonds over the top and let them toast slightly.

SALLY'S ONE-DISH SUPPER OR LUNCHEON

We agreed with Mother that Sally was a good cook.

6 ounces (about 1³/₄ cups) cut macaroni	3 tablespoons flour
¹/₂ pound sausages	1¹/₂ cups milk
1 green pepper	¹/₂ pound cheese
3 tablespoons butter	Salt and pepper

Boil the macaroni in a large amount of rapidly boiling, salted water, uncovered, until tender; drain, rinse with hot water and drain again. Leave 5 or 6 sausages whole and cut the remaining into ¹/₂-inch pieces; fry together until richly browned; remove from dripping.

Remove stem end and seeds from green pepper and cut pepper into ¹/₄-inch-thick slices; add to the sausage dripping and fry gently until pepper is tender. Arrange the cooked macaroni, half the green pepper and the sausage pieces in layers in a greased casserole. Melt the butter; remove from heat and blend in the flour; gradually blend in the milk; cook, stirring constantly, until thickened.

Shred the cheese and reserve ¹/₂ a cup for topping. Add the remaining cheese to the cream sauce and stir until the cheese is melted; season to taste with salt and pepper. Pour sauce over the macaroni mixture in the casserole. Top the casserole with remaining green pepper and fried whole sausages. Bake uncovered in a 350-degree oven for 20 minutes. Sprinkle with the ¹/₂-cup of cheese, return to the oven and bake until the cheese is melted—about 10 minutes longer.

WIENER-VEGETABLE CASSEROLE

This is one of those handy-dandy one-dish recipes that can be contracted or expanded and substituted to suit your needs. If you keep a package of frankfurters and peas frozen in your fridge, it's perfect for an emergency—or otherwise.

3 cups sliced potatoes	1 teaspoon salt
1 cup sliced carrots	Pepper to taste
1 or 2 onions, sliced	2 tablespoons flour
¹/₂ cup cut-up celery tops or stalks	1¹/₂ cups milk
2 tablespoons cut-up parsley	6, 8, 10 or more frankfurters
	Bacon slices to cover

Grease a casserole—or a deep flat baking dish with a lid if you want more surface. Spread half the potatoes in the bottom, sprinkle with flour, salt and pepper; arrange the other vegetables over the potatoes, sprinkle them the same way, then put the rest of the potatoes over the top. Pour milk over all—enough to almost cover, but not too close to the top of the dish. Arrange wieners on top and bacon slices covering the wieners. Cover and cook at 375 degrees for 50 minutes. Uncover for 10 minutes to crisp the bacon. The wieners will be puffy and brown when you take them out of the stove; they shrink unless you gobble them quickly.

LEFTOVER MEAT CASSEROLE

A good follow-up after a Sunday dinner—with many variations.

2 cups cooked meat cut in pieces (more if you like)
1 cup diced celery
An onion or two that went with your roast
1 cupful of leftover vegetable
1 can of tomato soup
1 can mushroom soup
3 cups cooked noodles
1 teaspoon salt
Pepper
1 cup meat broth or gravy
1 cup breadcrumbs
1/2 cup grated cheddar

Arrange the meat and vegetables and noodles in alternate layers— with noodles on top. Blend the soups and the gravy and pour into the casserole. Sprinkle grated cheese mixed with breadcrumbs over the top and bake in a 350-degree oven for an hour or so. It's good enough for company.

GEROLT FLAISCH (Meat Roll)

Bevvy says this makes a little meat go a long way:

Meat filling:

1 1/2 cups chopped cooked meat—or more
2 tablespoons minced onion
5 tablespoons gravy
Seasonings
Biscuit dough:
2 cups flour
4 teaspoons baking powder
1/2 teaspoon salt
5 tablespoons shortening
2/3 cup milk

Mix the biscuit dough ingredients in the order given and roll 1/4 of an inch thick. Spread with the meat filling. Roll up like a jelly roll and cut in slices 1 inch thick. Place pieces in a buttered baking pan. Dot with butter, bake in 450-degree oven about 15 minutes. Serve with additional gravy poured over it—or one of your own ingenious sauces—like mushroom or tomato soup.

CASSEROLE FOR CAROL AND PAUL

Some of the most surprisingly good dishes are made of leftovers. In late August I impulsively invited a young couple for dinner. I had some cooked green beans left from my Sunday dinner and 4 cooked cobs of corn, tomatoes, onions and a piece of pork sausage frozen in my fridge. Enough for a casserole, I decided.

I cut the corn from the cobs, sliced up a couple of onions, added the green beans, enough cut-up tomatoes to give plenty of moisture, salt, pepper and parsley. I boiled and browned the sausage before cutting it up into bite-sized pieces and mixing it with the vegetables in a buttered casserole. (I might have used cut-up wieners.) I covered it all with a thick layer of grated cheese mixed with corn flakes, put it in the oven at 350 degrees for about half an hour—till the top was crusty and golden—then served it with hot buns and a salad. Those kids ate every bit of what looked like enough for five or six people.

BEVVY'S ALLES TZSAMMA (All together in One Dish)

You could hide a few leftovers in this too if you wished.

Slice a layer of raw, peeled potatoes into the bottom of a buttered casserole; then a layer of sliced onions, green beans or peas (or both), a layer of ground beef or hamburger meat, slices of green pepper and, topping all, a thick layer of fresh tomatoes (or canned) to give moisture to the dish. Sprinkle salt and pepper over the various layers. Bake in a 300-degree oven for about an hour. And there's your nourishing, tasty meal—with a lettuce salad.

LEFTOVER CHICKEN DISH

Whenever I have a roast chicken dinner I always hope there'll be enough of everything left over to make this delicious dish the next day. Into a well-greased oven dish cut up into bite-size pieces the chicken—and dressing, if there is some. With it mix plenty of leftover gravy or make a sauce by blending milk, chicken soup or bouillon powder and flour—it will thicken as it cooks. Over the chicken mixture spread your leftover vegetables—or canned ones. Remash your leftover potatoes with plenty of butter and cream or milk and spread smoothly over the top and dot with butter. Cover the dish and bake it at 350 degrees, or thereabouts, for about 45 minutes; remove the lid and let the potatoes brown a bit before serving. With a green salad and leftover cranberries you'll have a wonderful meal.

BYE-BYE SHORTCAKE

This is a tasty way to use up leftover chicken or turkey—and fancy too.

Biscuit dough:

2 cups flour	5 tablespoons shortening
4 teaspoons baking powder	$^2/_3$ cup milk
$^1/_2$ teaspoon salt	

Blend the ingredients in the order given. Roll out the dough on a board to $^1/_2$-inch thickness; cut out rounds with a drinking glass; cut a round hole in half the rounds—like a doughnut. Brush whole rounds with melted shortening, place holey rounds on top and bake in a 450-degree oven for 15 minutes.

While the biscuits are baking make the meat sauce:

2 tablespoons butter	2 cups cooked meat, cut
6 tablespoons flour	in pieces
Salt and pepper	2 tablespoons parsley, cut up
2 cups milk or milk and	
gravy	

Melt the butter; add the flour, salt, pepper, and slowly the milk and gravy; stir till it thickens. Add the meat and parsley. When the biscuits are baked, deftly separate the holey biscuit rounds from the whole rounds. Pour meat sauce over the lower half of the biscuit, put biscuit ring on top and put a spoonful of cranberry sauce or jelly in the hole as a garnish. Add a salad and you have a good meal.

PORK PIE

One of the best ways to use leftover pork.

$2^1/_2$ cups, more or less, cold	1 cup—more or less—
roast pork cut in cubes	leftover gravy
2 medium-tart apples, cored	Pastry to cover
and sliced	Salt and pepper

Grease a shallow baking dish and put into it alternate layers of pork and apples. Season each layer with salt and pepper. Pour the gravy over all and cover the dish with pastry. Prick or slash the crust to let steam out during baking. Put in a 400-degree oven until the crust starts to brown; reduce heat to 350 degrees and bake another half hour.

NOODLES AND HAM

There's nothing unusual about this but it tastes good.

2 cups cooked ham, chopped	²/₃ cup grated cheese
2 cups noodles, cooked	2 cups thin white sauce

Put a layer of noodles in a greased oven dish. Add a layer of ham, cover with well-seasoned white sauce and sprinkle with cheese. Repeat layers of noodles, ham and white sauce until all the ingredients are used. Sprinkle cheese on top—mixed with a few breadcrumbs. Bake in a 350-degree oven for 30 minutes.

STUFFED SQUASH

You could use leftover squash as well as leftover meat with this.

3 pepper squash	2 tablespoons tomato
2¹/₂ cups soft bread crumbs	ketchup
1 cup cooked meat	A few drops of Worces-
Minced onion—much or	tershire sauce
little	Soup stock or water or
Salt and pepper	broth to moisten
2 tablespoons melted butter	

Wipe the squash and cut in half crosswise. Remove the seeds and stringy portion, then place a little butter in the hollowed halves and sprinkle with salt and pepper. Cover and bake in a 400-degree oven for 30 to 45 minutes until almost tender. Mix up the meat stuffing and fill up the squash. Return to the oven for about 15 minutes and serve hot, hot, hot.

LEFTOVER ROAST

If you have quite a lot of the roast left over after dinner, put it into an earthenware pot or casserole with a heavy, tight lid; pour the gravy over it and the leftover onions that went with the roast; you might put in carrots and any other mild vegetables too. Refrigerate. Next day, or a couple of days after, pop the pot into a 325-degree oven for not quite an hour—it just needs to be there long enough to be thoroughly heated. Because the pot is tightly covered the meat will have no leftover meat flavour; it will be like a delicious pot-roast—which is what it may have been in the first place.

HANDY COTTAGE PIE

For those last bits of meat that nobody wants cold.

2 cupfuls of diced cooked meat—beef, pork, veal, lamb or fowl	1 can vegetable soup diluted to make 2 cups
2 tablespoons of butter	Mashed potatos and gravy if there is any leftover
3 tablespoons flour	

Melt the butter, add the diced meat and cook until lightly browned. Add the flour and stir until well blended. Gradually add leftover gravy and the vegetable soup; cook, stirring constantly until the mixture thickens. You might add some parsley or herbs if you like. Turn into a baking dish and cover the top thickly and roughly with fluffy mashed potatoes. Bake in a 375-degree oven for about 15 minutes until nicely browned.

HAM LOAF

You'll be proud of this. It can be served hot or cold.

3 tablespoons butter	1/2 cup breadcrumbs
5 tablespoons brown sugar	1/4 cup milk
3 slices of pineapple	2 eggs
1 1/2 pounds of cooked, ground ham	Seasonings

Melt the butter in the loaf pan in which you are going to bake the loaf, add the sugar, stir until it is melted, then put in the pieces of pineapple which should cover the bottom of the pan. Mix the ham, eggs beaten slightly, add the crumbs, milk and pepper; spread on top of the sugar and pineapple and bake in a 350- to 400-degree oven for about an hour.

BETSY BRUBACHER'S SPAGHETTI

Wonderful to make when you have to feed a lot of people—it's easy, expandable, and everyone loves it with a green salad and a red wine.

1 pound of spaghetti	4 cupfuls of tomatoes
1/4 cup salad oil	2 teaspoons salt
4 medium-sized onions, sliced	1/2 cupful of cheese, grated or cubed
2 small green peppers, cut up	5 or 6 bay leaves

Cook the long strings of spaghetti in boiling, salted water until tender. Drain. Cook the sliced onions and peppers in the cooking oil, gently, until partly cooked; add the tomatoes and salt and cook till the onions are tender. Add the cheese to the drained spaghetti and put it into an ovenware serving dish. Pour the tomato mixture over it, inserting the bay leaves where you can pick them out before you serve the spaghetti. Spread bacon slices over the top of the spaghetti and put the covered dish into a 250- to 300-degree oven, leaving it as long as you need to. If it dries out a bit you can always add more tomato juice. Before serving take off the lid to crisp the bacon (you may need to grill extra bacon).

QUICK AND EASY

(for two or three)

At a supermarket one day I decided to try some Canadian sardines; they were cheap, so I bought half a dozen cans. On opening a tin I found silver, soft-bellied fish of various sizes that I didn't like at all served on leaf lettuce as I do the neat, firm, more expensive little Norwegian sardines. What to do with six cans of home-grown fish? My thrifty, patriotic soul inspired me to invent this way of using them:

Sardines from 1 can	**3 or 4 eggs**
2 tablespoons butter	**A sprinkle of cayenne**
2 tablespoons flour	**pepper**
1 teaspoon flavoured salt	**2 sliced tomatoes (optional)**
1 cup milk	**Thin slices of cheese**
1/2 cupful of cheddar chunks	
(optional)	

Empty the sardines into a greased pie plate. With a knife slit the fish through the belly and easily remove the vertebral bones and anything else you see there that you don't like the look of. Spread the fish halves flat on the bottom of the pie plate and over them pour a medium-thick cream sauce made of the butter, flour, salt and milk, with or without the cheddar chunks stirred into it. Break the eggs on top of the sauce, cover them with the slices of cheese and sprinkle with salt and cayenne. Put the dish into a 400-degree oven and leave it there until the eggs are firm, then under the broiler (if necessary) till the cheese is bubbly. To make the dish look attractive you might arrange a ring of tomato slices around the rim; if they are winter tomatoes lay them on and bake them along with the rest. To serve, neatly slip sardines, sauce, egg and tomato onto a piece of buttered toast on each plate.

This has been a great success; Canadian sardines are often on my shopping lists.

QUICKER AND EASIER

But not as good.

Pour undiluted mushroom or tomato soup into a pie plate; break eggs on top, spoon some soup over them, sprinkle with a mixture of grated cheese and bread crumbs and put the pan into a 350-degree oven till the eggs are firm, the soup bubbly, and the top is golden-brown. Serve on buttered toast or hot biscuits.

SARDINE-STUFFED EGGS

I discovered this to be another good way to use Canadian sardines. Cut hard-boiled eggs in half, remove the yolks. With a fork blend the yolks with sardines, a sprinkling of cayenne, salt, and enough mayonnaise to make the mixture creamy. Fill the egg whites with the mixture and garnish with parsley. Serve on lettuce with tomato slices, cucumbers, celery—and so forth.

STUFFED EGGS IN JELLY

This is a jellied luncheon salad the girls will remember. It uses Canadian sardines.

1 tin Canadian sardines, boned	2 tablespoons plain gelatine
6 hard-boiled eggs	$1/2$ cup cold water
3 tablespoons mayonnaise	$1/2$ cup dry white wine
2 sprigs finely cut parsley	3 cups well-seasoned
2 teaspoons lemon juice	chicken broth or broth
Pepper and salt to taste	made with chicken-base
	powder or cubes

Soften the gelatine in cold water, dissolve in hot broth, add wine and let cool. Cut the peeled eggs in half lengthwise and carefully remove yolks. Mash the egg yolks and sardines together, making a smooth paste with the mayonnaise, lemon juice, salt, pepper and parsley. Fill the egg whites with the mixture and arrange the halves in a ring mould. (You may have some left for seconds in another mould—or bowl.) Pour the gelatine mixture over the eggs, filling the mould. Chill until firm then turn out on a plate with lettuce leaves, cucumber and zucchini slices, tomato wedges, bits of carrot, radish, celery, olives, or whatever, prettily arranged inside and around the ring. Pass mayonnaise, and if you've made hot cheese biscuits or buns you've got yourself a meal.

VARIATIONS

Instead of the Canadian sardines you might mince a few anchovies with the egg yolks. Or you might use grated blue cheese.

CONNIE'S QUICKIE

This is super. Connie served it at a luncheon shower she had for me and I've been making it ever since.

Simply put thick slices of tomato on a piece of hot buttered toast. On each slice put a half, or a quarter, of a hot hard-boiled egg. Sprinkle with salt and pepper, then cover with hot cheese sauce and put strips of fried bacon or crisp bacon bits on top.

ANOTHER EASY ONE

To use up those miserable winter tomatoes.

Butter a custard cup, put half a tomato in the bottom, break an egg over it, sprinkle it with salt and pepper, then about half an inch of cheese cubes mixed with breadcrumbs. Put it in the oven till the egg is firm. Serve on buttered or grilled cheese toast.

LEVAVASCHT MIT BUNS (Headcheese Burgers)

Very quick and tasty.

Split hamburger rolls and on each half tailor to fit a slice of headcheese or liverwurst; slip under the broiler and brown it or let it become bubbly. Relish or slices of onion and tomato, raw or broiled, on top gives you a lunch.

HOT BOLOGNA

Bologna seems to have more flavour when it is heated.

Simply boil some water and put the ring (or part ring) of bologna into it until it is thoroughly heated; peel off the casing. With a salad and hot rolls you don't need more.

FRIED LARGE BOLOGNA SLICES

This is a budget-stretcher, and it's good too.

Nick the edges of bologna slices so they won't curl. Dip them in milk, sprinkle them with salt and pepper, dip them in fine bread crumbs, then into beaten egg with an added spoonful of milk. Coat again with the crumbs and pan-fry in melted dripping, turning carefully to brown each side—or dip in melted dripping and brown under the broiler. Try it with a salad and hot rolls.

FRIED NOODLES

Sometimes Mother served these instead of potatoes with chops, chicken or steaks, but mostly we had them with cold meats and a salad for supper.

Sometimes butter is merely allowed to melt over the hot, boiled noodles and they are covered, before serving, with browned buttered crumbs, or sprinkled with parsley.

To fry noodles: melt two tablespoons of butter in a pan and pour the boiled noodles into it; to keep them separate and slippery, stir them around in the pan until they are golden.

Or pour the noodles into the butter in the pan and put on a lid, letting the noodles become brown on the bottom, very, very slowly; then flip the whole mass over and let the other side become golden too. You may need to add more butter. The noodles will become one piece, which can be cut to serve.

DEUTSCHER NOODLE RING

You can have this for "fancy," trimming it up as much as you like.

1 cup noodles	**Salt and pepper to taste**
3 tablespoons flour	**1¹/₂ cups milk**
¹/₄ or ¹/₂ pound cheese	**2 eggs, well beaten**

Boil the noodles in salted water and cook till tender. Drain and put into a well-greased ring mould. Melt the butter, add the flour and blend. Stir in the milk and stir constantly until the sauce thickens. Add the cheese, cut in cubes. Reserve half the sauce to use later. To the remaining sauce add the well-beaten eggs and mix well. Pour the sauce over the noodles, set the mould in a pan of hot water and bake in a 350-degree oven for about 45 minutes. Unmould on a large platter, fill the centre with vegetables, meat or seafood, then pour the remaining hot cheese sauce over the noodle ring.

SCHNITZEL OIYAKUCHA (Ham and Bacon Omelette)

A Mennonite omelette—very tasty.

¹/₄ pound bacon, cut in pieces	**4 eggs, beaten slightly**
¹/₄ pound chopped ham	**4 tablespoons milk or cream**
4 onions, sliced	**Salt and pepper**

Fry the bacon until crisp; remove it from the pan and fry the ham in the bacon drippings until tender. Remove the ham and add it to the bacon. Fry the onions in some of the bacon drippings until soft and brown. Return the bacon and ham to the pan and mix with the onion. Beat the eggs and milk and seasonings together and pour them over the mixture in the pan. Cook slowly for 3 minutes. Serve on toast. With a salad or sliced tomatoes.

POTATO PANCAKES

To make these delicious, wonderful things as they should be made, you must have a wife, a maid or a truly loving mother who will stand over the kitchen stove and fry them while you eat them as they come out of the frying pan, crisp, sizzling, and golden, with lacy brown edges. In our family potato pancakes are the whole meal; we don't want anything else after we've each eaten at least a dozen, drowned in maple syrup.

5 or 6 medium-sized potatoes	**1 teaspoon salt**
3 eggs	**¹/₄ cup milk**
5 or 6 tablespoons flour	**Fat for frying**

You must grate the peeled raw potatoes on the coarse side of one of those old-fashioned tin graters with rough holes; don't think you'll make it easy by using a shredder, food chopper, or grinder; they are too coarse, making the potatoes sloppy and starchy—I've tried all three and they don't work. You must grate the potatoes, always remembering as your arm becomes limp, that nothing in this world tastes much better. (Of course if you have a blender, you have heaven on earth.)

You must work quickly: don't let the potatoes stand when you've grated them or they'll turn rosy, then black, the starch will settle and you'll have an unusable mess. Stir up the grated potatoes, break the eggs into them, add the salt, flour, and milk.

Put 3 or 4 tablespoons of lard or vegetable shortening into a large frying pan; let the fat become hot, then drop small ladlefuls of the rather runny batter into it, spreading fairly thin in 4- or 5-inch rounds. Let them fry quickly—watch them every second; when the centre looks dry and the bottom is golden, turn them over and brown the other side. Flip them onto the plate of each eager eater who will be hovering round to devour them smothered in maple syrup. (My mother's German cleaning woman prefers hers with apple sauce, my neighbour has them with sausages—we think those are desecrations.) DON'T, please don't pile them up and keep them hot or they'll become limp and grey as an unbleached damp dish cloth.

ELDERBERRY BLOSSOM PANCAKES

This is a rare delicacy that can be had only during the brief days when the elderberry bushes are blooming—late in June or the first week in July.

Kitchener-Waterloo pancake enthusiasts spot in advance the wild elderberry bushes that grow along the country roadsides and, early in the morning while they are fresh, pick the clusters of blossoms, one for each anticipated pancake. They hurry to the nearest picnic spot, make a fire, mix up a batch of pancake batter in a bowl, dip a cluster of blossoms, head first, into the batter and put it gently into hot shortening in a frying pan. While the pancake is cooking, the stem and veins are carefully snipped off with scissors, the pancake is turned and fried to a golden brown on the other side and eaten with maple syrup, bacon and coffee. They have a nutty, almost meat-like flavour that is unusual and delicious.

BUTTERMILK PANCAKES

Good on their own—with syrup, elderberry blossoms, or with any berries you'd like to try added to the batter.

2 cups flour	1 egg, well beaten
1 teaspoon baking soda	2 cupfuls buttermilk or
1/2 teaspoon salt	sour milk
1 tablespoon sugar	1 1/2 tablespoons melted
	shortening

Into the sifted dry ingredients add the egg beaten into the milk, then the melted shortening. (If you must use sweet milk, substitute

3 teaspoons of baking powder for the soda, and sweet milk for the sour.) Melt and heat some fat in a frying pan and ladle the batter into it in thin 4- or 5-inch rounds. Let fry till golden, flip, and brown on the other side. Or you might fry them on an electric grill without fat.

MENNONITE EGG TOAST

This is easier to make than pancakes, wonderful in an emergency or when you're alone and need nourishment that you can also enjoy. You can double, triple or quintuple the recipe if your arithmetic is up to it.

1 beaten egg	**2 or 3 slices of bread**
²/₃ cup milk	**Butter**
Pinch of salt	

Beat the egg, add the milk and salt and beat till they're blended. Soak the bread in the mixture, one piece at a time. Melt 2 teaspoons of butter in a frying pan and carefully slide the soaked bread into it. Fry, not too quickly, till it's brown on both sides and the centre is soft and set. You can use this with bacon, catsup, relish, cheese, cold meat; some people sprinkle it with sugar and cinnamon, others spread it with jelly or jam; I pour lots of corn or maple syrup over mine.

OIYA BROTE (Bread Omelette)

Egg bread or bread omelette that will help cover your bones.

¹/₂ loaf of day old bread	**3 eggs, beaten light**
¹/₂ cup butter (see what	**¹/₂ cup milk**
I mean?)	**Salt and pepper**

Cut the bread into cubes and brown them in the butter in a frying pan. Beat the eggs, add milk and seasonings to taste; pour them over the bread in the pan and fry until brown. Serve with a sauce or a salad.

FRENCH TOAST SANDWICHES

These hot sandwiches are ideal to serve at a luncheon with a green salad or sliced tomatoes. The sandwiches can be made ahead of time with any fillings you like: grated cheddar, chopped ham, chopped chicken, tuna, chopped egg. You might use leftover sandwiches.

1¹/₂ cups of sandwich filling	**3 tablespoons mayonnaise**
6 slices of bacon cut into bits	**12 slices of bread, spread with butter**
1 teaspoon grated onion (optional)	**2 eggs**
³/₄ teaspoon dry mustard	**Salt and pepper**
3 teaspoons cut-up parsley or celery	**1 cup milk**

Fry bacon bits until crisp, then drain on absorbent paper. With your sandwich filling blend the onion, mustard, parsley, mayonnaise and the bacon bits. Spread one side of the buttered bread thickly with the mixture and top with matching slice of bread— in other words, make a sandwich. Beat the eggs in a broad, shallow dish; mix in the salt, pepper and milk. Dip the sandwiches in the mixture, first on one side, then the other, till they have absorbed some of the milk. Fry them in a little melted butter until golden brown on both sides. Serve hot.

PAHNHAAS

Pahnhaas means "pan rabbit", though there is no rabbit in it. This is a popular old-timer. Mother eats hers with maple syrup poured over it but Bevvy serves it with relish or a salad.

2 cups cornmeal	**1 teaspoon salt**
4 to 6 cups boiling water (enough to make a stiff porridge with the cornmeal)	**A piece of liverwurst**

Mother buys liver sausage, eats what she wants of it and uses the rest for Pahnhaas—at least two inches of sausage with 2 cupfuls of cornmeal. It can be made with ground meat or head cheese as well.

Mother boils the cornmeal, water and salt in a big kettle because it spurts up when it's boiling and she doesn't want it to spatter her stove. She adds the liver sausage which melts as it is stirred into the porridge and keeps stirring till the mixture is thick enough to drop off the spoon in a lump and she can hardly stir it any more. She then presses it into a greased loaf pan and lets it cool. Next day she'll slice it ¹/₃ of an inch thick and fry it in shortening till it's crisp and deliciously brown on both sides.

FRIED CORNMEAL MUSH

Bevvy often makes cornmeal porridge in exactly the same way as Pahnhaas but without the meat; she fries and serves it with maple syrup or apple butter, not because it is economical but because it is so good.

FRIED OATMEAL PORRIDGE

Thick oatmeal porridge pressed into a loaf pan to set, then cut into pancake-thin slices and fried is another Mennonite favourite. "Till you've had it served with lots of fresh maple syrup," Bevvy says, "you don't know what a real treat you have missed."

Baking with Yeast

I haven't bought a loaf of bread for nine years. Ever since a librarian came to a pot-luck supper at my cottage, brought a loaf of home-baked bread and gave me the recipe for it, I've been making my own. My first loaves were heavy and soggy—I admit now—but I thought they were marvellous and kept inflicting them on all my relations till I learned better as I watched Bevvy Martin make featherlight bread that she said would stick to the ribs of her family while they worked in the barn and the fields. "If they eat store-bread," she says, "they're hungry again before they've milked more than one cow."

It wonders Bevvy—and me—what the commercial bakers put— or don't put—into their bread to produce such anaemic, sponge-rubber slices, while a delicious, gutsy loaf of bread can be made with nothing more than flour, yeast, water, and a modicum of salt, sugar and shortening.

Making bread is so easy. Though the whole process takes several hours because of the rising and baking, the actual business of mixing and kneading can be done in about 20 minutes.

"But you must have the knack," people say.

I think you need only an eager, experimental approach and the willingness to endure a few failures. What can you lose? A packet of yeast and two pounds of flour: with Canada producing millions of bushels a year that seems no great loss. Besides, you need not have a failure. People who bake bread develop a carefree, happy confidence.

Bread-making is a grand thing to do. Kneading is a kind of revelling: it makes one feel like a primitive, pioneer woman— unstarvable, self-sustaining and joyful. Bevvy sings happy hymns as she works with her yeast dough in the smooth old pine bread-trough her great grandmother brought in a Conestoga wagon to Waterloo County. My friend Clara May Ingraham in Neil's Harbour, Cape Breton, can't read or write but for fifty years she has been making great batches of moist, golden "buns o' bread" for her fisherman husband, thirteen children and boarders; and always her face has a special glow on her bread-making days. My own few shrinking loaves are nothing to boast of, but I like them, and I am brazenly proud of the tender, crusty little rolls my guests apologize for eating by the dozen.

Do I seem to be trying to talk you into making your own bread? I hope you don't mind. I simply enjoy making and eating it so much myself that I'd like everyone else to have the same pleasure. If, then, you can hardly wait to get started, I assure you again: you are ready for one of the great satisfactions of a lifetime. Good luck.

FINDING A WARM PLACE TO LET BREAD DOUGH RISE

The ideal rising temperature for bread dough is between 80 and 90 degrees Fahrenheit; if it is much cooler the rising is sluggish, if very much hotter the yeast might burn itself out. If the thermostat in your home is set at 80 you can put your bowl of dough anywhere. If your temperature is normal, a warm spot or high shelf in your kitchen might do, or you could turn on the heat in your oven at its lowest setting for 5 minutes, then turn it *off* and put the dough in. A friend of mine puts hers in the warming oven, set at its lowest. My mother puts her bowl of coffee-cake dough on a board on top of a radiator. I put mine on a sunny window ledge. In winter I put it on a shelf above an electric heating unit.

While visiting at a summer cottage I found a perfect rising-place on a cool day was the seat of my car parked in the sun. And one shivery morning in September I mixed my bread dough at dawn and went back to my warm welcome bed. Like the slap of a frosty wet fish the thought struck me that dough won't rise well in the cold. I got up, brought the covered bowl to my bed and tucked it under the electric blanket. Of course I slept again. Of course the dough rose. Very quickly.

You can see that finding a warm place to let your dough rise is no problem at all.

SOME HELPFUL THINGS TO KNOW ABOUT BAKING BREAD

Dough seems to rise better on a sunny day than on a dull one.

If you want to speed up your bread-making time to about $2^{1}/_{2}$ hours, you can use more yeast: 1 packet of yeast to each cup of liquid, or 1 packet to each 3 cups of flour.

Warm your mixing bowl with hot water before you pour in the lukewarm water to dissolve the yeast.

Instead of plain water in the basic recipe you can use milk, buttermilk, sour milk, fruit juices or potato water. Water gives a crisper crust; milk is more nutritious and makes a browner crust but must be scalded and cooled before using. Potato water will give a coarser, slightly larger loaf. One or two eggs can be used as part of the liquid; they add flavour, colour, and delicacy—they also make bread less elastic, and drier.

You may find that a stated amount of flour or liquid in a recipe seems exactly right at one time, but not at another; this is because the absorptive quality of the flour varies with temperature and humidity. All you do then is add a bit more flour or liquid until the dough is easy to handle. Better too moist than too dry. And *don't* be scared, you'll soon get the feel of it. Remember you're having fun. No one will spank you if your bread weighs a ton. It probably won't.

If you are interrupted while mixing or kneading your dough, don't worry about it: it will simply be easier to handle when you get back to it. Cover it if you're having a long-winded phone conversation.

If the dough has risen smooth and puffy above the rim of your bowl and you can't carry on with the process just then, don't let it run over and give you a sticky mess to clean up; simply punch the dough down with your hands and let it rise a second, third, or even a fourth time. It will rise more quickly each time.

You can tell if your dough has risen enough by sticking your finger deeply into it (the finger-tip test): if the dent stays, the dough is ready to be shaped into loaves.

If you want a glaze on your bread or buns, brush them before and just after baking with an egg yolk, white, or whole egg beaten and added to 1 or 2 tablespoons of water. Then too you can sprinkle them with poppy, sesame or celery seed.

If you want a hard crust, put a shallow pan of boiling water on the floor of the oven while baking your bread.

If your bread, richly brown in the oven and smelling like heaven, seems to be baked, take it out and tip it out of the pan, onto a rack; if then you discover that its bottom is pale, or if it does not give a hollow sound when you flick it with your finger, put it back in the pan and into the oven to bake a few minutes longer; no harm is done by the interruption—bread is much more accommodating than cake.

NEIL'S HARBOUR WHITE BREAD (Basic)

I've read dozens of recipes for making bread and I've tried quite a few but I don't like any as well as the one I got from Clara May in Neil's Harbour and have changed to suit my own hurried way. It is so good and so easy—try it some day when you're going to be home for 3 or 4 hours. You'll have 3 loaves or 6 buns o' bread.

Into a large, warmed, pottery bowl (10 inches across and 6 inches deep) pour:

	1 cup lukewarm water
In the water dissolve:	**1 teaspoon white sugar**
Over the water sprinkle:	**2 tablespoons yeast granules (2 packets)**

Let stand while you drink your breakfast coffee—10 minutes; by that time the yeast will have risen to the surface of the water. Stir till it's blended, making sure all the yeast is dissolved.

Into the yeast mixture stir:	**2 cups lukewarm water**
	1/2 cup white sugar
	1 heaping tablespoon salt
	1/2 cup salad oil or melted shortening
Beat, then stir in, 1 cup at a time:	**about 9 cups all-purpose flour**

Mix till it requires muscle (you might add another 1/2 cup of water to work in the last 2 cupfuls of flour); rest, then keep on mixing till the dough hangs together and is easy to handle but floppy and inclined to be moist.

Scrape the dough onto a well-floured surface, sprinkle it with flour and knead it, that is, gather the dough together in your hands then push it firmly away with the heels of your palms. Keep turning the dough, sprinkling on more flour—you might use a whole cupful. Keep kneading for several minutes—longer if you find it good therapy—till the dough seems smooth and elastic, though it might still have a few sticky spots.

Plop the dough back into the bowl, rub over it the dough that has stuck to your hands, and a sprinkling of flour. Loosely cover the bowl with waxed paper, a dish towel, or a piece of dry-cleaner's plastic, then a nice heavy sweater. Put the bowl in a warm, draughtless place and let the dough rise 1 to 2 hours when it should be double its original size, puffed up smoothly over the top of the bowl. Use the finger-tip test (see page 138).

Punch the dough down with your hands to get rid of air bubbles. Divide the dough into 3 or 6 parts; scoop out one part, dredge it with flour and shape it into a loaf or into a round, big, fat bun—as they do in Neil's Harbour. (I prefer the buns o' bread because the loaf can be torn apart to make two small loaves; also, when sliced with the torn part up, a slice fits better into my toaster.) Put the loaf or 2 buns into a thickly greased loaf pan, and do the same with the other portions of dough.

Cover the pans and let the dough rise again in the warm place till it is smooth and round over the tops of the pans—about an hour and slightly more.

Bake in a 400-degree oven for about 20 minutes. The baking smell will be divine. When the loaves are brown, top and bottom, remove them at once from the pans to a rack and let them cool, away from a draft—and from all impatient onlookers who love bread, hot from the oven, with butter melting into it. Oh Boy!

Though this bread is so popular that it won't last long if you make it accessible, you can easily freeze it and keep it.

If you like, you may vary each loaf that you make, or use some of the dough to make buns.

From this Basic Neil's Harbour Bread recipe you can make many interesting and delicious variations.

VARIATIONS:

RAISIN BREAD

Everyone loves raisin bread.

If you want three loaves of raisin bread you have simply to add a pound or so of raisins to the bread dough when you are mixing in the flour. If you want only one or two loaves you can add the raisins after the dough has risen and you've divided it: knead in a cupful of raisins per loaf, then put your loaf into the greased pan to rise.

FRUIT LOAF

Delicious and fancy.

Add 1 or 2 cups of mixed candied fruit, chopped fine, 1 or 2 cups raisins, 1 cup chopped nuts to the basic dough; or knead 1/3 of the amount into individual loaves. Glaze the top.

CHEESE BREAD

Need I exclaim? You know how good cheese bread is.

Mix 2 or 3 cupfuls of shredded, sharp cheddar or chunks of cheese into the basic bread dough, or knead 1 cupful into each loaf.

ONION BREAD

So good with salads. Or meats. Or cheese. Or anything.

Mix 2 or 3 cupfuls of minced onion, or slightly sautéed sliced onions, or 1 or 2 packages of onion soup-mix into the basic dough, or knead one-third of the amounts into each loaf. (If you use the soup mix omit the salt in the recipe.)

HERB BREAD

Wrap this in foil and serve hot, with or without garlic butter.

To basic dough add 1 teaspoon each of savory and marjoram, 1/2 teaspoon each of thyme or sage, basil, oregano, dill seed, celery seed, and 1 tablespoon of fresh cut-up parsley. OR you might like to try one or two different herbs in each of the 6 buns o' bread.

SPICE BREAD

Try it toasted with apple butter, honey or jam.

Add 1 teaspoon each of cinnamon, cloves, and 1/2 teaspoon nutmeg or ginger when you mix your flour.
Or knead spices into individual loaves.

CINNAMON ROLL

Lovely for afternoon tea—or any time.

Roll the dough for 1 loaf an inch thick and about 6 by 9 inches. Spread melted butter over the dough; then sprinkle it generously with white or brown sugar and cinnamon—raisins and chopped nuts too if you like. Roll it as you would a jelly roll and put it into a well-greased bread pan to rise. Bake at 400 degrees for about 30 minutes.

FRUIT ROLL

This is a beauty.

Roll the dough for 1 loaf an inch thick and about 6 by 9. Spread melted butter over the dough; then spread chopped candied fruits —or fresh fruits or jam over it. Roll it as you would a jelly roll, seal it carefully round the edges and put it into a well-greased pan to rise until doubled. Bake at 400 degrees for about 30 minutes, till done.

CHEESE ROLL

Quite special.

Roll the dough for 1 loaf an inch thick, about 6 by 9, dot it with chunks of cheddar or spread 1 cup of grated cheese over it. You might like to sprinkle on it celery seed or any pet flavour you may have (parsley is nice too). Roll it up like a jelly roll and fit it into a well-greased loaf pan to rise. Bake at 400 degrees for ¹/₂ an hour.

ONION ROLL

Do the same as you did with the Cheese Roll, using 1 cup of sautéed, sliced onions or a combination of onions and cheese, or onions sprinkled with celery salt or sage.

These *variations* require substitutions in the Neil's Harbour recipe.

BUTTERMILK BREAD

My absolute favourite. Whenever I have buttermilk, or sour milk that is fairly far advanced, I use it to make this tantalizingly cheesey bread; when it is toasted I savour every buttery mouthful.

To achieve this delight I merely substitute buttermilk or sour milk for the 2 cups of water in the Neil's Harbour Bread recipe; if I don't have 2 cupfuls of milk I use what I have with water to make up the difference, first scalding the milk, then adding the sugar, salt and shortening and letting it cool to lukewarm.

TOMATO-CELERY BREAD

If you want to mystify people, try this. It's nice for snacks.

In the Neil's Harbour Bread recipe (or half of it) substitute warm tomato juice for the water and add 1 or 2 tablespoons of celery seed. Sprinkle each loaf with seed before baking, making the seeds stick by brushing the top of the loaf with slightly beaten egg.

ORANGE RAISIN BREAD

An easy way to make something special.

Use warm orange juice instead of water in the Neil's Harbour recipe (or half of it). Add 1 or 2 tablespoons of grated orange rind and 1 or 2 cupfuls of raisins. 1/2 or 1 cupful of nuts too, if you want it to be even better.

DARK BREADS

By substituting darker flours for the all-purpose white flour in the Neil's Harbour basic white bread recipe you can experiment blithely and might achieve miracles. But there are a few things you should know before you start down that floury path.

1. Dark breads take longer to rise than white breads; where all-white might take 1 1/2 hours, the dark might take 2 hours or more; to tell when it has risen enough use the finger-tip test (see page 138).

2. Dark breads don't double in bulk; the finished loaves will be smaller, more compact; you might want to use smaller loaf pans.

3. Whole-wheat flour is the only one that can be substituted completely for white flour. All other flours should be combined with at least an equal quantity of all-purpose or whole-wheat flour, alternating them in the mixing.

4. You might substitute brown sugar for white in the basic recipe, and a half-cup of molasses as part of your liquid.

WHOLE WHEAT BREAD

Supposed to be less caloric and more nutritious than white bread. In Neil's Harbour recipe use whole wheat flour instead of all-purpose. That's all.

GRAHAM FLOUR BREAD

Use half graham and half all-purpose flour in Neil's Harbour basic white bread recipe. Into individual loaves you might like to knead 1 cup chopped mixed candied fruits, or pitted, chopped dates and 1 cup chopped nuts.

OATMEAL BREAD

One time in Edinburgh I bought a loaf of oatmeal bread, hot from the oven. I had an English friend with me and we ate the whole loaf before it was cold. I've never been able to make a loaf that tasted as good—though this is a fair attempt.

2 cups rolled oats (I prefer the coarse)	1/2 cup lukewarm water
	1 teaspoon sugar
2 cups boiling water	2 packets of yeast
1/2 cup molasses	chopped nuts (optional)
1/2 cup brown sugar	raisins (optional)
1 tablespoon salt	About 6 cups all-purpose
1/2 cup shortening	flour

Pour the boiling water over the rolled oats, stir, add the molasses, salt, brown sugar and shortening. Let stand till lukewarm, then add yeast dissolved in lukewarm water with white sugar. Proceed as in Neil's Harbour bread. Nuts or raisins (or both) may be added with the flour or kneaded into individual loaves. Bake at 400 degrees for about 35 minutes.

RYE BREAD

Use half rye and half all-purpose flour in basic white bread recipe, and use 1/2 cup molasses as part of the liquid.

ROLLS AND BUNS

Made with the same basic bread dough, they take less time to rise and to bake and seem a little more special. One batch of dough makes two loaves and one pan of buns; sometimes I make the whole batch into rolls, varying their shapes and their flavours.

PAN ROLLS

Easiest to make; soft, fluffy, with only a top and bottom crust.
After the dough has risen sufficiently in the bowl grease a square cake pan with lots of shortening and in it, side by side, place 16 or 25 little balls of dough about the size of golf or ping-pong balls. To get them round, dredge a piece of dough with flour, pull it into a long sausage shape, then break or cut off bits into flour; push a piece of dough through the circle made with a thumb and index finger, smoothing roundly into a ball. When the pan is filled put it away under wraps again till the dough has risen to double its size, nice and puffy. Pop the pan into a 425-degree oven for 10 to 15 minutes till the buns are that beautiful colour, top and

bottom. Cool them on a rack as soon as they come from the oven; serve hot or reheated. If you're going to pass them to people away from the table you might let butter melt onto their tops and you won't need to butter their tender sides when you pull them apart.

HAMBURGER AND HOT-DOG BUNS

These will make hot dogs and hamburgers sing. And they freeze better than those crumby store buns.

Roll the risen dough about 1/2 an inch thick; for the hamburger buns take a fairly large-rimmed drinking glass and with it cut the dough into rounds; for the hot-dog buns cut the rolled dough into strips, cut the strips into hot-dog lengths; taper at the ends. Place the buns, not quite touching, on greased cookie sheets. Cover and let rise. Bake in a 425-degree oven from 10 to 15 minutes. Cool on a rack. When people eat these they'll probably ask if you'll bake some for their next party because hamburgers and hot dogs never tasted so good.

CHELSEA BUNS

Bevvy calls these **STICKY BUNS**.

One day at brunch at my cottage, a man guest ate 15 of my Chelseas; I was flattered—but his wife was so embarrassed that she left the table.

For a 9-inch square cake pan of buns use 1/3 of the Neil's Harbour White Bread recipe. On your floured kitchen counter roll out the once-risen dough to about 1/3-inch thickness, about 7 inches wide and as long as it stretches to make the right width and thickness. Melt half a cup of butter in the cake pan (I prefer a pyrex one), spread 2/3 of the butter over the dough. Sprinkle about 1 cupful of brown sugar over the dough and 1/2 a cupful over the melted butter in the pan. Sprinkle the dough with cinnamon and a cupful of raisins. Bits of finely chopped orange rind and half a cup of nuts are nice too. Now roll up the dough as for a long, wobbly, jelly roll; cut inch-wide slices and place them cut-side up in the pan. You might have more than enough. Let the buns rise till they're double their original size; bake them in a 400-degree oven for about 20 minutes—watch them, they're precious. When they're a luscious, sticky, shiny, butterscotch brown take them out and carefully tip them onto a rack by putting the rack over **the pan** and then turning it upside down over waxed paper; scrape up all the good taffy and dot it over any bare spots on the buns. Eat the buns while they're lukewarm.

One afternoon my mother and three of her girl friends ate twenty-three after a game of bridge. Now you'll be thinking for sure I'm a bun-counter; I guess I am, but only because it pleases me when people enjoy them that much.

VARIATIONS

Chelsea buns can be made in individual muffin tins—if you don't mind washing dishes.

Or: After rolling the dough and spreading soft butter over it, cover it with any kind of jam, or currants, dates, candied peel, honey, peanut butter, ground baked ham, cheese, onions, herbs, chocolate bits, walnuts, chili sauce or fruit relish, catsup, barbecue sauce—whatever you like; roll it up like a jelly roll, cut in inch-thick pieces and place them touching on a greased pan or in muffin tins. Let rise and bake at 400 degrees for about 15 minutes.

VARIATIONS FOR ROLLS

Rolls can be made of any of the dough that is used for bread, white or dark. You can experiment with various trimmings. One morning I made 10 different kinds of buns simply by using a teaspoon of butter and a teaspoon of jam, honey, coconut and sugar, bacon bits, relish, and so on, in the bottom of muffin tins with a blob of dough on top. You should have seen how quickly they disappeared when a family of relatives came—everyone wanted to taste one bun of each kind, then several of their favourites.

ANOTHER VARIATION

After the dough has risen in the bowl divide it into as many parts as you have fancies to experiment with. Mix or knead into the dough, shape as you please, let rise again and bake at 400 degrees for about 15 minutes.

Cinnamon, cocoa mixed with sugar, nuts, raisins or currants, dates and walnuts, cheese, crumbled crisp bacon, chopped fruit, crushed pineapple, chopped peel, candied ginger, cranberries: what else have you?

VARIATIONS IN SHAPE

CLOVER LEAF—put 3 small balls of dough together in greased muffin tins.

TWIN ROLLS—put 2 small balls of dough together in greased muffin tins.

CRESCENT ROLLS—roll the dough about ¼ inch thick, cut in pie-shaped pieces; roll each piece from the wide outside edge toward the point. Curve slightly to make the crescent. You can roll jam into it if you like.

POCKET-BOOK ROLLS—cut out rounds of dough, butter one side and fold the other side over.

That's all I can think of but don't let me limit you—you probably have dozens of ideas I've never thought of; I have a tendency to stick to a good thing—my dear old basic recipe.

MRS. BRUBACHER'S CHEESE LOAF

I bought a loaf of this at the Kitchener Market and Mrs. Brubacher gave me her recipe. It is light and cheesey and irresistible — especially if it is warm or toasted.

In a saucepan mix and boil for 1 minute:
1³/₄ cups water
2 teaspoons salt
¹/₂ cup cornmeal

Remove from heat, add and stir in:
2 tablespoons butter
¹/₂ cup molasses

Into a large bowl pour: **¹/₂ cup lukewarm water**
In the water dissolve: **1 teaspoon white sugar**
Over water sprinkle: **1 tablespoon yeast granules (1 package)**

Let stand 10 minutes until yeast dissolves, then stir till yeast is blended.
To yeast mixture add cornmeal mixture (when it has cooled to lukewarm).

One cupful at a time, add: **5 cups all-purpose flour**

Stir until dough is right for kneading, adding more flour if necessary. Knead on surface covered with corn meal. Put the dough back into the bowl and let rise till double its bulk.

Cut into ¼-inch pieces: **³/₄ pound cheddar**

Take the risen dough from the bowl and knead the cheese into it a bit at a time till all the cheese has been added. Shape into loaves, put into 2 greased loaf pans and let rise again till the dough is nicely rounded over the top of the pans. Bake at 350 degrees for about 1/2 an hour—or until the loaves are crusty and brown, top and bottom.

CORNMEAL BREAD

This has a gritty texture and a corny, bacon flavour that complements a green salad; it is especially wonderful when toasted.

Into a large bowl pour:	**1/2 cup lukewarm water**
In the water dissolve:	**1 teaspoon white sugar**
Over water sprinkle:	**1 tablespoon yeast granules (1 package)**

Let stand 10 minutes until yeast dissolves, then stir till yeast is blended.

To yeast mixture add:	**2 tablespoons melted bacon fat (or butter)**
	1/2 cup lukewarm milk
	2 tablespoons honey (or sugar)
	2 teaspoons salt
Blend; then stir in:	**2 cups all-purpose flour**
Beat until smooth, add:	**1/2 cup cornmeal**

Add enough additional flour to make a dough stiff enough to knead. Knead until smooth then let rise in the bowl in a warm place until doubled. Shape into a loaf and put it into a greased loaf pan. Cover and let rise again until doubled. Bake in a 375-degree oven for about 30 minutes till it is crusty and brown.

LIBRARIAN'S BREAD

This is the recipe, exactly as it was given to me, with which I started baking bread. No wonder it was soggy and didn't rise very high. But I thought it had a wonderful flavour.

Mix:

4 cups whole wheat flour	**1 cake yeast dissolved in**
4 cups white flour	**1/4 cup water**
1/2 cup white or brown sugar	**1 quart of lukewarm water**
1 tablespoon salt	**or less (I'd say now at**
	least 11/2 cups less)

Cover with wax paper and towel for 1½ to 2 hours. Stir it down, put it into greased pans and let rise again. Bake at 350 degrees for 45 to 50 minutes.

Try it and see what I mean.

STONE-MILLED OR CRACKED-WHEAT BREAD

This crunchy, moist, chewy bread will make you a compulsive eater.

3 cups boiling water	½ cup lukewarm water
2 cups cracked wheat	1 teaspoon white sugar
½ cup shortening	2 packets yeast
1 tablespoon salt	5 or 6 cups all-purpose flour
½ cup brown sugar	

Pour the boiling water over the cracked wheat. Add the shortening, brown sugar and salt. Let cool to lukewarm then stir in the yeast which has been dissolved in the ½ cup lukewarm water with the white sugar. Stir in the flour one cup at a time till you can handle the dough—it should be quite moist. Turn out on a well-floured board and knead until smooth—it will be too soft to be as elastic as Basic White Bread. Return to the bowl and let rise in a warm place till it has almost doubled in bulk. Punch down and shape into loaves; place in greased pans and let rise until the dough reaches the tops of the pans. Bake in a 400-degree oven for about 45 minutes. Cool on a rack.

PORRIDGE BREAD

This is a good one to try when you have porridge left over on a winter morning.

3 cups thick oatmeal porridge	¼ teaspoon soda
2 cups molasses	2 packets of yeast
1 teaspoon salt	½ cup lukewarm coffee
4 teaspoons nutmeg	1 teaspoon sugar
	All-purpose flour

Dissolve the sugar and yeast in the coffee. Mix all the other ingredients, then stir in the yeast mixture. Add enough all-purpose flour to make a dough that is easy to handle. Knead the dough and let it rise till doubled in bulk. Shape into individual loaves, let rise again, then bake in a 400-degree oven for about 30 or 40 minutes. Cool on a rack. Serve warm with plenty of butter.

MOTHER'S COFFEE CAKE

People who've eaten them say my mother makes the best coffee cakes they've ever tasted; they are light, moist and covered with a baked-on crusty brown-sugar topping that sometimes forms deep little wells of candy. Over the years Mother must have given away hundreds of coffee cakes to friends and relations, while she herself has enjoyed all she kept to the last stale crumb, dunked in coffee.

In:	**1/2 cup lukewarm water**
Dissolve:	**1 teaspoon white sugar**
Over the mixture sprinkle:	**1 package of yeast (1 table-**
Let stand 10 minutes.	**spoon)**
In a double boiler scald:	**1 cup milk**
In a mixing bowl put:	**1/3 cup sugar**
	1 teaspoon salt
	2 eggs, well beaten

Pour scalding milk into mixture and stir until sugar is dissolved.

Cool to lukewarm, then add:	**1 cup lukewarm water and the yeast mixture**
Sift and add:	**3 cups all-purpose flour**
Beat mixture till smooth.	
One at a time, keep adding:	**3 1/2 cups more flour, mixing well to make a soft dough**

Because Mother doesn't like getting her hands sticky with dough, she keeps stirring and stirring instead of kneading the dough for a few minutes on a floured board. Mother puts the dough in the mixing bowl on a board or a pile of newspapers on her radiator to keep warm and to rise till the dough has doubled; then she divides it in 4, puts it into greased cake pans, square or round, and lets the dough rise again till doubled.

Carefully then, before baking, she puts on the topping: 1/4 cup melted butter, 1 cup brown sugar and 1 tablespoon cornstarch, blended together over very low heat, thinning it if necessary with a bit of cream. While this mixture is warm, she spreads it gently over the puffy tops of the coffeecakes, sprinkles a little brown sugar over top, then she spreads over that some "crumbs" made of 2 tablespoons soft butter, about 3/4 cup brown sugar and 1/2 cup flour. She sprinkles that with cinnamon then puts the cakes in the oven at 375 degrees for about ¹/₂ an hour (till they are done), watching them towards the last.

KUCHA (Basic Dough)

From this fine, sweet, almost cake-like yeast dough, rolled out fairly thin, can be made a variety of delicious desserts, coffee cakes, butter horns, turnovers, crescent rolls, schnecken, kipfel, or nut rolls. Bevvy says it's appreciated at weddings, or funerals, or whenever a lot of folks come together to eat.

2 cups scalded milk	1 packet of yeast (2 if you're
¹/₂ cup butter or margarine	in a hurry)
³/₄ cup sugar	About 6 cups all-purpose
2 teaspoons salt	flour
Yolks of 2 eggs—or 1 whole	Grated rind of ¹/₂ a lemon
egg	(optional)

Sprinkle the yeast granules over ¹/₂ cup of the scalded milk cooled to lukewarm; let stand about 10 minutes then stir till dissolved. To the rest of the scalded milk add the butter, sugar, salt and the lemon rind. When cooled to lukewarm, add the beaten egg yolks; stir in the yeast mixture and enough flour to make the dough easy to handle—it is better to put the dough into the fridge to stiffen than to put in too much flour. Knead the dough until smooth and elastic. Cover and let it rise in a warm place until doubled in bulk—it will take at least 2 hours.

Now is the time to divide the dough for whatever you want to make of it: 1 dessert fruit kuchen and 2 dozen kipfel, or a coffee cake and a batch of butter horns—whatever you fancy; the whole batch of dough would make enough fruit kuchen for 35 servings—or it would make 40 rolls. OR you could make 1 or 2 things and put the rest of the dough in a tightly covered bowl (that would allow some rising) into the fridge for 24 hours; then shape it as you please, let rise and bake.

PLAIN KAFFEE KUCHA

After the Kucha dough has risen in the bowl spread some of it an inch thick in a shallow buttered pan or pie plate. Cover and let rise again. Melt enough butter to spread over the dough, sprinkle it with sugar, cinnamon, chopped nuts or coconut; or crumbs made of ¹/₄ cup butter, ¹/₂ cup brown sugar and ¹/₄ cup flour, with a sprinkling of cinnamon and dabs of cream. Bake in a 400-degree oven for about 15 minutes.

FRUIT KUCHA

These refreshing, not-too-rich dessert squares of fruit-covered Kucha have as many variations as there are varieties of fruit.

After the Kucha dough has risen in the bowl, roll some of it as thin as you can and fit it into a well-greased flat pan or cookie sheet, 12 by 12, or thereabouts—the size doesn't matter. In parallel rows on top of the dough lay segments or halves of apples, peaches, plums, cooked prunes, apricots; or spread fairly generously over the dough pitted cherries, blueberries, strawberries, raspberries, seedless grapes—or whatever. Beat an egg slightly, add a tablespoon of cream or rich milk, and enough white sugar to make a thick, runny mixture that you can dribble over and around the fruit without having it run over the edges of the dough. Bake the Kucha in a 425 oven for 25 to 30 minutes; watch it till the crust is slightly brown on the bottom and the fruit is softish.

Now: remember the egg whites you had left from the Kucha dough? Beat them stiff, add 4 or 5 tablespoons of sugar and spread the meringue over the fruit. Return to the oven long enough to slightly gild the meringue. Cut into squares, 4 by 4, if you want to serve them on a plate with a fork; or cut them smaller if they are firm enough to be held in your hand. Either way they'll be lovely good eating.

SCHNECKA (SNAILS)

When Kucha dough has risen, roll some of it to 1/4 inch thickness in an oblong 9 by 18, or thereabouts. Spread with softened butter, sprinkle with sugar, cinnamon, and raisins or firm, fresh berries. Roll like a jelly roll, cut into inch-pieces and brush sides with melted butter. Place side by side in a well-buttered pan; brush tops with butter, sprinkle with sugar and cinnamon and let rise until light. Bake at 375 degrees for about 25 minutes. Watch them. Cool on a rack.

OR, if you want more bother and even more commendable results, try baking the Schnecka in muffin tins with a teaspoon each of butter, honey or corn syrup, and a tablespoon of brown sugar with several neatly arranged nuts in the bottom of each section of the muffin tins. Let the Schnecka rise till more than double in bulk, then bake in a 375-degree oven for about 25 minutes till nicely browned. Let cool for a moment, then remove Schnecka carefully.

TURNOVERS

After Kucha dough has risen roll some of it ¼ inch thick, cut it into 4-inch squares and put a tablespoon of jam or pie filling in the centre of each square. Fold one corner over to the opposite corner and pinch the edges tightly together. Place on a greased sheet, let rise again, then bake in a 400-degree oven until nicely browned.

KIPFEL

After Kucha dough has risen roll some of it ¼-inch thick, cut into 3-inch squares and put a tablespoon of jam or pie filling in the centre of each square. Pinch together the 4 corners of the square over the filling, wetting the edges and pinching them tightly to keep juices from running out. Place on a greased baking sheet, let rise again and bake in a 400-degree oven until faintly browned.

CRESCENT ROLLS

After Kucha dough has risen roll some of it into 9-inch rounds ¼ inch thick. Spread with softened butter then cut the round into 4 pie-shaped sections. Roll each section from the wide end to the opposite point. Curve to crescent shape, put on a greased pan, let rise again till puffy—about 2 hours. Bake at 400 degrees for about 15 minutes.

BUTTER HORNS

After the Kucha dough has risen roll some of it into 9-inch rounds ¼ inch thick (or roll all of it if you want about 40 butter horns). Spread with softened butter, then with a jam or nut filling (made by creaming 4 tablespoons butter with ⅔ cup sugar and ⅔ cup finely ground, blanched almonds or ground hazelnuts; add just enough slightly beaten egg to make a spreadable paste). Cut the 9-inch Kucha round in 4 pie-shaped wedges. Roll each section from the wide end to the opposite point. Curve to crescent shape. Put on a greased tin, let rise again till puffy—about 2 hours. Bake at 375 degrees about 20 minutes. You can ice these with a plain butter icing (see Index, Icings) if you want them fancy.

FASTNACHTS

The Lutherans call these Fastnachts and are supposed to eat them on Shrove Tuesday; the Mennonites call them Raised Doughnuts and will eat them any time. They're wonderful, warm or cold, with maple syrup, or sprinkled with sugar.

1 packet of yeast dissolved in	1 cup sugar
1/2 cup warm water with	1 cup water that the potatoes were boiled in (lukewarm)
1 teaspoon sugar	
1 cup hot, mashed potatoes	1 cup all-purpose flour

Mix potatoes, sugar, potato water and flour; add yeast dissolved in water. Let rise in a warm place for several hours.

Then add:

1 cup sugar	3 eggs beaten
1 cup lukewarm water or milk	1 teaspoon salt
3/4 cup melted butter	About 5 cups sifted flour for stiff dough

Mix all together, cover and let rise in a warm place for an hour or two—till the dough has doubled in size. Knead lightly, adding more flour to make a stiff dough. Now, according to all my instruction, you're supposed to let the dough rise again for another hour or two, but that means you'd be fussing with these things all day; figure it out: this would be its third rising, with another to come; I think at this point I'd be reckless and divide the dough in thirds and start rolling it out. What matters if you do have a few larger holes in your fastnachts? Take your choice, rise or roll. I'd try rolling the dough to about 3/4-inch thickness. Fastnachts have a traditional diamond shape; cut them into diamonds with a knife. Another essential is to cut a slit across the top of each fastnacht with a sharp knife. Let the fastnachts rise, covered, in a warm place, till they're springy to the touch; when they're quite fat and puffy, drop them with the raised side down into fat that is hot enough to brown a bread cube—375 degrees. If you don't want that many fried cakes you might try baking some in a hot oven as rolls.

DAMPFNODEL (Steamed Dumplings)

The last time I had supper with Bevvy and Dave, he said, "Did you ever have Dampfnodel yet? That is the best; that is really, really good."

Bevvy told me it is a dessert she makes on the day she bakes bread; she uses some of the bread dough. As soon as it has risen in the bowl to double its size, she works tablespoonfuls of the dough into smooth round balls and lets them rise on a board until they are puffy.

Meanwhile she combines the ingredients for a syrup:

3 cups water	**Butter the size of an egg**
2 cups brown sugar	**1 cup of raisins—sometimes, not always**

When the dumplings have risen to double their size she boils the syrup for 5 minutes then carefully drops in the dumplings, one at a time, covering and cooking slowly for 25 to 30 minutes without lifting the lid.

After trying them myself I can see what Dave means.

Biscuits, Muffins, Quick Breads and Fat Cakes

"We call fat cakes all those things like doughnuts and fritters and fetschpatze that we fry in deep fat," Bevvy tells me. "And oh my, they are good. When we have them it's always for supper, dunked in maple syrup while they're real fresh, maybe even a little bit warm yet, and we all eat so many that we don't want anything else."

Biscuits and muffins too are served warm and eaten with plenty of butter and jam at Bevvy's and my Mother's tables. They both like to experiment with them by adding various fruits, bacon, cheese or whatever strikes their fancy and suits the occasion. If there are ever any left over they can be frozen and freshened again in the oven.

Quick and easy to make are the fruit and nut breads. They don't need any icing, have a rich wonderful flavour, and they'll stay moist for a week. They can be served warm with butter melting into them, or cold and sliced thin with a cup of coffee or tea. They are delicious when toasted and perfect with fruit for dessert. I like to keep one always in the freezing part of my fridge: it can be so easily sliced, buttered and thawed when a welcome visitor drops in.

MRS. MENNO MARTIN'S FET KUCHA (Fat Cakes)

These won a prize at a local baking competition. They have that indescribable, old-fashioned flavour.

1 pint sour cream	Flour to make a soft dough
1 pint sour milk	3 eggs, beaten
2 teaspoons soda	1 teaspoon salt
3/4 teaspoon cream of tartar	

Beat the eggs, blend in the sour cream and milk; stir in the sifted dry ingredients. Roll 3/4-inch thick, cut in strips 1½ by 4 inches with a knife and bake in hot, deep fat. Delicious with maple syrup.

BEVVY'S DOUGHNUTS

Rich and very good.

1 cup sour cream or sour milk	**1 teaspoon cream of tartar**
3 eggs, beaten	**2 teaspoons soda**
¹/₂ teaspoon salt	**Several cups of flour to make a soft dough**

Stir all together in the order given. Roll ³/₄ of an inch thick on a floured board. Drop into hot lard (375 degrees) and bake till brown on both sides. Drain on brown paper. Shake in a bag with powdered sugar, or eat plain with syrup.

FETSCHPATZE (Fat Sparrows)

Called this, Bevvy says, because of the odd shapes they take when the batter is dropped in hot lard. I once ate nine at a sitting.

1 egg, beaten	**1 cup sour cream or sour milk**
A little salt	
Flour to make a stiffish batter	**1 rounded teaspoon of soda**

You simply mix them up and drop tablespoonfuls of the batter into lard or shortening that will brown a bread cube (375 degrees). Let them become just past golden brown all round, drain them on brown paper for a minute or two, then see if you can resist less than nine—dunked in maple syrup.

MOTHER'S POTATO DOUGHNUTS

They have a delicate, different flavour and stay moist for days— not like most doughnuts that are good for only a few hours.

2 cups hot mashed potatoes	**2 tablespoons butter**
2 cups sweet milk	**5 teaspoons baking powder**
2 cups white sugar	**1 teaspoon vanilla**
Flour to make a soft dough —probably 5 cupfuls	

Mix potatoes, sugar, butter, milk and vanilla, then stir in the sifted flour and baking powder. Roll out ³/₄-inch thick, cut into small rounds, fry in hot shortening (375 degrees) until they are golden brown. Drain, then drop into a bag with icing sugar and shake till the doughnuts are coated.

RAISED DOUGHNUTS

When you make bread or Kucha dough take some of the risen dough and roll it into a sheet about ¹/₂-inch thick and cut it into rings or oblongs. Let stand until nearly doubled in size—fat and puffy, then fry in deep, hot fat (375 degrees). Drain on paper and roll in powdered sugar or eat with maple syrup. If you like you can cut a slit in these and put it some jam or jelly. But why bother?

APPLE FRITTERS

When Mother made these we didn't want anything else that would waste our space.

2 or 3 apples	2 tablespoons sugar
1 cup flour	1 beaten egg
1 teaspoon baking powder	1 cup milk
¹/₂ teaspoon salt	

Peel the apples and carefully remove the core without breaking the apple; cut the apple into round slices about ¹/₄-inch thick. Beat the egg well, add the sugar, salt, then the milk alternately with the sifted flour and baking powder. You might need a bit more flour to make a fairly thick batter. Dip the apple slices into the batter, making sure they are well coated on both sides. Fry the rings in deep fat at 375 degrees till the fritters are golden all around. Don't prick them or they'll absorb fat; drain them. You may dust them with sugar and cinnamon or eat them as we did with maple syrup poured over them.

BEVVY'S EPPEL KICHLE (Apple Fritters)

Instead of using the round, carefully cut slices of apple in her fritters, Bevvy chops up her apples—about 1¹/₂ cupfuls—adds them to the batter and stirs them in before dropping spoonfuls of batter into deep hot fat.

PASCHING PUFFA (Peach Fritters or Puffs)

Peach Fritters served with whipped or ice cream make a super dessert.

¹/₂ cup sugar	3 teaspoons baking powder
¹/₃ cup butter	¹/₂ teaspoon salt
2 eggs, well beaten	1¹/₂ cups chopped peaches
1 cup milk	—fresh or canned
¹/₂ teaspoon vanilla	¹/₂ teaspoon lemon juice
2 cups flour	(optional)

Cream the butter and sugar, add the eggs and beat together thoroughly. Sift the dry ingredients together and add alternately with the milk. Fold in the peaches, lemon juice and vanilla. Drop by teaspoonfuls into hot fat (375 degrees) and fry until golden brown. Drain on paper. Serve with whipped or ice cream, or sprinkled with powdered sugar.

FUNNEL CAKES

Bevvy's children always stand near the stove to watch the fun while she makes these.

2 eggs, well beaten	**1 teaspoon baking powder**
3 tablespoons sour cream	**$^1/_2$ teaspoon salt**
Not quite 2 cups milk	**3 cups flour**
$^1/_2$ teaspoon soda	

Measure the sour cream into a cup and fill the cup with milk, then stir the milk into the beaten eggs. Sift the dry ingredients into the egg-milk mixture and beat until smooth. If the batter isn't runny you will have to add more milk. Heat deep fat till it browns a cube of bread, or reaches 375 degrees. Pour the batter into a small pitcher so it will be easier to handle.

Now comes the fun. Put your finger over the spout of a funnel and pour about 3 tablespoons of the batter into the funnel, take off your finger and let the batter run into the hot fat, swirling the funnel around and around so the batter forms a lacy pattern or concentric circles about 3 to 6 inches in diameter. Bevvy says it's best to make the swirls from the centre out. The frying becomes quite an art as you learn to make quick twists and turns of the funnel, covering and uncovering the opening. It's not as hard as it sounds.

Fry them until they are golden brown, drain them on paper towels, and serve hot, sprinkled with powdered sugar.

BANANA FRITTERS

Mother usually made these for company and we had to finish them up before bed-time because the bananas inside them would turn black if kept longer. Happy day!

1 egg, beaten slightly	**1 teaspoon soda**
$^1/_2$ cup white sugar	**Flour to make a stiff dough**
1 pinch of salt	**(try 1$^1/_2$ cups)**
$^1/_2$ cup sour cream	**1 teaspoon maple flavouring**
1 cup buttermilk	

Beat the sugar into the egg, add the salt, maple flavouring, and sour cream; then alternately add the buttermilk and soda sifted with flour to make quite a stiff dough. Cut bananas into ³/₄-inch slices, drop into batter, coat well with batter and drop into hot fat (365 degrees) till nicely browned all around. Drain on paper and dredge with powdered sugar. They're wonderful.

BUTTERMILK COFFEE CAKE

Easy to make, tender—and everyone wants the recipe, Bevvy tells me.

2¹/₄ cups flour
1 teaspoon salt
¹/₂ teaspoon cinnamon
1 cup brown sugar, firmly
   packed
³/₄ cup granulated sugar
³/₄ cup lard
¹/₂ cup walnuts, coarsely
   chopped

1 teaspoon soda
1 teaspoon baking powder
1 teaspoon cinnamon
   (additional)
1 egg, slightly beaten
1 cup buttermilk or sour
   cream

Sift flour with salt and the ¹/₂ teaspoon of cinnamon into a large bowl. Add sugars and shortening and mix until all is well-blended and feathery (in your electric mixer). Take out ³/₄ cup of this mixture for topping and to it add the nuts and the 1 teaspoon of cinnamon; mix and set aside. To the remaining mixture, add soda, baking powder, egg and buttermilk; mix until smooth. Spoon mixture into a greased pan, sprinkle the reserved topping over it and press it down lightly. Bake in a 350-degree oven for about 30 minutes—or until it tests done. Cut into squares and serve warm or cold. It is moist and tender and wonderful (even if it drops in the middle as mine did the first time I tried it).

FLORENCE HONDERICH'S SOUR CREAM COFFEE CAKE

Served warm, this is a treat for breakfast—or any time.

¹/₂ cup butter or margarine
1 cup white sugar
2 eggs, beaten
1 teaspoon vanilla
1 cup sour cream
1 teaspoon soda

1³/₄ cups sifted cake flour
2 teaspoons baking powder
Topping:
¹/₂ cup brown sugar
1 tablespoon cinnamon
¹/₂ cup finely chopped nuts

Blend butter and sugar, add eggs and vanilla; beat well. Combine sour cream and soda (the cream should double in volume but probably won't), add alternately with sifted flour and baking powder to creamed mixture. Spread half the batter in a greased cake pan 9 by 9. Sprinkle with half the topping mixture. Cover with remaining batter and sprinkle the rest of the topping on top. Bake at 350 degrees for 45 minutes. If there's any left after you serve it, it can be wrapped in foil and reheated.

MOTHER'S DATE BREAD

A good keeper.

Beat together till creamy:	1/2 cup white sugar
	1/2 teaspoon salt
	Butter the size of an egg
Combine and add to first mixture:	1 1/2 cups cut-up dates
	1 cup walnuts, chopped
	1 cup boiling water
	1 teaspoon soda
Then add:	1 1/2 cups flour
	1 teaspoon baking powder

Pour into a loaf pan and bake at 375 degrees till it tests done— about 45 minutes. Slice, butter, and serve.

SUSAN MACMAHON'S CURRANT SODA BREAD

This was handed down by my Irish great-grandmother. There's no wonder that it survived. Try it with Irish coffee.

1/4 cup sugar	1/4 cup butter (or margarine)
1 teaspoon salt	1 egg, slightly beaten
4 cups all-purpose flour	1 3/4 cups sour milk
1 teaspoon soda	2 cups currants
3 teaspoons baking powder	1/4 teaspoon nutmeg

Combine all the dry ingredients, including the currants. Add the shortening and work in until crumbly (I let my electric mixer do it—wouldn't Susan have loved that?) Mix the egg with the milk, add to the dry mixture and stir until blended. Turn out on a floured board and knead for a couple of minutes till smooth. Divide the dough in half and form each part into a round loaf;

press each loaf into a greased pie plate. With a sharp knife cut about an inch deep into the tops of the loaves as if you were cutting a pie. Sprinkle sugar on top of the loaves. Bake in a 375-degree oven for about 40 minutes. Butter and eat hot. It stays moist for several days.

MOTHER'S JOHNNY CAKE

This was a supper treat, served hot from the oven, slathered with butter and drenched with maple syrup. (Of course we were just skinny little girls in those days.)

³/₄ cup butter	1¹/₄ cup milk
1 cup sugar	1 cup cornmeal
3 eggs	2 cups flour
Cinnamon	3 teaspoons baking powder

Mix butter and sugar, beat in the beaten eggs, stir in the sifted dry ingredients alternately with the milk. Pour into a greased cake pan, sprinkle with cinnamon and bake in a 350-degree oven for half an hour—or till it tests done.

BEVVY'S BRAN BREAD

"Wonderful easy" to make, moist and delicious.

1 cup brown sugar	2 cups buttermilk or sour
2 cups bran	milk
2 cups flour	1 cup raisins
1 teaspoon salt	¹/₂ cup coarsely chopped
2 teaspoons soda	nuts

Mix sugar and bran with sifted flour, soda and salt. Add milk and stir in raisins and nuts. Pour into a loaf pan 9 by 5 and bake in a 350-degree oven for almost an hour.

MUSTARD HOT BREAD

"Maybe somebody started making gingerbread and put in mustard by mistake," Bevvy told me. Anyway, it's a winner.

¹/₂ cup shortening	1 teaspoon cinnamon
¹/₂ cup sugar	¹/₂ teaspoon ground cloves
1 egg, well beaten	1 teaspoon salt
2¹/₂ cups sifted flour	1 cup molasses
1¹/₂ teaspoon soda	1 cup hot water
1 teaspoon dry mustard	

Cream the shortening and sugar till smooth, then the egg till well blended. Sift the flour, spices, mustard, soda and salt. Combine the hot water and molasses and add to the creamed mixture alternately with the flour mixture. Pour into a well-greased cake pan 9 by 9 and bake in a 350-degree oven for about 35 minutes. Serve while it is still warm in thick buttered slices. Your guests will protest about putting on pounds but they'll all take three or four slices.

GRAHAM FRUIT BREAD

Light, smooth, delicious and easy to mix. Recipe makes 2 loaves.

1 cup all-purpose flour	1/2 cup walnuts, chopped
2 teaspoons baking powder	1 cup buttermilk or sour
1 teaspoon salt	milk
1/2 cup sugar	1 cup sweet milk
2 cups graham flour	1/2 cup molasses
1/2 cup raisins or dates	1 teaspoon soda

Sift the white flour with baking powder, sugar and salt; add and stir in the graham flour, nuts, and raisins or dates. Add milk and stir until the mixture is just blended. Beat the soda into the molasses with a fork until it is foamy, then quickly add to the other mixture and stir until blended—no more. Turn into 2 greased loaf pans and bake in a 350-degree oven for 45 minutes.

BANANA LOAF

There are times when there is a special on bananas at the local supermarket and I can't resist buying one of the fat yellow bundles. All that for thirty-six cents—why not? But I usually find that bananas have a nasty habit of turning brown rather more quickly than I can eat them and I'm happily forced to make this lovely banana loaf.

2 ripe bananas—about 1	2 cups sifted flour
cupful, mashed	2 teaspoons baking powder
1/4 cup shortening	1/2 teaspoon soda
1/2 cup sugar	1 teaspoon salt
2 eggs	1 teaspoon almond
1/2 cup sour milk or	flavouring
buttermilk	

Sift the flour, baking powder, soda and salt. Cream the shortening and sugar, add eggs and mix well; add the mashed bananas and flavouring to the milk and add alternately with the flour mixture to the creamed mixture. When well blended pour into a greased bread pan and bake at 350 degrees for 45 minutes to an hour. Let cool and spread slices with butter.

MOLASSES GRAHAM BREAD

Flavourful and moist and super served hot with butter melting into it—but it's good cold too.

¹/₄ cup sugar	¹/₃ cup shortening—could be
2 cups flour	vegetable oil
1¹/₂ teaspoon soda	2 eggs, beaten
2 teaspoons salt	1³/₄ cups sour milk or
1 teaspoon baking powder	buttermilk
1³/₄ cups graham flour	³/₄ cup molasses

Sift dry ingredients and cut shortening into them. Blend eggs, milk and molasses; pour into dry mixture and stir just enough to blend all together. Pour into 2 greased loaf pans and bake in a 350-degree oven for about 40 minutes. This keeps well—can be frozen and reheated.

LEMON OR ORANGE BREAD

Read this recipe and try to resist it.

Rind cut from 2 oranges or	¹/₄ cup shortening, melted
3 lemons	4 teaspoons baking powder
¹/₂ cup chopped walnuts	¹/₂ teaspoon salt
¹/₂ cup coarsely chopped,	³/₄ cup milk
pitted dates	1 teaspoon vanilla
1 cup white sugar	2 cups flour

Cut rind in thin narrow strips, cover with water and simmer till rind is tender—about 15 minutes. Drain water off rind and discard it. Combine rind, sugar and ¹/₂-cup of water in a saucepan; simmer over low heat, stirring constantly until liquid thickens and will sheet from a spoon. Cool. Sift flour, baking powder and salt together into a bowl. Make a well in the dry ingredients and stir in the cooked rind, syrup, milk, vanilla and melted shortening. Stir in the nuts and dates. Turn batter into a well-greased loaf pan and bake in a 350-degree oven for about an hour. Let loaf stand in its pan 15 minutes on a cake rack, then turn out and finish cooling on the rack. Slice and butter.

BISCUITS WITH VARIATIONS

Biscuits have a standard formula but you can enjoy experimenting with all sorts of things.

2 cups flour	**¹/₄ cup butter or margarine**
3 teaspoons baking powder	**²/₃ or ³/₄ cup milk**
¹/₂ teaspoon salt	

Sift the flour, baking powder and salt. Cut in the shortening till the mixture is crumbly. Stir in the milk, using just enough to hold everything together. Drop the dough on a floured board, handling it lightly—or kneading it a few times. Roll it about ¹/₂ an inch thick and cut it in 2-inch rounds—or be lazy and simply drop tablespoons of the dough on a greased cookie sheet. Bake in a 450-degree oven for 12 minutes.

The flavour of this basic recipe can be greatly improved by replacing some of the milk with cream or various juices, or an egg or two.

If you want a sweet dough add ¹/₄ to ¹/₂ a cup of sugar.

You can use sour milk instead of sweet—substituting 1 teaspoon of soda for the baking powder.

You might use 1 cup of white flour and 1 cup of graham flour, or whole wheat, or rye, or oatmeal, and so forth.

To any of these variations add nuts or raisins (or both), dates, currants, blueberries, cranberries—or what have you?

How about adding a cupful of minced or fried onions?

Grated cheese or chunks of cheddar melting in the biscuits is hard to beat.

Sometimes I put in a cupful of cheese and a cupful of raisins, and either drop spoonfuls of the dough on cookie sheets or smooth out the whole mass of dough in a cake pan and cut it in squares after baking—it's delicious with marmalade or a fruit salad.

You might try adding crisply fried bacon bits.

Or peanut butter, honey, herbs, celery seed, bits of cooked ham, mint, watercress, parsley.

Try everything, anything—it's so easy, fun and surprising.

AUNT ELLIE'S TEA BISCUITS

Aunt Ellie had white hair, mischievous blue eyes, a budgie bird that sat on her head; and she made the best tea biscuits that anyone ever tasted.

4 cups flour	1 cup lard
1 teaspoon soda	2 cups sour milk or
1 tablespoon baking powder	buttermilk
1 cup sugar	1 cup currants (optional)
1 teaspoon salt	

Mix the dry ingredients and the shortening till the mixture is crumbly. Add the sour milk and mix with a spoon just enough to make sure everything is connected. Drop spoonfuls of the thick dough on a buttered sheet pan, sprinkle with a bit of sugar and bake in a 400-degree oven for about 15 minutes—keep watching till they are golden brown on the edges. Serve them warm; they're so rich they hardly need butter; with the currants in them they don't need jam either.

MOTHER'S AFTERNOON TEA CAKES

We got only what was left of these after the company ladies had gone home; never enough!

1/2 cup white sugar	2 teaspoons baking powder
1 1/2 cups flour	1/2 cup raisins or currants
1/2 teaspoon salt	2 tablespoons milk
1/2 cup butter	1 beaten egg

Sift the dry ingredients and work in the butter. Add the raisins or currants. Mix lightly into a dough by adding the milk with the egg. Form into small balls, sprinkle with sugar and bake at 375 degrees till they are slightly browned.

HOT GINGER SCONES

Easy to make and very good with apple sauce.

2 teaspoons ground ginger	2 tablespoons shortening
2 cups flour	2 tablespoons corn syrup
4 teaspoons baking powder	3/4 cup milk
1/8 teaspoon salt	

Sift together the dry ingredients; cut in the shortening, then stir in lightly the milk which has been blended with the corn syrup.

Drop tablespoons of the batter on a greased cookie sheet and bake at 425 degrees for about 15 minutes.

ADA'S CRISP BISCUITS

These are so thin and crisp they can be gobbled in one heavenly bite.

2 cups flour	1/3 cup butter, or margarine
2 teaspoons baking powder	3/4 cup milk
1 teaspoon salt	

Mix in the order given. Roll out to 1/4-inch thickness. Cut in small rounds and bake 12 minutes in a 400-degree oven—or hotter if you're willing to risk it.

BRAN GEMS

Bevvy's family loves these.

1/2 cup brown sugar	1/2 cup flour
Butter the size of an egg	1 teaspoon soda
1 egg, beaten	Bran to make a spongy
1 cup sour milk or buttermilk	dough

Mix in the order given, drop into greased gem pans and bake in a 400-degree oven.

FRUIT ROLLS

Bevvy says these are popular at a barn-raising.

2 cups flour	2 tablespoons sugar
4 teaspoons baking powder	2 tablespoons lard
1/2 tablespoon salt	2/3 cup milk or water

Mix in the order given. Roll 1/4-inch thick and spread with mixture of:

2 tablespoons soft butter	1/3 cup brown sugar
1/2 teaspoon cinnamon	1/3 cup currants

Spread the mixture on the dough, roll like a jelly roll and cut in 3/4-inch slices. Place in greased pans and bake in 350-degree oven for 15 minutes.

BLUEBERRY CUP CAKES

Bake these in paper baking cups, they look so professional.

¹/₄ cup shortening	2 cups flour
1¹/₂ cups sugar	4 teaspoons baking powder
2 eggs, well beaten	1 teaspoon salt
1 teaspoon vanilla	2 cups fresh blueberries
1 cup milk	¹/₄ cup additional flour

Cream shortening, add sugar gradually, then well beaten eggs and vanilla; blend well. Stir in the milk alternately with the sifted flour, baking powder and salt. Mix well. Add the blueberries, sprinkled with the ¹/₄-cup of flour. Fill paper cups ²/₃ full. Bake in 375-degree oven for about 25 minutes. I'll bet these would be good with cranberries too.

CHEESE ROLLS

Get up early some Sunday morning and—but no!— you don't have to get up early to treat them to these on a Sunday morning; they'll be baking while you're frying the sausages, bacon, and scrambled eggs.

2 cups bread flour	2 tablespoons shortening
5 teaspoons baking powder	³/₄ cup milk
1 teaspoon salt	1 cup grated cheese

Mix and sift the dry ingredients, cut in the shortening and add liquid gradually, mixing to a soft dough. Roll thin on floured board and sprinkle with the cheese. Roll up like a jelly roll, cut in 1-inch pieces and bake on a greased cookie sheet in a 450-degree oven for about 12 minutes.

ORANGE RAISIN MUFFINS

For after-church company in Bevvy's house.

2 cups flour	¹/₃ cup orange juice
³/₄ teaspoon baking soda	¹/₂ teaspoon grated orange
¹/₂ teaspoon salt	rind
¹/₃ cup sugar	²/₃ cup sour milk
¹/₂ cup raisins	¹/₃ cup shortening, melted
1 egg	

Sift together the flour, baking soda, salt and sugar, add the raisins. Combine the well beaten egg, orange juice, rind, sour milk and melted shortening. Turn wet ingredients into the dry and mix only until dry ones are dampened. Fill greased muffin tins ²/₃ full. Bake in a 400-degree oven for about 20 to 30 minutes. Keep your eye on them.

OATMEAL MUFFINS FROM SELENA'S GRANDMOTHER

Chewy and moist. And lots of them.

2 cups brown sugar	8 cups flour
1 cup lard	5 teaspoons soda
1 pint molasses	2 teaspoons allspice
1 cup hot water	3 teaspoons cinnamon
2 cups oatmeal	2 teaspoons cloves

Bevvy's recipe gives no directions for making these. I think the best way would be to cream the sugar and lard, add the molasses and mix well. Pour the hot water over the oatmeal, stir into butter mixture, then add the sifted flour, soda and spices. Since they are called muffins I would expect to put the dough into muffin tins but Bevvy's little black book says, "Roll nearly ¹/₂-inch thick and cut with a small cutter; beat an egg and rub on each cake before baking."

GERMAN BUNS

Popular at Mennonite funerals.

4 cups flour	**Filling:**
1 teaspoon salt	1 egg, beaten
1 cup white sugar	1 cup brown sugar
1 teaspoon soda	¹/₂ cup flour
2 teaspoons cream of tartar	
¹/₂ cup butter	
¹/₂ cup lard	
1 egg, beaten	

Sift dry ingredients, work in shortening, blend egg with milk and add just enough to other mixture to make a soft dough. Roll out on a floured board and cover with filling; roll up like a jelly roll, cut into ³/₄-inch-thick pieces and put on a cookie sheet to bake in a hot oven.

BELFASTS

Graham gems to serve with apple butter.

1 cup sugar	2 cups graham flour
1/2 cup butter	1/4 cup white flour
1 cup buttermilk	1 teaspoon soda
1 egg	1/2 teaspoon salt
1/2 teaspoon cinnamon	1 cup raisins

Blend sugar and butter, blend milk and egg, sift dry ingredients and add alternately with milk to butter mixture. Add raisins. Bake in gem tins in 350-degree oven for 30 minutes.

LAZY CAKES

3/4 cup butter and lard mixed	4 cups flour
1 1/2 cups sugar	1 teaspoon soda
3 eggs	1 teaspoon cream tartar

Blend shortening and sugar, add eggs and beat well together. Mix in sifted dry ingredients and make into small flat buns. Roll buns in sugar and bake in a 400-degree oven about 20 minutes.

Cookies

Bevvy bakes batches of cookies every week, she puts them on her table three times a day, and whenever Lyddie and Amsey have a hungry feeling between meals they reach into her cookie jars and help themselves to a plump ginger cookie or a handful of pfeffernusse. Almost half of Bevvy's little black book is made up of cookie recipes: most of them use oatmeal or molasses, spices, or raisins; the rest are plain sugar cookies, kisses or squares.

My sister Norm has a kitchen drawer full of clippings and hand-written recipes. Almost every time I go to her house she seems to be taking a pan of cookies from the oven. She says, "Oh, kid, try one of these, they're a new kind." But we don't stop at one.

As soon as my cookie jar is empty I make a new batch and seldom the same kind twice, except at Christmas when I always bake those that Mother and Daddy made when I was a little girl. One day in the week before Christmas Mother would cut up dates, nuts, cherries and candied peel; we'd have an early supper, clear the big square kitchen table and, from recipes of her grandmother's, Mother would measure out the ingredients, put them into her big blue bowl while Daddy would mix them together. Mother said she needed his muscles to do all the stirring. When Mother thought the consistency was right, Daddy would roll out the dough. Mother would shape the cookies with fancy cutters, and decorate them with red and green sugar or nuts. If I was quiet and good I was allowed to put the currant buttons and eyes on the gingerbread men and to taste the first cookies that came from the oven, before they sent me happy and dreaming to bed.

CHRISTMAS COOKIES

When I was young, unconfident, and eager for praise, I'd bake dozens and dozens of cookies at Christmas, all pretty, fussy little things, nine or ten different kinds—then I'd invite friends in to eat and admire them.

NEW ORLEANS JUMBLES

These look like little Christmas wreaths—with a good flavour.

1 cup shortening	Grated rind of 1 orange and
1 cup sugar	1 lemon, or ¹/₄ pound
1 egg	mixed, finely chopped
	peel
	3 cups flour

Cream shortening, add sugar and grated rind—or chopped peel. Work the flour into the mixture, break the egg into the dough and work it in thoroughly—sometimes I seem to need 2 eggs. Dredge a board with sugar and on it roll small pieces of dough, as in shaping small bread sticks. Join the ends to make rings about 1¹/₂ inches in diameter. Bake on a greased tin in a 375-degree oven until firm—but not coloured.

When they were cold I'd ice them with a soft butter white icing (see Index), to which I'd add a very, very little bit of green colouring; then I'd sprinkle them with those tiny multicoloured round candy trimmings to make them look like wreaths.

If you don't want to make an impression you can shape the dough into thin rolls, keep it in the fridge for several hours, cut it into thin slices and bake till firm.

CHOCOLATE MACAROONS

Tasty. Mine are sometimes tough—but always good to eat.

2 egg whites	1¹/₂ cups shredded coconut
1 cup sugar	1¹/₂ squares unsweetened
¹/₂ teaspoon salt	chocolate, melted
¹/₂ teaspoon vanilla	

Beat the egg whites until stiff, then fold in the sugar, salt and vanilla and beat till they form peaks. Work in the coconut and melted chocolate. Drop by teaspoonfuls on a greased, floured baking sheet and bake in a 275-degree oven for about 20 minutes.

LEP COOKIES

There hasn't been a Christmas in my life without lep cookies and I hope there never will be; I prefer them to all the rich fancy ones. Mother's recipe, which she got from her grandmother, makes eight cookie jars full; this is only one quarter of that amount:

2 eggs	1 cup sour cream
³/₄ cup brown sugar	¹/₂ pound almonds, blanched
1 pint baking syrup	and sliced
(molasses)	1 teaspoon soda
³/₄ teaspoon cloves (ground)	8 ounce package citron peel,
³/₄ teaspoon cinnamon	chopped
¹/₂ teaspoon nutmeg	8 ounce package mixed peel,
1 teaspoon aniseed	chopped
(optional)	7 cups flour

Stir everything together but the flour. Heat the mixture to luke-warm in a heavy pot or in the top of a double boiler, stirring continuously. When warm, stir in the flour; then put the mixture into a cool place for a day or two. The mixture will then be thick enough to roll—the cold seems to thicken it. Take a good large spoonful out of the pot at a time (leaving the rest in the cold) and roll it about 1/6th of an inch thick on a floured board; cut with a cookie cutter—the fruit will make it impossible to be fancy about shapes; I use a drinking glass as a cutter. After cutting the cookies, brush the tops with egg white to make them shiny, and press an almond into the centre.

The lep cookies are crisp at first, later they become chewy. They'll keep fresh-tasting long after all the other cookies have become stale.

PFEFFERNUSSE

Neat little balls; hard as pebbles for the first week—you can't bite them, you just have to suck them, or dunk them in coffee as the old-timers do; the dunking gives them a special flavour. They soften with age.

2 eggs, separated	¹/₂ teaspoon white pepper
1 cup white sugar	1 grated lemon peel
1 teaspoon cinnamon	(optional)
¹/₂ teaspoon cloves	2 cups flour

Blend the egg yolks and sugar then fold in the stiffly beaten egg whites. Stir in the spices, pepper and flour. Mix well and knead slightly on a floured board—the dough is quite stiff. Form into balls, small enough to pop into your mouth. Place them on a greased cookie sheet and let stand overnight to dry. Bake in a

350-degree oven for about 15 minutes, but watch them—they shouldn't be brown. If you keep them in a tight container for two or three weeks they'll soften, but you can hurry the process by putting a quartered apple with them overnight.

SNOW DROPS

These melt in your mouth—in one bite. Some people call them Mexican Mice or Wedding Cookies.

⁷/₈ cup butter	1 cup nuts, chopped
4 tablespoons icing sugar	2 teaspoons vanilla
2 cups cake flour	1 teaspoon water

Beat butter till creamy, add sugar, then stir and blend in the flour, nuts, vanilla and water. Chill until firm enough to shape with your fingers into small, date-shaped pieces. Bake at 400 degrees for 10 minutes, but watch them—remember they're *snow* drops, not coals, or even golden cookies. Roll in sifted icing sugar as soon as you remove them from the oven.

PARTY SHORTBREAD

They almost melt in your hand.

¹/₂ pound butter	2 cups sifted flour—less 2
¹/₂ cup icing sugar, sifted	tablespoonfuls
	2 tablespoons cornstarch

Replace 2 tablespoons of flour with 2 tablespoons cornstarch and sift together. Cream butter, add sugar gradually and blend in the flour with your hands—you may need a bit more flour. Roll into cylinders and put in a cold place overnight. Slice about 1/3 of an inch thick and bake on a buttered pan in a 300-degree oven, watching like a hawk; don't leave them too long, you don't want them brown. When cold, ice them with rich butter icing (see Index), flavoured with almond, and put an almond on top—or flavour icing with vanilla or rum and press a whole walnut or pecan into the icing in the centre of the cookie. Handsome.

CHOCOLATE SHORTBREAD

My own invention—and how I boasted about that when my friends asked for the recipe. Very simple—it doesn't require genius. Just add 2 squares of melted unsweetened chocolate to the butter in the PARTY SHORTBREAD recipe, ice with chocolate butter icing made by adding melted chocolate to left-over butter icing after you've iced the white shortbread. Put a walnut on top.

GOOD OLD-FASHIONED SHORTBREAD

These improve with age if you store them in a crock under your bed.

1 cup brown sugar	1 cup lard (not shortening)
1 cup butter (not margarine)	4 cups all-purpose flour

Blend sugar, butter and lard; add flour gradually. Dough is quite stiff. Knead it as long as it takes to become smooth. Roll out on lightly floured board—thick or thin, as you like. Cut into shapes or squares and bake at 350 degrees for about 10 minutes—until they are a pale gold. Don't ice, just eat.

SUGAR COOKIES

No child should grow up without sugar cookies at Christmas. Mother would cut hers into sheep and rabbits with curranty eyes, Kriss Kringles with tiny red candies for buttons, reindeer, and a man and woman in flat-hatted clerical dress (whose heads and small feet were always bitten off first).

1/2 cup butter	2 cups flour
1 cup sugar	3 teaspoons baking powder
2 eggs, beaten	1/2 teaspoon salt
1/2 cup milk	1/2 teaspoon vanilla

Cream butter; add sugar, eggs, then sifted dry ingredients alternately with milk and vanilla. Roll very thin and cut into fancy shapes—or plainer ones if it isn't Christmas. Decorate. Bake at 350 degrees till they're pale but done—10 minutes. Watch! You don't want them to burn after doing all that decorating.

ANISEED COOKIES

We children used to call these Annie Seed Cookies and wonder who Annie was. We liked the slightly licorice flavour. Mother says they make best when mixed on a sunny morning.

1 cup powdered sugar	1 teaspoon baking powder
3 eggs, separated	1 1/2 tablespoons crushed
1 teaspoon lemon juice	aniseed
2 cups all-purpose flour	

Beat the egg yolks until thick, the egg whites until stiff, and combine the two. Gradually fold in the sifted powdered sugar and lemon juice. Sift the flour and baking powder and add them and the aniseed to the batter. Drop from a teaspoon about an inch apart on a greased cookie sheet. Let stand on sheets overnight at room temperature. Bake at 325 degrees until the cookies begin to colour. They'll have a meringue-like top and soft bottom.

SAND COOKIES

Mother makes these dainty little cookies for special occasions; over the years she must have made thousands—with infinite patience.

1 cup butter	Topping:
1 scant cup light brown	White of 1 egg
sugar	$1/4$ cup white sugar
2 eggs (1 separated)	Almonds
2 tablespoons cold water	Cinnamon
$3^1/_2$ cups flour	
2 tablespoons baking	
powder	
$1/_2$ teaspoon cinnamon	

Blend butter and sugar, add 1 egg and yolk of the second egg, then water and flour sifted with baking powder and cinnamon. Roll thin as paper, cut with a pretty little cutter. For topping: mix white sugar with $1/_2$ a teaspoon of cinnamon; beat egg white slightly; blanch almonds and slit them in half. Brush each cookie with egg white, put a half-almond in the centre, sprinkle cookie with sugar-cinnamon mixture; place on greased cookie sheets and bake in a 350-degree oven till lightly browned—not very long.

HAZELNUT MACAROONS

Mother always made these for Christmas; very special.

1 pound shelled hazelnuts	$3^1/_2$ cups fine white sugar
Whites of 2 large eggs	$1/_2$ cup flour

Put the nuts in the warm oven to dry till the brown skins come off; then roll or chop them till they are very fine indeed. Beat egg whites till stiff, gradually add the sugar and flour mixed together, then the rolled nuts. On a lightly floured board, roll the dough about $1/_4$-inch thick; cut into bars, place on greased cookie sheets, ice with meringue, decorate with cherries or press half a nut into centre; bake about 15 minutes in a 300-degree oven.

BUTTERSCOTCH MACAROONS

Quite festive looking—and tasty.

2/3 cup packed brown sugar
4 tablespoons butter
2 tablespoons water
1/3 cup chopped nuts or
    raisins (or both)
1/4 cup chopped candied
    cherries

1/3 teaspoon salt
1 teaspoon vanilla
2 cups rolled oats
1 tablespoon cornstarch
2 egg whites, beaten stiff

Cook sugar, butter and water slowly together, stirring, for 5 minutes. Add nuts, cherries, salt, vanilla, rolled oats and cornstarch. (You can substitute a cupful of coconut for a cupful of rolled oats if you like.) Mix thoroughly—the mixture will be crumbly. Beat the egg whites till stiff, but not dry, and fold them into the mixture. Drop mixture by spoonfuls, an inch apart, on greased pans. Bake in a 300-degree oven for about 20 minutes. Remove from pan while hot—using a buttered knife.

BUTTERSCOTCH BRITTLES

More people asked for this recipe than any other at my last year's Christmas party.

3/4 cup shortening
    (I used chicken fat)
3 cups brown sugar
1/2 tablespoon soda,
    dissolved in
1 tablespoon warm water

3 cups sifted flour
1 cup molasses
1 cup grated coconut
1 cup chopped walnuts or
    pecans

Cream the butter and sugar; add the soda and water to the molasses; sift flour and add to the butter mixture alternately with the molasses; stir vigorously. Fold in the coconut and nuts. Let stand overnight in a cold place; next day drop by teaspoonfuls on a greased, floured sheet. Bake at 350 degrees for 10 to 15 minutes.

    I hate to tell you but the first time I tried these they ran together on the pan and scrunched up into a long narrow blob too hard to bite, when I tried to remove them. Finally I made little balls of the dough, rolled them in flour and put them far apart on the pans. I had to take them off the pans at just the right moment—not immediately but while they were still hot.

MANDEL KUCHA (Almond Wafers)

Like crisp gold lace—with toasted-almond flavouring.

1 cup sugar	Topping:
1 cup butter	1 egg white, beaten
2 egg yolks	1 tablespoon water
1¹/₂ cups all-purpose flour	1 cup shredded almonds
¹/₄ teaspoon salt	¹/₂ cup sugar
Grated rind of half a lemon	2 teaspoons cinnamon

Grate the lemon rind and mix it with the sugar, cream the sugar with the butter and beat in the egg yolks, one at a time. Add the flour gradually, sifting it into the batter to make a rich dough. Form into little balls, half the size of a walnut, and flatten them with the bottom of a glass dipped in flour. Blanch the almonds and shred them lengthwise. Beat the egg white slightly with water and brush it over the cookies. Mix the ¹/₂-cup of sugar, the cinnamon, salt and almonds, and sprinkle the mixture thickly over tops of cookies. Bake in a 350-degree oven until golden.

ALMOND MACAROONS

Puffy and light—they'll keep for weeks if you hide them from the madding crowd.

¹/₂ cup butter	2 teaspoons cream of tartar
¹/₂ cup lard	¹/₂ teaspoon salt
¹/₂ cup white sugar	¹/₄ pound almonds, put
¹/₂ cup brown sugar	through chopper
1 egg	³/₄ teaspoon extract of bitter
2 cups flour	almond
1 teaspoon soda	

Cream the butter, lard, brown and white sugars; beat in the egg and stir in the rest of the ingredients. Roll pieces about as big as acorns in your hands and put them on a greased, floured sheet. Bake in a 350-degree oven.

FILLED OATMEAL CRISPS

Not fancy, but a bit fussy. They always get raves.

2¹/₂ cups rolled oats finely ground through food chopper	¹/₄ teaspoon salt
	¹/₂ cup shortening
	1¹/₂ cups light brown sugar
1 teaspoon soda	¹/₂ cup sour cream
1 teaspoon baking powder	

Mix oats with soda, baking powder and salt. Cream shortening with sugar and blend in oats mixture. Add sour cream and work into a stiff dough. Chill for at least 2 hours. Roll very thin on a lightly floured board, cut and lift *carefully* onto greased baking sheets—the dough is very tender. Bake in a 400-degree oven for 8 minutes—watch it! Remove from pans. When cold, put two cookies together with a thin layer of the following delicious filling:

¹/₂ pound seeded dates	¹/₂ cup walnuts, finely ground
¹/₂ pound figs	
1 cup brown sugar	1 tablespoon butter
2 tablespoons boiling water	1 teaspoon grated orange rind
2 tablespoons lemon juice	

Cut dates and figs into small pieces, mix in saucepan with sugar, water, lemon juice and nuts. Cook gently about 15 minutes—until thick and clear, stirring often. Add butter and orange rind, then cool. I don't spread this on the cookies until I'm ready to serve them or they'll become soft. I like them crisp, with that soft tasty filling squishing between them. These are really terrific.

BESSIE'S GINGER WALNUT COOKIES

The kind you can't stop eating—crunchy, rich—nippy when you hit a piece of ginger.

²/₃ cup butter	2 cups flour
2 cups brown sugar	2 teaspoons vanilla
2 teaspoons soda, dissolved in	¹/₂ cup cut Chinese ginger
	¹/₂ cup chopped pecans or walnuts
4 tablespoons boiling water	

Buy the crystallized ginger that comes in packages at the supermarkets—I use a whole package, cut up not too finely. Mix the dough in the order given, form into balls smaller than a walnut. Press down with a floured fork. Top each with a green or red cherry and bake in a 325-degree oven for about 15 or 20 minutes. Watch: they brown quickly.

TEMPTERS

Crisp coconut cookies with chocolate chips—and nuts if you like.

<table>
<tr><td>1/2 cup shortening</td><td>1 1/2 teaspoons baking</td></tr>
<tr><td>1 cup white sugar</td><td>   powder</td></tr>
<tr><td>1 egg, beaten</td><td>1/2 teaspoon salt</td></tr>
<tr><td>1 teaspoon vanilla</td><td>1/2 cup chocolate chips</td></tr>
<tr><td>1/4 teaspoon almond extract</td><td>1 cup cut-up shredded</td></tr>
<tr><td>2 tablespoons milk</td><td>   coconut</td></tr>
<tr><td>2 cups pastry flour or</td><td>1/2 cup nuts (optional)</td></tr>
<tr><td>   1 3/4 all-purpose</td><td></td></tr>
</table>

Cream shortening until light and fluffy, blend in sugar; beat in egg, vanilla, almond extract and milk. Mix in the dry ingredients (sifted together), 1/3 at a time, combining well after each addition. Mix in the coconut and chocolate chips (and nuts). Drop teaspoonfuls of dough onto greased cookie sheets, press flat with a wet fork. Bake in a 350-degree oven until golden—about 12 minutes.

GUMDROP COOKIES

Colourful, chewy and crisp—pretty on a plate.

<table>
<tr><td>1/2 cup shortening</td><td>1/2 teaspoon salt</td></tr>
<tr><td>1/2 cup brown sugar</td><td>1/2 teaspoon soda</td></tr>
<tr><td>1/2 cup white sugar</td><td>1 teaspoon baking powder</td></tr>
<tr><td>1 egg</td><td>1/2 cup coconut</td></tr>
<tr><td>1 cup rolled oats</td><td>1/2 cup gumdrops, cut up</td></tr>
<tr><td>1 cup corn flakes</td><td>   (no black)</td></tr>
<tr><td>1 cup flour</td><td></td></tr>
</table>

Cream shortening and sugar together. Add egg and beat until fluffy. Sift flour, salt, soda and baking powder, add to creamed mixture and beat until well blended; then add gumdrops, coconut, rolled oats and corn flakes. Blend into dough and drop teaspoonfuls onto greased baking sheets, about 2 inches apart. Bake at 350 degrees for 15 minutes. I put one bit of gumdrop on top of each cookie before baking, and when I served them I put some of the whole gumdrops on the plate with the cookies for added colour.

CURRANT WAFERS

Thin as net on the edges, with a thicker, curranty part in the centre.

¹/₂ cup shortening (butter)	¹/₂ teaspoon soda
¹/₂ cup sugar	1 cup flour
2 eggs	1 cup currants
¹/₂ cup sour cream	1 teaspoon vanilla

Cream butter and sugar and stir in the lighly beaten eggs. Dissolve soda in sour cream, mix with the egg-and-butter mixture, sift in flour. Dredge currants in a very little flour and fold into batter with vanilla. Drop from teaspoon onto greased cookie sheet—at least 3 inches apart because they'll spread. Bake at 350 degrees for 10 minutes. Remove from sheet while hot. If you'd rather have cookies that are less fragile, add another cup of flour.

MELTING MOMENTS

Need I say more?

³/₄ cup brown sugar	¹/₂ teaspoon soda
1 cup butter, melted	¹/₂ teaspoon cream of tartar
1 unbeaten egg	1 cup chopped nuts
1 teaspoon vanilla	(optional)
2¹/₂ cups pastry flour	

Blend butter and brown sugar, then unbeaten egg and vanilla; beat well together. Add sifted dry ingredients (and nuts). Drop by teaspoonfuls on greased cookie sheet and bake at 350 degrees for a few minutes.

IRRESISTIBLE COOKIES

Sometimes they're chewy, sometimes they're crisp—always they're big and wonderful.

1 cup butter	1 teaspoon soda
2 cups brown sugar	1 teaspoon baking powder
1 cup raisins, chopped	2 cups flour—enough to roll
1 tablespoon corn syrup	1 teaspoon cinnamon
4 tablespoons sour milk	

Cream the butter and sugar together; add the corn syrup and raisins, then the sour milk with the soda dissolved in it; sift in the flour, baking powder and cinnamon. Roll out (not too thin), cut with a round cutter—or drinking glass—and bake at 350 degrees till they're your favourite shade of brown. Then hide them.

PEANUT BUTTER COOKIES

Kids love these—and so do I.

1/2 cup butter	1 egg
1/2 cup brown sugar	1 1/2 cups flour
1/2 cup white sugar	1/2 teaspoon soda
1/2 cup peanut butter	1 teaspoon vanilla
1/2 teaspoon salt	

Mix in the order given. Flatten teaspoonfuls of dough on greased cookie sheets, or make into rolls, chill and slice. Bake at 350 degrees for about 10 minutes.

BUTTERSCOTCH RAISIN COOKIES

Norm makes these often and they don't last long.

1 cup butter or shortening	4 cups flour
2 cups brown sugar	1 cup coconut
2 eggs	1 cup chopped walnuts
1 teaspoon cream of tartar	1 cup raisins
1 teaspoon soda	1 teaspoon vanilla

Mix in the order given (the dry ingredients sifted together); pack in a loaf pan and let stand overnight in the fridge. Cut in slices and bake in a 350-degree oven till golden.

SCRUNCHIES

Chocolate chips and peanuts make these very more-ish.

1 cup butter	1/2 cup chocolate chips
1 1/4 cups brown sugar	(more if you love
2 tablespoons milk	chocolate as I do)
1 egg	1 3/4 cups flour
1/2 cup chopped salted	2 teaspoons baking powder
peanuts (or a whole cup)	1/4 teaspoon soda
	1/2 teaspoon salt

Blend butter and sugar, beat in milk and egg, then add peanuts and chocolate chips. Chill for 10 minutes. Sift and add the dry ingredients and blend until well combined. Drop teaspoonfuls onto greased sheet. Bake in 375-degree oven about 8 to 10 minutes.

PEANUT BUTTER CRISPY COOKIES

Norm has so many quick-to-make cookie recipes—these are as quickly eaten!

1 cup brown sugar	1 teaspoon vanilla
1/2 cup corn syrup	2 cups rice crispies
1/2 cup peanut butter	1/2 cup walnuts

Dissolve the sugar, syrup and peanut butter on the stove—slowly; then add the vanilla, crispies and walnuts. Mix quickly and pat into a greased, square cake pan. Don't bake. Ice with chocolate butter icing and cut into squares—if they last that long.

FUNERAL COOKIES

Not a bit funereal but the quickest thing to make and take to a suddenly bereaved friend who might need to have "something on hand."

2 cups white sugar	3 cups rolled oats
1/2 cup shortening	1 cup coconut
1/2 cup cocoa	1/2 cup walnuts
1/2 cup milk	1 teaspoon vanilla
1/2 teaspoon salt	1/2 cup raisins (optional)

Mix rolled oats, coconut, walnuts (and raisins). Bring the sugar, shortening, cocoa, milk and salt to a rolling boil—no more than that; Remove the saucepan from the heat, add the vanilla, then the mixed dry ingredients. Stir all quickly together to a crumbly mass and drop spoonfuls of it onto your kitchen counter (or waxed paper), working quickly before it cools and hardens. The dropped cookies may be a bit ragged: let them be, there isn't time to repair them till you've dropped all of the mixture. Press the cookies together with your fingers while they're still warm to give them a more regular shape and to be sure they hang together.

If you want a change you can use only a third of a cup of shortening in the boiled part and when you take it off the heat stir in, until melted, a third of a cup of peanut butter (and use peanuts instead of walnuts).

CHINESE CHEWS

I don't know what is Chinese about these; Mother often made them when she entertained ladies.

2 eggs, beaten	1 heaping teaspoon baking
1 cup brown sugar	powder
1 cup chopped walnuts	1/2 teaspoon salt
3/4 cup flour	

Add the sugar to the beaten eggs, then the fruit and nuts, the flour sifted with the baking powder and salt; mix well. Spread the dough in a buttered pan and bake in a 350-degree oven. When golden, remove it, cut it into narrow strips and roll the strips in icing sugar.

BUTTERSCOTCH SQUARES

Chewy and buttery—Norm makes these often.

¹/₄ cup butter	1 teaspoon baking powder
1 cup brown sugar	1¹/₄ teaspoons vanilla
1 egg	¹/₂ cup nuts
³/₄ cup flour	

Cook butter and sugar till well blended. Cool to lukewarm and add unbeaten egg; beat well. Add flour and baking powder, then vanilla and nuts. Spread the dough on a greased pan, bake 25 minutes in a 350-degree oven, then cut into squares.

CHEWY BROWNIES

The best I've ever tasted.

¹/₂ cup butter	1 cup walnuts
1 cup brown sugar	1 teaspoon vanilla
1 egg	¹/₂ cup flour
¹/₂ cup cocoa	Pinch salt

Mix the ingredients in the order given and bake at 350 degrees for 20 minutes in a greased cake pan. The Brownies, cut in squares, will be soft and seem to be not finished—but that's the secret of their fudginess. They never get stale—at Norm's house they are often eaten before they have a chance to get cold.

If you want the brownies even more chocolatey, use 2 squares of melted chocolate instead of cocoa.

MERLE'S CHEESE PATTIES

Merle makes these for cocktail parties. She says they're grand.

1 cup grated cheddar	1 teaspoon salt
¹/₂ cup butter	1¹/₂ cups sifted flour
¹/₂ teaspoon cayenne pepper	

Mix thoroughly, using your hands. Chill slightly, then shape the dough into balls the size of a marble. Put them on a buttered cookie sheet with a blanched almond pressed on top of each one. Bake at 350 degrees for a few minutes—but not till they're brown.

BELLE'S CHEESE COOKIES

These have a nippy crispness that makes you eat more and more as you sip a slight drink.

1/4 cup soft butter	1 cup grated old cheese
1/4 teaspoon salt	1/2 cup crushed rice crispies
2 grains cayenne	1/2 cup all-purpose flour

Mix thoroughly, shape into balls, put them on a buttered cookie sheet and flatten them slightly with a fork. Bake at 375 degrees for 8 to 10 minutes.

OATMEAL COOKIES

You can't beat a good oatmeal cookie: flavourful, rich, not too sweet, fine texture, keeps well. After going through my cookie recipes I found that over thirty require oatmeal. A number have similar ingredients and are prepared in the same way. You might pick your own favourites or make your own variations or substitutions from these:

OATMEAL DROP COOKIES

	CRISP	MY FAVOURITE	CHEWY	BEVVY'S BEST
Shortening	3/4 cup	1 cup	1/2 cup lard	1 cup bacon fat
Brown sugar	1 1/2 cups	2 cups	1 cup	1 cup
Eggs		2, beaten		
Vanilla or rum		1 teaspoon		1 teaspoon
Sour milk or buttermilk (or water)	6 tablespoons	5 teaspoons	1/4 cup water	2 tablespoons warm water
Salt	1 teaspoon	1 teaspoon	1/2 teaspoon	pinch
Rolled oats	3 cups	3 cups	2 cups	3 cups
Raisins		1 cup	1 cup	
Walnuts		1 cup		
Flour	1 1/2 cups	2 cups	1 cup	1 1/2 cups
Soda	3/4 teaspoon	1 teaspoon	1 teaspoon	1 teaspoon
Cinnamon		1 teaspoon		

Blend the shortening and sugar; add vanilla, (eggs), milk or water, salt; mix in the rolled oats, (cinnamon) raisins, (walnuts); then the flour and soda sifted together. Drop teaspoonfuls on greased cookie sheets, flattening each cookie with a fork (you don't want them thick). Bake at 350 degrees until lightly browned—8 to 10 minutes. Don't pile them in layers in your cookie jar until they are completely cold or they'll lose their crispness.

ROLLED OATMEAL COOKIES WITH FILLING

	TRILBY'S	LOVINA'S	MOTHER'S	BEVVY'S
	With filling baked in:		Filled after baking:	
Shortening	1 cup	1 cup	1 cup	1 cup
Sugar	1 cup white	1¹/₂ cups brown	1 cup brown	1 cup brown
Flour	2¹/₂ cups	2 cups	2 cups	3 cups (almost)
Soda	1 teaspoon	1 teaspoon	1 teaspoon	3 teaspoons baking powder
Salt	¹/₂ teaspoon	¹/₂ teaspoon	¹/₂ teaspoon	¹/₂ teaspoon
Rolled oats	2¹/₂ cups	3 cups	2 cups	2 cups
Milk or water	1 cup sweet milk	¹/₂ cup water	¹/₄ cup sour milk	¹/₂ cup sweet milk

Cream shortening and sugar together. Sift dry ingredients together and stir them into the creamed mixture along with the rolled oats and milk or water. Chill if the dough is too sticky to roll. Roll out to ¹/₈ of an inch thickness. For Trilby's and Lovina's cookies use a cutter about three inches in diameter; put a teaspoon of the filling on one side, fold the other side over and pinch the filling into the cookie; place on a greased cookie sheet and bake at 350 degrees till golden brown. For Mother's and Bevvy's use a small cutter and bake on greased cookie sheets at 350 degrees for about 10 minutes. When baked and cooled, put them together in pairs with date filling between—when you are ready to serve them, or they'll become limp.

DATE FILLING

2 cups cut-up dates
¹/₂ cup sugar, brown or white

¹/₂ cup water
2 tablespoons lemon or orange juice (optional)
1 teaspoon vanilla

Cook together slowly, stirring until thick—about 5 minutes. This keeps well in the fridge.

SCOTTIES

These are hard at first, but good eating for a long time.

1³/₄ cups flour	1 cupful sliced dates
¹/₄ teaspoon salt	¹/₂ cup chopped nuts
2 teaspoons baking powder	¹/₂ cup shortening
¹/₂ teaspoon cinnamon	1 cup sugar
¹/₄ teaspoon nutmeg	1 egg, beaten
¹/₄ teaspoon cloves	2 tablespoons milk
1³/₄ cups rolled oats	

Sift together the flour, salt, baking powder and spices; add the dates, nuts, and oatmeal; mix well. Cream the shortening, add the sugar gradually, then the egg. Work in the dry ingredients with the milk (you may need a bit more milk). Drop by teaspoonfuls two inches apart on a well-greased baking sheet and bake in a 400-degree oven for almost 10 minutes.

BROWN OAT COOKIES

A bit crumbly—with richness.

³/₄ cup shortening	³/₄ cup coconut
1 cup white sugar	³/₄ teaspoon soda
¹/₂ cup brown sugar	1 teaspoon baking powder
1¹/₂ cups all-purpose flour	1 teaspoon salt
1¹/₄ cups rolled oats	1 egg, beaten

Blend shortening and sugar, then beat in the egg. Work in the dry ingredients with your fingers, if necessary. Break into small pieces, press with a fork on a greased baking sheet. Bake at 350 degrees till pale gold. You may put in a few nuts, if you like, or put one on top. If the dough is too dry work in a teaspoon or two of water.

BUTTER MEAL COOKIES

This is one of my standbys; I make them whenever I have chicken fat on hand—no other shortening gives them quite the delicacy.

¹/₂ cup chicken fat	2 cups flour
1 heaping cup brown sugar	2 cups quick rolled oats
2 teaspoons vanilla (almost)	A good pinch of salt
¹/₄ cup boiling water, to which you have added:	
1 scant teaspoon soda	

Blend the fat with the sugar; add the vanilla, boiling water and soda. Mix in well the flour, oats and salt. Drop in spoonfuls on a greased cookie sheet and pat out as thin as possible, using your hand or a fork dipped in flour. Bake in a 350-degree oven till golden brown—just a few minutes.

OATMEAL CARAMEL COOKIES

Quick and easy: the first recipe I pasted in my book when I was married. Delicious.

$^1/_2$ cup melted butter	2 cups rolled oats
1 cup brown sugar	$^1/_2$ teaspoon baking powder
1 teaspoon vanilla	

Mix all together and press down in a greased, floured cookie tin with sides (they're really just crumbs at this stage). Bake in a 400-degree oven and they'll all melt together till they're golden and the smell is divine—just a few minutes (watch them carefully). As soon as you take them from the oven cut them in squares and remove them from the pan while they're hot. They'll be crisp and scrummy. Their thickness depends on the size of your pan—they're good $^1/_2$ an inch thick, better and more of them if they are thinner.

From here on the recipes for cookies are Bevvy's.

ORANGE DROP COOKIES

It's nice to have these to vary your flavours when you serve a plateful of cookies.

$^3/_4$ cup shortening	1 tablespoon grated orange
$^1/_4$ cup butter	rind
$1^1/_2$ cups brown sugar	1 teaspoon vanilla
2 eggs, beaten	1 cup sour milk
1 cup chopped dates	$3^1/_2$ cups flour
1 cup nuts, chopped	$^1/_4$ teaspoon baking powder
$^1/_4$ cup orange juice	1 teaspoon soda

Cream shortening, sugar; add eggs, orange juice, rind, vanilla and sour milk. Add sifted dry ingredients, then dates and nuts. Drop from a teaspoon onto greased cookie sheet. Bake in a 350-degree oven for 15 minutes. To make them look pretty you might put a paper-thin cross of orange rind on each cookie, or half a walnut.

THIMBLE COOKIES

One delicious bite.

1/2 cup butter or margarine	1 egg white, unbeaten
1/4 cup sugar	3/4 cup nuts, cut fine
1 egg yolk, slightly beaten	Red jelly or jam
1 cup flour	

Cream the butter; add the sugar gradually and cream until light. Add the egg yolk; mix well and work in the flour. Form into small balls; dip the balls into egg white, then roll in the nuts. Place on greased cookie sheet and press fairly flat with the bottom of a glass. Bake in a 300-degree oven for 5 minutes. Remove from oven and make an indentation in centre of each cookie with a thimble; bake about 15 minutes longer. Cool and fill the thimble holes with a tart jelly or jam just before serving.

DATE SQUARES

You never get tired of this old favourite.

1 1/2 cups rolled oats	1 cup brown sugar
1 1/2 cups flour	(or 1/2 cup)
1 teaspoon baking powder	1 cup butter
—or soda	1/4 cup chopped walnuts
1/4 teaspoon salt	(optional)

Cream butter and sugar; add flour and baking powder sifted together, then the oats. Pat half the crumbly mixture into the bottom of a greased square pan, spread the date filling over it and cover with the remaining oats mixture. Or distribute the mixture and filling in several layers, topping with oat mixture. Bake in a 350-degree oven for about 45 minutes.

DATE FILLING

For one layer filling:

1 pound dates, stoned and cut up	1 cup water
1/2 cup sugar (or 1 cup)	1 teaspoon vanilla

To the dates add water and sugar; cook until soft but not dry. Cool, add vanilla and spread over the crumb mixture.

These squares, loaded with delicious calories, are a complete dessert, topped with whipped or ice cream. You might try them with different fillings—jam, or raisins, instead of dates; Bevvy says ground-cherries are good too.

LEBKUCHEN

Fruity, cakey squares, improved by a bit of icing.

1/4 cup shortening	2 cups flour
1/2 cup brown sugar	1 tablespoon cocoa
1 egg, beaten	1/2 teaspoon cinnamon
1/2 cup molasses	1/2 teaspoon cloves
1/2 cup hot coffee	1/2 teaspoon allspice
1/2 teaspoon soda	1/2 pound mixed peel
1/2 teaspoon salt	1/2 cup chopped nuts

Cream the shortening and sugar, add egg and mix well. Add molasses; dissolve soda in hot coffee and add. Sift flour and cocoa with spices and salt and stir into the first mixture alternately with mixed fruit and nuts. Grease a large cookie sheet; spread the batter to 1/2-inch thickness on the sheet, allowing for spreading. Bake in 350-degree oven for 20 minutes. Cool, ice with soft butter icing (see Index), and cut into squares. You could ice the cakes all around with a butter icing moistened with strong coffee, or cocoa.

BEVVY'S BUTTERNUT SQUARES

Have you seen any butternuts lately? When we were kids Daddy used to take us into the country, stop our Briscoe at the side of a bush and we'd wander around till we came to a butternut tree with sticky green nuts lying under it. At home we'd spread the nuts on papers in the attic till they became hard and dry, then Daddy would open them for us with a hammer. (For these squares I now use pecans.)

	Topping:
1 cup dark brown sugar	
1 cup butter	1 well beaten egg
1 well beaten egg	1/2 cup dark brown sugar
2 cups flour	1 cup coarsely chopped nuts

Cream the shortening and sugar, add the egg and mix well. Work in the flour gradually, then spread the mixture in a thin layer on a greased baking sheet. For the topping brush on the well-beaten egg; sprinkle 1/4-cup of the brown sugar over it, then the chopped nuts and the rest of the sugar. Bake in a 350-degree oven for 20 to 25 minutes. Cut into squares when slightly cooled.

CHOCOLATE CRISPIES

If you want something good but haven't much time to fuss, try these:

2 squares melted chocolate	1/2 cup sifted flour
1/2 cup butter or shortening	1 teaspoon vanilla
1 cup sugar	1/2 teaspoon salt
2 eggs	1/2 cup chopped nuts

To melted chocolate add butter, sugar, eggs, flour, vanilla and salt; beat well and spread on a greased baking sheet. Sprinkle nuts on top and press down a bit so they'll stick. Bake at 350 degrees till firm; cool slightly and cut in squares.

TOASTED BEECHNUT COOKIES

But who has beechnuts in these days? We used to spread blankets under the trees in the bush and Daddy would shake down the nuts. Mother patiently opened them with a sharp knife and toasted them in the oven. If you haven't a beech tree handy you could use toasted almonds.

4 tablespoons shortening	1/2 teaspoon salt
1/2 cup sugar	4 tablespoons milk
2 egg yolks (or 1 whole egg)	1 teaspoon lemon juice
1 1/2 teaspoons baking	(optional)
powder	2 cups toasted nuts
1 cup flour	

Cream the shortening, add sugar and beaten yolks, then lemon juice. Sift the flour with the baking powder and salt; add, with milk, to mixture. Add toasted nuts. Drop by spoonfuls on to greased tin. Bake at 350 degrees for 10 minutes.

CHEWY MOLASSES COOKIES

Bevvy makes these big and round.

3/4 cup shortening	1 teaspoon salt
1 cup sugar	1 teaspoon soda
2 eggs, beaten	2 teaspoons cinnamon
1 cup molasses	1 teaspoon ginger
4 cups flour	3/4 cup cold, strong coffee

Cream shortening and sugar, add eggs and molasses; beat well. Add sifted dry ingredients alternately with coffee. Drop from a teaspoon onto greased cooky sheet and bake in a 350-degree oven for 15 minutes. It makes a lot. Put a walnut on top for a prize.

DANIEL'S GINGER CRINKLES

Hard, with cracks in their sugar coating, and very tasty.

³/₄ cup lard	¹/₂ teaspoon salt
1 cup brown sugar	1 teaspoon cinnamon
1 egg	1 teaspoon ginger
4 tablespoons molasses	¹/₂ teaspoon cloves
2¹/₄ cups flour	White sugar
2 teaspoons soda	

Blend lard and sugar; add egg and molasses and beat until blended. Sift flour, salt, soda and spices; add to creamed mixture and blend thoroughly. Put the dough in a cold place till it is well chilled. Shape into balls the size of hickory nuts, roll them in white sugar and put 2 inches apart on a greased baking sheet, pressing them a bit flat with a fork. Bake at 350 degrees for 12 to 15 minutes. Wonderful with apple sauce.

HENRY'S HOCHZICH KUCHA (Wedding Cookies)

1 cup lard	¹/₂ teaspoon salt
1¹/₂ cups brown sugar	¹/₂ cup water
2 eggs, beaten	3 teaspoons soda
1 cup baking molasses	1 teaspoon cream of tartar
¹/₂ teaspoon nutmeg	Flour enough to roll
	(try 3 to 4 cups)

Mix in the order given—sifting the dry ingredients together. Roll and cut in heart shapes. Bake in a 350-degree oven until golden.

GINGERBREAD MEN

How the children love these with their curranty eyes.

¹/₃ cup butter	¹/₃ teaspoon salt
¹/₃ cup brown sugar	1 teaspoon ginger
1 egg, well beaten	3 cups flour
3 teaspoons baking powder	²/₃ cups molasses

Cream shortening and sugar, add the egg. Sift dry ingredients together and add alternately with the molasses to the first mixture. Roll out ¹/₄ of an inch thick. With a small round (shot) glass cut the head. The body is cut with a glass somewhat larger. Cut the arms and feet with a knife. Join the parts by moistening the edges with egg white and pressing them together to make them stick. Press currants or raisins into the little men for eyes, mouth and buttons. Bake for 10 minutes at 400 degrees. Let the children dress up the gingerbread men with frosting if you want them to have some real fun.

SHORT CAKES

I'm copying this straight from Bevvy's book.

>   **1 quart flour**
>   **A good handful of lard (How do you like that?)**
>   **1¹/₂ cups sugar**   **1 cup currants**
>   **1 teaspoon soda**   **2 teaspoons baking powder**
>   **Buttermilk to roll out**

JAM JAMS

These are chewy and have a tantalizing old-fashioned flavour. I think it's the lard that does it.

>   **1 cup lard**   **4 cups flour**
>   **1 cup brown sugar**   **2 small teaspoons soda**
>   **2 eggs**   **1 teaspoon lemon or vanilla**
>   **6 tablespoons molasses**

Blend lard and sugar, then molasses, vanilla and egg. Add flour sifted with soda. The dough is easy to handle. Roll it quite thin and cut into rounds. Bake on a greased sheet at 325 degrees for 7 minutes then look—it might take a minute more for the cookies to turn crisp and brown. While they are still warm put two together with apple butter or jam spread between them. They become soft and keep well.

RIGGLEVAKE KUCHA (Railroad Cookies)

Light part: **Dark part:**
>   **1 cup sugar**   **1 cup sugar, brown**
>   **1 egg**   **1 cup butter**
>   **1 cup butter**   **1 cup molasses**
>   **¹/₂ cup milk**   **¹/₂ cup water**
>   **2 teaspoons baking powder**   **2 teaspoons soda**
>   **¹/₂ teaspoon vanilla**   **¹/₂ teaspoon vanilla**

Enough flour in each part to make dough easy to handle.

Mix the light and dark parts in separate bowls. Blend the sugar and butter for both parts. For the light part beat in the egg then alternately add the milk, vanilla and baking power sifted with flour. For the dark part add to the butter-sugar mixture the molasses, water and vanilla alternately with enough flour.

Break off pieces of dough from both dark and light parts, shape them into rounds and roll them separately about 1/8 inch thick. Put one on top of the other, roll up like a jelly roll and slice off pieces as thinly as you can. Place on greased cookie sheets and bake at 350 degrees till done.

A Cake in the House

Mother loves cake: she'll eat it for breakfast, dinner, and supper. "No use letting it get stale," she explains, but as soon as a cake is all gone she'll say, "I haven't a cake in the house," and immediately bake another one.

In Bevvy's household a cake seldom lasts a day; then Salome stirs up another from the many recipes in Bevvy's little black book where only the ingredients are listed.

In interpreting Bevvy's and Mother's recipes here I've suggested standard directions. I've tried many of them and they work— almost always. When I bake a cake I believe in being precise about things like soda and baking powder, and fairly accurate about proportions of liquid and dry, but I can't imagine messily measuring three tablespoons of butter when it's so easy to simply slice a sliver off the pound.

What if a cake doesn't come out of the oven high and light as a piece of foam rubber or a cake mix? If it's a little bit flat it is sure to be moister and you can easily fluff it up with great gobs of icing. You might be the best meat cooker and potato boiler in the world but you know it's the woman who turns out those cakes with the fluffy pink icing sprinkled with little silver balls and multicoloured doodads that gets all the praise.

I've shied away from Bevvy's recipes that call for more than three eggs; those Mennonite farmers' wives with whom she swapped her recipes didn't have to economize, they just went into the chicken pen, pulled an old hen off the nest and found half a dozen eggs they could cheerfully break into a batter. For a reason other than economy I've also eliminated recipes that call for cupfuls of cream.

In all my own cookbooks I've written a large S in the margin beside the cakes that are made with sour milk; I think they are moister and more flavourful. Besides they give me a good way to use up the sour milk I make a point of keeping on hand—it mustn't be kept too long, and I naturally wouldn't throw it away.

I had cake for breakfast this morning; I had cake for lunch and for dinner; tomorrow I'll have to bake another. I like to keep a cake in the house.

1-2-3-4 CAKE

This is Mother's most fool-proof light cake.

1 cup butter	1 cup cold water or milk
2 cups sugar	2 teaspoons cream of tartar
3 cups flour	1 teaspoon soda
4 eggs	1 teaspoon vanilla

Cream butter, add sugar and blend, beat in the eggs; sift the cream of tartar and soda with the flour twice before adding to the batter alternately with the milk and vanilla. (Put in a cup of raisins or walnuts for variety.) Pour into a large buttered and floured cake pan or two layer pans, and bake in a 350-degree oven: 45 minutes for the large cake pan, 30 for the layer pans. Test it.

Mother usually iced it with a plain butter icing, but sometimes, glory of glories, she made Mocha Cakes.

MOCHA CAKES

These were Mother's pride and joy. To this day people who came to parties at our house forty years ago ask me, "Does your mother still make those marvellous Mocha Cakes?" She does.

When Mother's 1-2-3-4 cake in a large pan was completely cold she would cut it in 2-inch squares, each of which she would carefully ice, top and sides, with a rich butter icing. Immediately, before the icing could set, she would sprinkle generously on all sides, or dip the cake on all sides into, very finely chopped almonds which she had previously browned in butter. You never tasted such cakes. A lot of bother, mind you, blanching and hand-chopping, and buttering all those nuts—but think of enjoying a deserved reputation for doing it throughout all those years.

MAPLE SYRUP CAKE

Two layers of sweetness and light!

$^1/_2$ cup shortening	2 cups cake flour
$^3/_4$ cup maple syrup	$^1/_2$ teaspoon salt
2 eggs, beaten	$2^1/_2$ teaspoons baking powder
1 teaspoon vanilla	$^1/_2$ cup butternuts or
$^1/_2$ cup sugar	walnuts, or pecans

Blend the shortening, sugar, syrup, eggs and vanilla. Sift the flour, salt and baking powder, stir in the nuts and add all to the blended mixture. Pour into greased, floured layer pans and bake at 375 degrees for 20 minutes. Cool a few minutes then carefully turn cakes onto racks to become cold. Put together with soft Maple Icing and ice all over.

GUM DROP CAKE

Bevvy bakes this for special events—like a wedding, or a gebuts-dag—(birthday).

1 cup white sugar
1/2 cup butter
2 eggs, well beaten
1 cup milk
1 pound gum drops (no black ones) cut up

2 teaspoons baking powder
1 teaspoon nutmeg
1 teaspoon cinnamon
2 1/2 cups flour

Blend the butter and sugar, beat in the eggs; alternately add the milk and sifted dry ingredients, then the gum drops. Bake in a greased pan at 350 degrees for 45 minutes. Ice with a white icing and decorate with gum drops. It will be a hit.

CHERRY CAKE

This cake when prettily iced makes a delicious dessert.

1/2 cup butter
1 cup granulated sugar
2 eggs, separated
1/2 cup milk
2 cups flour
1 1/2 teaspoons baking powder

1/2 teaspoon salt
1 cup maraschino cherries, cut in halves
2 tablespoons maraschino cherry juice

Cream the butter; add the sugar gradually, then the yolks of the eggs, well beaten, the milk and the dry ingredients, mixed and sifted. Fold in the stiffly beaten whites of eggs; add the cherries and juice and bake in a 350-degree oven for about an hour. (You can cut down on the cherries if you think a cupful is too great an extravagance.) Slather it at the last minute before serving with whipped cream, or ice it with a butter icing

GEBURTSTAG KUCHA (Birthday Cake from Rebecca Weber)

Snow white and light as a feather; baked in layers.

$^1/_2$ cup butter	$1^1/_2$ cups ice water
2 cups white sugar	1 teaspoon vanilla
$3^1/_2$ cups flour	$^1/_2$ teaspoon almond extract
1 teaspoon salt	4 egg whites beaten stiff
3 teaspoons baking powder	

Add sugar to the butter and beat until light. Sift dry ingredients and add alternately with ice water and flavourings, beating thoroughly after each addition. Fold in the beaten egg whites. Pour into greased layer pans and bake at 350 degrees for about 30 minutes. Cover with Angel Feather Icing and be tactful about the number of candles.

COCONUT CLOUD CAKE (from Serena Shantz)

Pretty and good; you can easily cut the recipe in half if you don't want a layer cake.

$^3/_4$ cup shortening	3 cups sifted flour
$^3/_4$ teaspoon salt	$4^1/_2$ teaspoons baking
$1^1/_2$ cups sugar	powder
2 cups milk	1 teaspoon almond extract
3 eggs, separated	1 cup dessicated coconut
1 teaspoon vanilla	

Cream butter, add sugar and beaten egg yolks and 1 egg white; continue beating. Sift flour with baking powder and salt, mix with coconut and add alternately with milk and flavourings to butter mixture. Pour into greased layer-cake pans and bake in 350-degree oven for about 30 minutes. Cool; remove from pans to a rack and ice with Angel Feather Icing (see Icings), sprinkle shredded coconut generously on top and sides of cake after you've iced both the layers and put one on top of the other.

CARROT CAKE

Wende Machetzki, the darling bride who works in Kitchener's Provident Mennonite book store where you can browse, sit in front of a charming real fireplace and have a free cup of coffee, gave me her favourite cake recipe. "I don't call it carrot cake because people don't want to even taste it then. I call it Wednesday cake or whatever day of the week I baked it on," she told me.

2 cups sugar	1¹/₄ cups vegetable oil
2 cups flour	4 whole eggs
3 cups finely shredded carrots	2 teaspoons cinnamon
	Pinch of salt
2 teaspoons baking soda	2 teaspoons vanilla

Mix dry ingredients together. Blend in oil, add eggs and carrots, then vanilla. Blend well and bake in 8-inch layer pans at 350-degrees for 35 minutes.

Icing:

8 ounces cream cheese	1 teaspoon vanilla
¹/₂ cup butter	1 teaspoon orange juice
1 pound icing sugar	1 cup finely chopped pecans

Blend cheese and butter, slowly add sugar, vanilla, orange juice and nuts. Ice only after cake is completely cold.

This cake is very moist and delicious, can easily be halved if you don't want a layer cake.

COMPROMISE CAKE

The only compromising thing about this cake is that, having made it, you'll be asked to make it again and again.

1 cup seeded raisins	2 eggs, separated
Rind of an orange	1 cup buttermilk or sour milk
¹/₂ cup nuts—walnuts or pecans	2 cups all-purpose flour
¹/₂ cup shortening	1 teaspoon soda
¹/₂ cup white sugar	¹/₂ teaspoon salt
²/₃ cup brown sugar	

Put orange rind and raisins through food chopper—or blender—running orange rind through more than once, if necessary, to have it very fine. Mix a small amount of the flour with the fruit. Cream the shortening, add sugar and blend well. Add egg yolks and beat well. Add alternately the buttermilk and remainder of flour sifted with soda and salt. Stir in the raisins, orange rind and nuts. Fold in the stiffly beaten egg whites. Turn into an 8-inch square greased pan. Bake in a 350-degree oven about 55 minutes. When cool, frost with a soft white butter icing flavoured with grated orange rind, or with penuche—for me there's nothing as good as penuche icing.

WEARY WILLIE CAKE

Easy and fun to make. Light, tender and delicious.

Into a measuring cup break the whites of 2 eggs, add enough soft butter to half fill the cup, then fill the cup with milk. In a mixing bowl measure 1½ cups flour sifted with 2 teaspoons baking powder and 1 cup sugar; turn into the dry ingredients the contents of the measuring cup and beat all together for 5 minutes. Add a teaspoon of any flavouring you like, I prefer almond, and bake the cake for half an hour in a 350-degree oven. The yolks of the eggs can be blended with powdered sugar to make an icing.

GRAHAM WAFER CAKE

Mother was thrilled with this very rich layer-cake recipe. She put lemon or cream filling between the layers and iced it with a fluffy white icing.

2 tablespoons butter
1¼ cups white sugar
2 eggs
Pinch of salt

1½ cups buttermilk or sour milk
32 graham wafers rolled and sifted
1 teaspoon soda

Blend the butter and sugar, beat in the eggs and salt; sift the soda with the finely rolled graham wafers and add alternately with the buttermilk. Pour into 2 greased layer pans and bake in a 350-degree oven till done.

BANANA CAKE

I've tried a lot of banana cake recipes and I'm sure this is the best. It stays moist, and with a penuche icing it's out of this world.

½ cup soft shortening
1½ cups sugar
2 large eggs
2¼ cups flour
1 teaspoon baking powder
¾ teaspoon soda

1 teaspoon salt
¼ cup buttermilk or sour milk
1 cup mashed ripe bananas
½ cup chopped walnuts or pecans

Cream together until fluffy the shortening and sugar; beat in thoroughly the eggs. Sift together the dry ingredients and stir them in alternately with the milk, bananas and nuts. Pour into the greased and floured cake pan, 13 by 9, or two layer-pans; bake at 350 degrees until the cake tests done—about 25 to 30 minutes for the layers, 40 to 45 for the long pan. For the layer cake you can spread whipped cream and sliced bananas for a filling and slather whipped cream over the top with slices of banana round the edges—a scrumptious company dessert. If you're making it in the long pan, ice it with penuche. I'd even favour icing the layers with Penuche Icing.

EPPEL DUNKES KUCHA (Dunking Apple Cake)

Tastes good, stays moist—you wouldn't need to dunk it.

1/2 cup butter	1/2 teaspoon cloves
1 cup white sugar	1 teaspoon cinnamon
1 egg	1 cup raisins
2 cups flour	1 cup warm apple sauce
1 teaspoon soda	3/4 cup chopped walnuts
1/2 teaspoon salt	(optional)

Soften the butter, add the sugar and egg and blend well. Stir in the apple sauce. Sift the dry ingredients and to them add the raisins and walnuts. Stir into the first mixture. Pour into a greased oblong cake pan and bake at 350 degrees for about 40 or 45 minutes. I like mine iced with a baked-on topping.

SAUERKRAUT CHOCOLATE CAKE

Leftover, cooked sauerkraut makes this cake moist and delicious.

2/3 cup butter	2 1/4 cup flour
1 1/2 cups white sugar	1/2 cup cocoa
3 large eggs	1 teaspoon baking powder
1 teaspoon vanilla	1 teaspoon soda
1 cup water	1/2 teaspoon salt
2/3 cup drained sauerkraut	

Blend butter and sugar, beat in the eggs, one at a time; add water alternately with sifted dry ingredients, then stir in the sauerkraut and vanilla. Pour batter into two greased layer-cake pans and bake in a 350-degree oven for 30 minutes. Cool on racks and ice with Mocha icing. Strangely enough, the cake doesn't taste of sauerkraut.

MARBLE CAKE

My Auntie Clara used to put pink or green colouring in one-third of this cake and we thought it was miraculous.

3/4 cup butter	4 teaspoons baking powder
2 cups sugar	2 squares grated chocolate
4 eggs	1 teaspoon cinnamon
1 cup milk	1 teaspoon vanilla
3 cups cake flour	A very little colouring

Cream the butter, add the sugar and blend; add the eggs, one at a time, beating them in. Add the flour mixed with the baking powder and the milk, stirring till smooth. Put 1/3 of the dough into another bowl and mix well with the chocolate, cinnamon and vanilla. In another bowl add the colouring to another 1/3. Finally, into a greased tube pan spoon alternate layers of the white, dark and coloured. Bake at 350 degrees for 45 minutes.

ANGEL CAKE

I have never baked a real angel cake. With a foolproof commercial angel cake mix I make a tall gorgeous synthetic creation and brazenly enjoy the exclamations that come when I produce it beautifully decorated with Angel Feather Icing and birthday candles or sparsely sprinkled with those tiny coloured candy bits.

PURE ANGEL CAKE

Of course if you want to try the real thing, here is Mother's recipe. Good luck.

1 cup egg whites (9-11 eggs)	1 cup sifted cake flour
1/4 teaspoon salt	(Swansdown)
3/4 teaspoon cream of tartar	3/4 teaspoon vanilla
1 1/4 cups sifted fine	1/4 teaspoon almond
granulated sugar	flavouring

Sift flour once, measure and sift four more times. Beat egg whites with salt; when foamy add cream of tartar and continue beating until eggs are stiff enough to hold up in peaks, but not dry. (Mother's recipe says to do this on a large platter with a wire whip or two forks—I hope you have an electric beater.) Fold in the sugar, 2 tablespoons at a time. Fold in the flour the same way, then the flavouring. Turn into an angel cake pan that is *not* greased and bake in a 375-degree oven for about 35 minutes— or until the top is brown and no imprint remains when you touch the top lightly with your finger. Invert on a funnel till cold.

CHOCOLATE ANGEL FOOD CAKE—merely substitute 1/4 cup cocoa for as much flour.

CHOCOLATE MOCHA ANGEL CAKE

My sister Norm says this is one of the easiest company desserts she makes: I say it's one of the best.

1 chocolate angel cake	1/2 cup white sugar
1 pint whipping cream— whipped	2 heaping tablespoons instant coffee powder

With a sharp knife slice chocolate angel cake horizontally into four layers. Dissolve the coffee powder in cream, whip till stiff, add sugar, then slather generously over each part of cake, putting it together again and covering the outside as well. Shave chips of semi-sweet chocolate over top and sides. Keep it cool till you are ready to serve it. It can be made a day ahead.

SUNNY SPONGE CAKE

Here's how to use up the egg yolks left from the Angel Cake; it keeps well and is nice for Trifle Pudding later on.

12 egg yolks (1 cup)	1/2 teaspoon salt
1 1/2 cups sugar	3/4 cup warm water
2 cups cake flour	1/2 teaspoon lemon juice or extract
2 teaspoons baking powder	
1 tablespoon orange or lemon rind (optional)	1/2 teaspoon vanilla

Beat the egg yolks until thick, gradually add the sugar; alternately beat in the water and flavourings with the sifted flour, baking powder and salt. Pour into an ungreased tube pan and bake at 325 degrees for almost an hour. Invert on a funnel till cold, then ice with a fluffy or soft icing. It's good with maple icing too.

AUNT MAGDALINE'S HURRY SPONGE CAKE

You can make Trifle Pudding with this cake too.

3 eggs	2 teaspoons baking powder
1¹/2 cups white sugar	1 teaspoon lemon or vanilla
2 cups flour	flavouring
¹/2 teaspoon salt	¹/2 cup water

Beat the eggs for 1 minute. Gradually add sugar and beat for 5 minutes. Add 1 cup of sifted flour and beat 1 minute more, then add 1/2 cup of water. Fold in remaining cup of flour sifted with baking powder and salt; stir in the flavouring. Pour into greased cake or tube pan and bake at 350 degrees for 25 to 30 minutes.

OATMEAL CAKE (from Mrs. Ammon Bauman)

Moist and marvellous, with a crispy, delicious icing baked on.

1 cup quick rolled oats	2 eggs, beaten
1¹/3 cups boiling water	1¹/3 cups all-purpose flour
¹/2 cup butter	1 teaspoon soda
1 cup brown sugar	1 teaspoon cinnamon
1 cup white sugar	1 teaspoon salt

Pour boiling water over the oats, stir and let cool. Cream together the butter and sugars, then add the eggs beaten till fluffy. Sift the dry ingredients and add them alternately with the soaked oatmeal until blended. Turn into a buttered 9 by 11 pan, bake at 350 degrees for about 35 minutes.

While the cake is baking mix the topping:

6 tablespoons melted butter	¹/2 cup coarsely chopped nuts
¹/2 cup brown sugar	¹/4 cup cream
¹/2 cup dessicated coconut	¹/2 teaspoon vanilla

While the cake is hot, carefully spread the topping over it smoothly. Broil 4 inches from the burner until just melted and bubbly, watching it all the time. Oh Boy!

UPSIDE-DOWN CAKE

Fruity, luscious and dripping with taffy; vary it with any fruit you like.

¹/2 cup butter or margarine	¹/2 teaspoon salt
1¹/2 cups sugar	2 teaspoons baking powder
2 eggs	1 cup milk
2¹/4 cups all-purpose flour	1 teaspoon vanilla

Upside-down topping:

¹/₃ cup butter	**Fruit to cover bottom of**
³/₄ cup brown sugar	**cake pan**

Soften shortening and add sugar gradually. Add beaten eggs and beat until the mixture is fluffy. Sift flour, salt and baking powder and add alternately with milk and flavouring, beating well after each addition. If you want a good, white, foolproof, moist, plain cake, you can stop right there; put it into a square pan and bake it at 350 degrees. But if you want to take a chance on making a super-dessert: melt ¹/₃ cup butter in your baking pan, sprinkle ³/₄ cup brown sugar evenly over the butter and arrange drained fruit in an attractive pattern on the butter-sugar base. You might try pineapple rounds with maraschino cherries and pecan halves, or large pitted prunes with walnut halves, peach or apricot halves, canned or raw, with cherries or blanched almonds, or apple slices, blueberries (even raspberries though they are rather soft). Bake at 350 for 45 minutes. Turn the cake upside-down while it is hot and patch up the fruity part if it needs patching. Serve it as soon as it's cool enough, with or without whipped, or ice cream.

Warning: Once I made a pineapple upside-down cake for a Spin-the-Wheel booth at a Rotary Carnival. Winners always chose the mile-high, eye-appealing, professionally-iced sponge cakes (dry as dust in the midriff, I'm sure) and left my luscious but flatter offering on the shelf.

UPSA-DAISY CAKE

This one is from the Lutheran Ladies' Aid cook book. It's tried and true.

4 tablespoons butter	**3 eggs, separated**
3 tablespoons sherry (may	**¹/₄ teaspoon salt**
be omitted)	**1 cup sugar**
1 cup brown sugar	**¹/₂ teaspoon vanilla**
8 to 12 pitted, cooked, large	**¹/₂ cup hot water**
prunes	**1 cup sifted cake flour**
12 walnut halves	**1 teaspoon baking powder**

Melt the butter in a deep, round cake pan. Add sherry if wished; spread brown sugar evenly over bottom. Arrange prunes and nuts over sugar. Set aside. To egg whites add salt; beat stiff with rotary beater; gradually beat in a half-cup of sugar. Using same beater, beat yolks very light; gradually beat in remaining sugar, vanilla and hot water. Add flour sifted with baking powder and beat smooth. Fold in egg whites, pour over prunes in pan, and bake in a 325-degree oven for about 40 minutes. Invert on a large plate: serve warm, with whipped cream.

CRUMB CAKE

Mother's life became joyful when she discovered this easy, self-iced cake.

1 egg	1¹/₂ cups flour
¹/₄ cup butter	1 teaspoon soda
1 cup brown sugar	1 teaspoon baking powder
1 cup buttermilk or sour milk	1 teaspoon vanilla or cinnamon

Crumbs:

1 cup brown sugar	¹/₂ cup flour
¹/₄ cup butter	

Cream the butter, add sugar, beaten egg, then the sifted dry ingredients alternately with the milk and vanilla. Pour the batter into a square greased and floured cake pan and spread the crumbs lightly over the top. Bake in a 350-degree oven for about 45 minutes till the cake tests done and the crumbs are golden.

THE BEST COCOA CAKE

With a smooth, moist texture, this really is a dandy. I've made it many times.

¹/₂ cup shortening	¹/₂ cup sour milk or buttermilk
2 cups brown sugar	1 teaspoon soda
2 eggs, well beaten	1¹/₂ cups flour
¹/₂ cup cocoa	1 teaspoon vanilla
¹/₂ teaspoon salt	
¹/₂ cup boiling water	

Cream the shortening, add the sugar and keep creaming. Add the well-beaten eggs and beat the mixture thoroughly. Dissolve the cocoa in boiling water and add the sour milk. Combine with the first mixture. Sift together the soda, flour, and salt, add to the other mixture and beat again—with vanilla. Butter a square cake pan, flour it, pour in the batter and bake in a 350-degree oven for about 45 minutes. Cool and frost with Soft Chocolate Icing.

DEVIL'S FOOD LAYER CAKE

This is a good big one; sometimes you need that kind.

1/2 cup butter	1 cup white sugar
2 eggs, beaten separately	1 cup brown sugar
3 1/2 cups flour	1 teaspoon baking powder
2 squares chocolate, melted	1/8 teaspoon cinnamon
1 teaspoon soda	1/8 teaspoon allspice
1 cup sour milk or buttermilk	1 teaspoon vanilla

Cream butter and sugar, add egg and melted chocolate. Sift flour, baking powder, and spices, then add to butter mixture alternately with milk in which the soda has been dissolved. Add vanilla and fold in the beaten egg whites. Pour into greased, floured layer-cake pans and bake in a 350-degree oven for 30 minutes. Especially good with an orange or date filling between the layers and a soft chocolate icing over all. (See Icings and Fillings.)

COUSIN LUCY'S SPICE CAKE

My father's white-haired Cousin Lucy was considered one of the finest cooks in Grand Rapids, Michigan. We thought so anyway.

1 cup white sugar	1 1/2 cups flour
Butter the size of an egg	1 teaspoon cinnamon
1 egg, slightly beaten	Pinch of allspice
3 tablespoons molasses	1/2 teaspoon baking powder
1 cup sour milk	1/2 teaspoon soda
1/4 teaspoon vanilla	

Soften butter, blend in sugar, egg, and molasses. Sift all the dry ingredients and add them to the egg mixture alternately with the milk and vanilla. Bake in a greased, square cake pan in a 350-degree oven for about 45 minutes. Give it a penuche icing—it deserves it.

MOTHER'S MAGIC SPICE CAKE

Mother was mortified when the hostess at a party for pre-schoolers told her I had refused a piece of birthday cake "because

I only like my mother's spice cake when it goes down in the middle like taffy."

1/2 cup butter	1 teaspoon cloves
2 cups brown sugar	1 teaspoon cinnamon
2 eggs	1/2 teaspoon nutmeg
3/4 cup sour milk	1 teaspoon soda
Flour for a cake batter	
(try 11/2 cups)	

Blend the butter and sugar, add the eggs and beat them in; sift the flour with the soda and spices and add them alternately with the sour milk. Pour the batter into a greased cake pan and bake in a 350-degree oven for about 40 minutes. If you're lucky it falls flat and you won't have to ice it.

BEULAH'S DATE AND COCONUT CAKE

Mother had great faith in Beulah's recipes, they usually turned out pretty well.

1 cup butter	1 cup coconut
1 cup brown sugar	1 cup walnuts, chopped
2 eggs, slightly beaten	coarsely
1/2 cup sweet milk	1 teaspoon soda
1 cup sour cream	11/2 cups flour
1 pound of dates, cut up	

Blend the butter and sugar, beat in eggs; alternately add the milk, cream and sifted dry ingredients with the dates, coconut and walnuts. Turn into a greased cake pan in a 350-degree oven till it tests done. Cover with toasted coconut frosting.

RUM AND DATE CAKE

Mother had to wangle this precious recipe from Mrs. Emil Schultz.

1 pound dates (1/2 pound is	1/2 teaspoon salt
better, Mother says)	1 teaspoon vanilla
1 cup walnuts, chopped	1 teaspoon water
1 teaspoon baking soda	4 tablespoons rum
1 cup boiling water	
1/2 cup butter	Icing:
1 cup brown sugar	1/2 cup soft butter
2 eggs	11/2 cups icing sugar
1 cup sifted flour	1 tablespoon rum

Chop dates and nuts, add soda to boiling water and pour over dates and nuts; let stand while preparing batter.

Cream butter and gradually add the sugar; beat eggs thoroughly and add to butter and sugar. Pour date mixture into this and mix well. Measure flour and sift with salt; add to mixture, adding vanilla last. Pour into greased pan and bake at 350 degrees for one hour. Remove cake from oven and pour over it the rum mixed with a little water. Allow to cool before icing. This keeps well and is moist and rummy and rich.

DATE OATMEAL CAKE (Mrs. Christian Eby's)

One of the best-tasting cakes I've ever eaten.

Sift together into a bowl:

¹/₂ cup flour	**1 teaspoon cinnamon**
1 teaspoon soda	**1 teaspoon cloves**

Pour 1 cup boiling water over 2 cups rolled oats, mix well, cool slightly, then blend in (using electric blender if you have one):

³/₄ cup butter or margarine	**1¹/₂ cups finely chopped**
2 cups brown sugar	**dates**
2 eggs	**1 cup coarsely chopped**
	walnuts

Pour oatmeal mixture into dry ingredients and mix well. Bake in 8-inch square pan at 350 degrees for 45 minutes, or until done. It is so moist and rich it hardly needs icing—but if you insist, use Penuche Icing.

JELLY ROLL

We always hung around to watch—and to eat—when Mother made a jelly roll.

3 large eggs, beaten	**1 teaspoon vanilla**
1 cup sugar	**1 cup flour**
5 tablespoons water	**1 teaspoon baking powder**
¹/₄ teaspoon salt	

Gradually add sugar to the thickly beaten eggs, continue beating and add water and vanilla. Sift dry ingredients together and beat them in until the batter is smooth. Pour into a flat, greased and floured pan, 15 by 10, lined with greased paper or foil. Bake at 375 degrees for 12 to 15 minutes—till the cake just tests done—overbaking makes it hard to remove the paper. Immediately turn the cake upside-down on a towel sprinkled with confectioners' sugar. Quickly and carefully pull off the paper. Spread the cake at once with jelly or jam or lemon honey (see Tarts). Roll up, wrap in a towel until cool and don't keep it too long before you serve it.

ANGIE'S RAVISHING RAISIN CAKE

This is a "keeper."

2^1/$_2$ cups seedless raisins
2^1/$_4$ cups boiling water
^{2}/$_3$ cup shortening
^{3}/$_4$ cup white sugar
^{3}/$_4$ cup brown sugar
3 cups all-purpose flour
1^1/$_2$ teaspoons salt
1^1/$_2$ teaspoons soda

^{1}/$_4$ teaspoon nutmeg
^{1}/$_2$ teaspoon cloves
1 teaspoon cinnamon
1 cup sour milk or
    buttermilk
1 cup coarsely chopped nuts
2 teaspoons vanilla

Boil the raisins in the water until there is almost no water left— no more than a couple of tablespoonfuls. Add the shortening and stir until it is melted, then the sugars and stir until they are completely dissolved. Add the sifted dry ingredients and nuts alternately with the milk and vanilla, beating well after each addition. Pour into two greased loaf pans and bake at 325 degrees for an hour—or until it tests done.

LIGHT CHRISTMAS FRUIT CAKE

My favourite; has a mild, fruity flavour.

^{1}/$_2$ pound butter
^{1}/$_2$ cup white sugar
3 eggs
^{1}/$_2$ teaspoon salt
1 pound white raisins
1 cup almonds, sliced
    lengthwise
1 cup mixed peel, cut or
    sliced thin
2^3/$_4$ cups flour
1 teaspoon nutmeg
1 teaspoon baking powder
1 cup additional almonds for
    topping

1 cup canned pineapple,
    cut up
^{1}/$_2$ pound candied red
    cherries, cut up
^{1}/$_4$ pound candied green
    cherries, cut up
1 teaspoon lemon flavouring
    (or juice)
1 teaspoon almond
    flavouring
2 teaspoons vanilla

Blend butter and sugar; add eggs, one at a time, and beat; add flavourings, sifted dry ingredients, fruit and nuts; mix well. Grease sheet of brown paper with shortening, fit carefully into a large loaf pan—or two smaller ones. Turn cake into pan, cover with cup of sliced almonds, pressed slightly into the dough to make them stick. Bake at 250 to 350 degrees for 3 hours.

AUNTIE'S DARK FRUIT CAKE

Mother never found a recipe for Christmas Cake that she liked better than this really old one.

1/2 pound brown sugar	1 teaspoon cloves
1/2 pound butter	1 teaspoon nutmeg
5 eggs, well beaten	1 pound raisins
1/2 cup wine or whisky	1/2 pound currants
1/2 cup medium baking syrup	1 cup almonds or Brazils, cut fine
1 teaspoon soda	1 cup lemon and citron peel, chopped
1/2 teaspoon baking powder	
2 cups sifted flour	1 cup dates, cut up
1 teaspoon cinnamon	1 cup candied cherries

Mother says you can put in more fruit and nuts if you like—but not less than 1 cup of each. Blend the butter and sugar, beat in the eggs, stir in the whisky and syrup, then the flour sifted with the other dry ingredients and spices. Now stir in the nuts and fruits—and stir and stir. Line a high, round or oblong pan—or two loaf pans—with double heavy waxed paper, also greased.

Bake in a very slow oven—about 300 degrees. Mother says to put two cookie pans in the bottom of the oven, below the cake, as it burns so easily on the bottom. Mother's aunt's directions say the cake should be baked for 3 hours but Mother doesn't think it takes that long.

After the cake has been cooled Mother drizzles some wine or whisky over it—how much you'd like to use depends on you.

ICINGS AND FILLINGS

BASIC BUTTER ICING

You can't make a mistake with a plain butter icing; plenty of beating makes it quite fluffy. There are also as many variations as you care to invent.

4 tablespoons soft butter
1¹/₂ cups icing sugar
Pinch of salt

1 to 2 tablespoons milk, cream, water, fruit juice or coffee
1 teaspoon vanilla, rum, or any flavouring

Cream the butter and gradually work in half the sugar. Add salt, liquid and flavouring, then work in the remaining sugar (or enough to make the icing spread easily). You can't miss: you just keep adding sugar or liquid until the spreadability is perfect. For layer cakes just double or triple the amounts. If you want it richer, add more butter.

CHOCOLATE BUTTER ICING

Add ¹/₃ cup cocoa or 2 ounces of melted chocolate to Basic Butter Icing.

COFFEE BUTTER ICING

Use strong coffee for the liquid or add a teaspoon or a tablespoon of instant coffee powder to the basic recipe. I like a combination of chocolate and coffee myself.

ALMOND BUTTER ICING

Almond flavouring added to Basic Butter Icing is all you need, but you might like to add toasted almonds as well—or sprinkle them on top.

ORANGE OR LEMON BUTTER ICING

Use orange juice or lemon juice as your liquid and flavouring, plus a teaspoon of grated rind.

LIQUEUR BUTTER ICING

Any liqueurs, rum, crème de cacao, crème de menthe, Cointreau, whisky, Tia Maria or whatever you have; a pleasant surprise and taste—as a flavouring, or even as the liquid in your icing.

COLOURED BUTTER ICING

Simply add a very little bit of fruit colouring to basic icing to get the colour you want. But be careful—shocking pink or indigo is not appetizing.

SOFT CHOCOLATE ICING

Richly chocolate in flavour, this foolproof icing stays soft, moist, glossy, and keeps the cake that way too.

2 squares unsweetened chocolate, cut in pieces —or ¹/₂ cup cocoa
1¹/₄ cups milk (or strong coffee)

4 tablespoons flour
1 cup white sugar
2 tablespoons butter

Add the chocolate to the milk in a double boiler and heat. When the chocolate is melted beat with a rotary beater until blended. Sift flour with sugar, add a small amount of chocolate mixture, stirring until smooth; return to double boiler, cook until thickened, add butter and vanilla. Cool and spread on cake. This amount makes enough to cover tops and sides of two 9-inch layers.

If you make it with cocoa, mix the sugar, flour and cocoa in a bowl while you heat the milk in the double boiler, then pour enough of the milk into the dry mixture to make it pour nicely into the scalded milk and carry on as I've told you above.

PENUCHE ICING

Soft, creamy, and delicious, my favourite on many cakes: spice, oatmeal, banana especially. Can be easily expanded to cover several layers—or eaten as candy.

²/₃ cup brown sugar
²/₃ cup milk

²/₃ cup butter
¹/₂ teaspoon salt

Stir over low heat, then bring rapidly to full boil, stirring constantly. Boil to 220 degrees, or exactly 1 minute. Remove from heat, beat until lukewarm, no longer glossy, and of the right consistency to spread. If by some fluke of fate it doesn't get thick enough, you can (1) boil it again, adding 2 tablespoons of cornstarch or flour to thicken it—or (2) enjoy scraping it off the plate as it runs down the sides of the cake.

ANGEL FEATHER ICING

There's nothing better for an angel cake or a layer cake than this almost foolproof and luscious icing; it doesn't dissolve, run away or get crusty; it stays tender and fluffy for days if anyone lets it last that long.

2 egg whites	**¼ teaspoon cream of tartar**
¾ cup sugar	**¼ teaspoon salt**
⅓ cup corn syrup	**1 teaspoon vanilla or other**
2 tablespoons water	**flavouring**

Put everything but the vanilla into the top of a double boiler with fast-boiling water below. Start beating immediately with a rotary beater or electric mixer until the mixture stands in stiff peaks. Remove from heat, add flavouring, and keep on beating until it is thick enough to spread easily. You'll be delighted and everyone will exclaim when they see the glorified cake.

BAKED-ON FROSTINGS

These are so simple to do and so good when toasted under the broiler. They give something special to many kinds of cake— plain white, spice, banana, oatmeal, even chocolate. Let your cake cool for about 5 minutes, spread the icing over the top, quickly, then put it under your broiler until it bubbles and becomes lightly browned—keep watching it all the time, it doesn't take long.

TOASTED COCONUT FROSTING

⅓ cup brown sugar	**¾ cup shredded coconut**
2 tablespoons cream	**(½ cup walnuts or pecans or almonds might be added)**

BAKED-ON MERINGUE ICING

2 egg whites, beaten stiff	**1 cup brown sugar**
Pinch of salt	**1 cup chopped nuts or**
¼ teaspoon cream of tartar	**coconut—or both**

Beat egg whites till stiff, adding salt and cream of tartar; a bit at a time, add the brown sugar, beating until smooth. Spread over cake and sprinkle with nuts or coconut—bake at 350 degrees until bubbly.

BAKED-ON MARSHMALLOW ICING

12 marshmallows	1/2 cup chopped nuts
1/2 cup brown sugar	

Cut the marshmallows in half, crosswise, place them on the unbaked, thick batter of your cake—(or on the baked cake that has cooled for 5 minutes)—mix the sugar and nuts and sprinkle over the marshmallows and bake on the cake or broil until slightly bubbly.

BAKED-ON BUTTERSCOTCH FROSTING

3 tablespoons butter, melted	4 tablespoons cream
3/4 cup brown sugar	1/2 cup coconut or chopped nuts

Mix, spread on cake while it is warm and put under the broiler until it begins to bubble.

LAZY BAKED-ON ICING

Sometimes when I'm in a hurry I simply sprinkle a fairly thick cake batter with a mixture of sugar and nuts—not too thick or it will sink. Or I make crumbs—with 1 cup of brown sugar, 3 tablespoons of butter and 3 tablespoons of flour—and spread them over the batter, or baked cake, and bake them or brown them.

BUTTERSCOTCH ICING

Mix 1 cup brown sugar, 1 tablespoon butter, 3 tablespoons milk in a saucepan and let come to a boil, no more. Take from stove and add enough icing sugar to make a mixture that is just right for spreading over your cake. Flavour with vanilla or rum. It will not harden.

FLUFFY MAPLE ICING

Boil 1 1/2 cups maple syrup until it spins a long thread; pour it slowly over the stiffly beaten whites of 2 eggs, whipping steadily during the process.

SOFT MAPLE ICING

1/4 cup soft butter	1/2 teaspoon vanilla
1/2 cup maple syrup	2 1/2 cups icing sugar

Blend butter, syrup and vanilla till smooth, then add gradually and blend in the icing sugar. Delicious, easy to spread—and it stays soft.

PEANUT BUTTER ICING

Blend ¹/₄ cup butter or margarine with ¹/₃ cup peanut butter and ¹/₃ teaspoon salt. Add 2¹/₄ cups sifted icing sugar and ¹/₂ cup strong cold coffee, alternately, a little at a time. Cream after each addition till smooth.

PEACH DESSERT ICING

Slather a plain light layer cake with whipped cream, between the layers and on top and sides, putting peach-halves between the layers, round the rim on top (either fresh or canned peaches will do).

MOISTENERS

If you have a cake that is going a bit stale, or if you want to keep a cake moist, you might try the following:

Dissolve ¹/₂ cup sugar in 1 cup of orange juice or in ³/₄ cup lemon juice and ¹/₄ cup water; dribble the mixture over a stale cake—or as soon as you take a cake out of the oven.

Some people use the same trick with rum and water; others use wine.

RAISIN FILLING

Delicious between the layers of almost any cake, but especially with spice or oatmeal cakes.

³/₄ cup sugar	1 cup raisins
3 tablespoons butter	1 cup water
1 tablespoon cornstarch	

Blend sugar and cornstarch, then the water. Add raisins and cook the mixture in a heavy saucepan or a double boiler until it is thick and clear. Remove from the heat, add butter and stir into mixture until it disappears. Spread between layers and on top of cake too if you like, it will keep it moist and give it a "wonderful-good" flavour.

ORANGE FILLING (for one layer)

Good between layers of an orange, raisin, spice, graham wafer or white cake.

Juice of 1 orange	Grated rind of $^1/_2$ orange
1 tablespoon cornstarch	3 teaspoons sugar
1 tablespoon lemon juice	$^1/_2$ cup hot water
1 egg yolk	1 tablespoon butter

Mix the sugar and cornstarch, add the egg yolk, then the fruit juices, orange rind and hot water. Cook in double boiler until of consistency to spread. Stir in the butter till blended.

CREAM FILLING (for two layers)

With bananas sliced over it, this will transform a light layer cake into a Banana Cream Pie.

2 cups milk	2 eggs, slightly beaten
1 cup sugar	2 tablespoons butter
$^1/_3$ cup flour	1 teaspoon vanilla or rum or
$^1/_4$ teaspoon salt	almond

Scald the milk. Mix the sugar, flour and salt and blend in the scalded milk. Stir and cook over low heat or in a double boiler until thickened. Quickly blend in the beaten eggs and stir over heat for 2 minutes more. Add butter and flavouring. Cool and spread.

DATE FILLING (for one layer)

1 cup chopped dates	1 tablespoon flour
$^1/_2$ cup sugar	$^1/_2$ cup water

Cook slowly together until thickened, stirring constantly. When almost cold, spread over the bottom layer of a cake. Some date addicts have been known to double the recipe and put a layer under the icing of a chocolate cake. Not me.

Pies and Tarts

Pie appears on Bevvy's table three times a day. Every Friday she and Salome bake twenty pies and store them away in the cellar. If company comes after church on Sunday the pies may all be used at once; if not there'll be enough pies to last through the week. Their variety is infinite: besides all the fruit, milk and mince pies there are sour-cream, raisin, tomato, schnitz, apple butter, cottage cheese, thick milk, funeral pie, and some made up on the spur of the moment to keep things from being wasted. It is not surprising that the Pennsylvania Dutch are credited with inventing the double-crust pie.

Without fail in the winter Bevvy makes shoofly, botzelbaum (somersault) or gravel pies. She calls them cake-pies because they have in them a touch of soda and their rather dry, crumbly-topped fillings stay moist in the basement yet do not soak into the crust. They are put on the table for breakfast and taste especially good dunked in coffee.

When I ask Amsey which pie is his favourite, he says, "Peach pie made with the peelings."

Bevvy smiles shyly, "We make it sometimes with the peelings after we did the canning. You know how sometimes the peaches don't peel too good and a little bit of the flesh sticks yet? Well we chust boil it with sugar and a little water till it's almost like jam then we put it in a baked pie shell and cover it with whipped cream or boiled custard."

Amsey rolls his big brown eyes, "And that really schmecks!"

May I add: my mother and sister Norm make wonderful pies too—and some of my own are not bad.

PIE CRUST

There are many ways to make pie crust: stick to your own method if you have one you like, or try this fairly rich, tender, easy way.

For a 9-inch double crust pie:

2 cups sifted flour	**²/₃ cup shortening**
1 teaspoon salt	**¹/₄ cup cold water—or less**

Sift flour with salt into a bowl. Cut in shortening with 2 knives, a pastry blender or your electric mixer, until particles are the size of small peas. (If you like you can double the recipe and store part in a covered jar in your fridge.) When ready to use sprinkle the flour-shortening mixture with ice cold water and mix lightly with a fork. Use only enough water to make a pastry ball that may be cleaned easily from the bowl. Roll on a lightly floured canvas or board.

The best church-social pie baker of Wilmot Township tells me that instead of water in her pie crust she uses sour cream with a ¹/₂-teaspoon of soda dissolved in it.

GRAHAM WAFER CRUST

Wonderful under a cream pie.

16 graham wafers (1¹/₂ cups)	**¹/₂ cup sugar**
1 teaspoon flour	**1 teaspoon cinnamon**
¹/₂ cup softened butter	

Finely crush the wafers then combine them with the remaining ingredients and blend thoroughly. Press a bit more than half the mixture firmly to the bottom and sides of a well-buttered pie plate. Sprinkle the remaining crumbs over the meringue that covers your cream pie. Bake in a slow oven—300 degrees—until lightly browned—about 20 minutes.

SCHNITZ PIE

Probably everyone in Waterloo County who makes schnitz pie has a slightly different version. I think my Mother's is the best but I'm darned if I can duplicate her "little handful" of this, that, or the other. I've tried here to reduce it to exact measurements for your enjoyment, but your guess could be as good (or better) than mine.

Pastry for one-crust, 9-inch pie

**5, or 7 apples—depending
  on the size needed to fill
  the pie plate
1 cup brown sugar
3 tablespoons soft butter**

**3 tablespoons flour
A sprinkle of cinnamon
Dabs of sour cream
Dabs of butter**

Peel and core the apples; cut them in segments about 1 inch thick on the round, outer side. Arrange the apples tightly-touching but not overlapping—the rounded side up like scallops around the edge of the pastry in the pie plate and throughout the bottom in a pattern of rounds. Blend the butter and sugar, then the flour and spread the resulting crumbs over the apples, being sure the apples on the outer edge get some of the mixture too. Dab cream over the crumbs, here and there, also the butter, and sprinkle the cinnamon over all. Bake for 15 minutes at 400 degrees, then at 350 degrees for about half an hour. But look before that—the apples should be tender, the crumbs and crust golden brown.

CREAM SCHNITZ PIE

This is richer than Mother's schnitz pie, but not quite so sweet.

Pastry for one-crust, 9-inch pie

**5 or 7 apples—depending
  on size
3 tablespoons flour
1/8 teaspoon salt**

**1 cup thick cream—sweet,
  sour, or on the turn
3/4 teaspoon cinnamon
1 cup sugar**

Combine 3/4 cup of the sugar, flour, salt and the cream and beat until smooth. Peel and core the apples, cut them in schnitz and arrange prettily and closely in the pastry shell. Pour the cream mixture over the apples. Mix the remaining 1/4 cup sugar with the cinnamon and sprinkle over the top. Bake at 425 degrees for 10 minutes, turn heat to 350 degrees and bake half an hour till the apples are soft and the filling is set. Watch it.

CREAM-AND-CRUMB SCHNITZ PIE

If you want to have it both ways, try this one.

Pastry for one-crust, 9-inch pie

Enough apples to fill up the pie shell	**¹/₃ cup flour**
1 cup brown sugar	**²/₃ cup cream—sweet, sour, or turning**
3 tablespoons butter	**³/₄ teaspoon cinnamon**

Mix butter, sugar and flour into crumbs. Sprinkle half in the bottom of the shell. Peel and core the apples, cut them in schnitz and arrange them on top of the crumbs. Mix half the remaining crumbs with the cream and pour the mixture over the apples. Finally, mix the cinnamon with the rest of the crumbs and sprinkle these over the top. Bake at 425 degrees for 10 minutes, then at 350 degrees for about half an hour. WOW!

DRIED SCHNITZ PIE

A good one for winter, Bevvy says.

Pastry for a two-crust, 9-inch pie

1 pound dried sour schnitz (apple segments)	**Juice and rind of 1 orange**
1 quart water	**2 teaspoons cinnamon**
	2 cups sugar

Put the schnitz and the water into a saucepan and cook to a soft pulp. Add cinnamon, sugar, orange juice and rind, blend well. Stand aside to cool. Fill the pie shell with the mixture and cover with top crust—making vents for steam. Bake in a 450-degree oven for 10 minutes, then at 350 degrees for 30 minutes.

DOUBLE-CRUST APPLE PIE

Is anything more popular than regular, old-fashioned apple pie, slightly warm, with a generous slab of nippy cheddar?

Pastry for a 9-inch double-crust pie

²/₃ or 1 cup sugar— depending on the tartness of your apples	**¹/₄ teaspoon nutmeg**
	¹/₈ teaspoon salt
2 tablespoons flour	**2 tablespoons milk or cream**
¹/₄ teaspoon cinnamon	**2 or 3 tablespoons butter**

Peel, core and slice enough apples to make 3 cupfuls. Combine the sugar, flour, and spices and mix them with the apples. Pour the combination into the pie shell, drip the milk and put dots of butter over the top. Cover with a top crust, fasten the edges firmly and make a fluted trimming. Cut a pattern of holes in the lid to let the steam escape. Bake in a 375-degree oven for 40 to 45 minutes until the crusts are a pale, golden colour.

DUTCH APPLE PIE

Easy to make and not rich.

Pastry for a one-crust, 9-inch pie

5 or 6 apples cut in quarters —unless the apples are huge	**1 cup sugar**
	1/2 teaspoon nutmeg or cinnamon
1 tablespoon flour	**2 tablespoons butter**

Sprinkle the flour and a 1/2-cup of the sugar, mixed together, on the crust lining the pie plate. Place the apples in a pattern over the sugar and flour. Cover them with the rest of the sugar, dot with butter and sprinkle with the nutmeg or cinnamon (or both). Bake in oven about 35 minutes, or until the apples are baked and a syrup has formed around them.

GREEN TOMATO PIE

The Mennonites make pies out of anything they happen to have around that needs eating; that's how they managed to invent so many wonderful recipes.

Pastry for one 9-inch crust with a lid

3 cups green tomatoes	**2 tablespoons flour**
3/4 cup brown sugar	**1 teaspoon cinnamon**
1/2 cup molasses	**1/4 teaspoon nutmeg**
1/4 cup water	

Remove the stem end of the tomatoes—don't peel them. Slice the tomatoes in thin rings, cover them with boiling water and let stand for about 10 minutes, then drain them. Arrange the tomato slices in the unbaked pastry shell. Combine the sugar, flour, spices, molasses and water; pour the mixture over the tomatoes and cover with the top crust. Bake at 425 degrees for 15 minutes, then at 350 degrees for 30 minutes.

SOUR CREAM RAISIN PIE

"Be reckless, forget about calories; you won't get this Pennsylvania Dutch specialty very often." Tell that to your guests.

Pastry for a one-crust, 9-inch pie

1 cup raisins—light or dark	1 cup sour cream
1 cup sugar	A pinch of salt
1 egg, beaten	1/2 teaspoon vanilla

Beat the egg, add the sugar and beat until the sugar is partially dissolved; add cream, raisins, salt and vanilla. Blend and pour into an unbaked pie shell. Bake at 400 degrees for 10 minutes; then at 350 degrees, or slightly less. Test as for custard pie— when a silver knife blade comes out clean from the centre of the pie it is done. If you want to make it even more luscious you can sprinkle walnuts or pecans over the top or cover the baked, cooled pie with whipped cream just before serving.

RAISIN CRUMB PIE

"It's always better to make two of these pies at a time," Bevvy says. "They go down so good."

Pastry for 2 one-crust, 9-inch pies

1 pound seeded raisins	1 cup milk
1 1/2 cups cold water	2 eggs, well beaten
3 cups brown sugar	2 tablespoons baking
2 cups flour	powder
1/2 cup shortening	

To the raisins add the cold water and a 1/2-cup of sugar; cook until the raisins are tender and plump. Set aside to cool. Mix the flour, remaining 2 1/2 cups of sugar and the shortening, crumbling well with the fingers. Take out 2 cups of the crumbs and set them aside; to the remaining crumb mixture add the eggs and milk, mix them well, then stir in the baking powder. Divide the raisin mixture between the two pies, pour the batter over them and sprinkle the top of both pies with 1 cup of reserved crumbs. Bake in a hot oven—400 degrees—for 10 minutes; finish baking at 350 degrees for about 35 minutes.

CHRISTMAS MINCE

Mother's mince pies are the best I've ever tasted: not too strong and sharp. She made the mixture a few weeks before Christmas; it was always gone soon after and we had to wait a whole year for more.

> 1 pound of beef, cooked well and chopped fine
> About a cupful of beef suet, chopped fine
> 1 pound of raisins. washed, dried and cut fine
> Currants—but not more than a cupful (Mother sometimes omits them)
> About a cupful of citron peel, cut fine
> 1/2 cup brown sugar
> 1/2 cup wine or whisky
> 1 teaspoon cinnamon
> 1 teaspoon of cloves and nutmeg together (careful here)
> Salt to taste
> About 1 cup cooked apple cider or a bit of beef broth instead of all cider
> 1 cup of apples, chopped and added to each pint of mincemeat before baking the pie

Mother says, "Taste it as you go along."

Put all the ingredients but the whisky into a kettle; bring to a boil and simmer for 15 minutes. Stir in the wine or whisky. Pack in sterilized jars. When you're ready to make the pies add the chopped apples and pour the mincemeat into a pastry-lined pie plate, cover with a top crust, seal, flute the edges, prick the top crust and bake at 425 degrees for 15 minutes, then at 350 degrees for half an hour. Serve hot.

FUNERAL PIE

It is traditional for the Old Order Mennonites and the Old Amish to have raisin pie at a funeral—perhaps because its rich crusty goodness lifts the spirits.

> Pastry for a two-crust, deep 9-inch pie

1 cup seeded raisins	Juice of 1 lemon
2 cups water	1/4 teaspoon salt
1 1/2 cups sugar	2 tablespoons grated lemon
4 tablespoons flour	rind
1 egg, well beaten	

Wash raisins and soak them in cold water for 3 hours. Drain. Combine the 2 cups of water, raisins, the blended sugar and flour, salt, lemon juice and rind, then the beaten egg; mix thoroughly and cook over hot water for 15 minutes, stirring occasionally till thick. Cool. Pour into pastry in pie plate; cover with a top crust or with criss-crossed narrow strips of dough. Bake in a 450-degree oven for 10 minutes, then at 350 degrees for 30 minutes.

If you prefer, you can pour the cooked raisin mixture into a BAKED pie shell and spoon whipped cream on each piece as you serve it.

Another innovation is to substitute 1 cup of orange juice for 1 cup of water, using the orange rind instead of the lemon.

OR substitute a cup of honey instead of using sugar.

Raisin pies should be nearly cool when cut—if they have become cold they should be slightly heated before serving.

Don't wait for a funeral to make this.

GREEN TOMATO MINCE MEAT

Mother canned this mixture in the fall and made the pies throughout the winter; we didn't like it as well as Christmas Mince, but it kept longer and was more economical.

1/2 peck green tomatoes (about 6 cupfuls)	**1 teaspoon cinnamon**
3/4 cup salt	**1 teaspoon ground cloves**
Boiling water	**1 teaspoon nutmeg**
5 to 7 cups white or brown sugar	**3/4 cup lemon or citron peel**
1 or 2 pounds raisins	**1 cup apple juice**
1 cup ground suet	**1 cup molasses**
1 tablespoon salt	**(1 cup chopped apples to each pint of prepared mince meat)**

Put the tomatoes through the grinder and add 3/4 cup salt. Cover with boiling water and let stand for 15 minutes. Drain off all the liquid; then add all the other ingredients but the apple and cook till thick and transparent. Seal in pint jars—no wax needed. When you want to make a pie, open a jar, chop up a cupful of apple and mix it with the mincemeat; taste it and add more sugar if you think it needs it. Pour the mixture into a pastry-lined pie plate, cover it with a pastry lid, making vents for the steam to escape. Seal the edges and bake the pie in the oven at 425 degrees for 15 minutes, then at 375 degrees for another 35 minutes.

NORM'S RHUBARB PIE

This pie has that refreshing, tangy rhubarb taste that tells you spring is here.

Pastry for a 9-inch pie with a lattice top

2 cups pink rhubarb	1 egg, beaten
3 tablespoons flour	1 cup sugar

Cut the rhubarb in pieces and distribute it evenly in the unbaked pie shell. Mix the flour, sugar and egg; beat the mixture and pour it over the rhubarb. Cover the top with lattice. Bake the pie for 10 minutes at 450 degrees, then at 350 degrees for 35 minutes.

RHUBARB MERINGUE PIE

This is rhubarb pie de luxe. My guests tell me it is the best rhubarb pie they've ever tasted: the credit goes to Mrs. Charlie Voelker, an old friend of my mother who gave me the recipe a long time ago.

Pastry for a 9-inch pie, fairly deep, single crust

2 eggs, separated	Cinnamon
2 tablespoons flour	2 or 3 cups cut-up rhubarb
3 tablespoons water	Boiling water to blanch the
1 cup sugar	rhubarb
3 or 4 tablespoons butter, melted	

Get the pink or red rhubarb if you can—it's supposed to taste better and it certainly looks prettier. Cut the rhubarb stalks into $3/4$-inch lengths; if the stalks are exceptionally fat you might split them. Measure the rhubarb into the pie plate so you'll know you have cut up enough to fill it. In a dish, scald the rhubarb with boiling water and let it stand in the water for 15 minutes (this is supposed to make it less acid or something equally beneficial— it also takes away some of the lovely pink colour). Drain the water off the rhubarb.

In a bowl, blend the melted butter with the sugar and flour; add the 3 tablespoons of water and the beaten egg yolks—the mixture should be smooth and runny. Spread the rhubarb in the pie shell and pour the sauce over it. Sprinkle it with cinnamon. Bake the pie at 425 degrees for 15 minutes, then at 325 degrees for about half an hour longer—or until the rhubarb is soft, the custard set, and the pastry golden. Make a meringue of the egg whites: beat the whites, add 3 tablespoons granulated sugar and $1/4$ teaspoon cream of tartar while you're beating. Spread it over the pie not too long before you are ready to serve it and either brown the top under the broiler, watching it every minute, or put it into the oven for 12 minutes at 325 degrees. Now share the pie and bask in the compliments that will be coming your way.

CRANBERRY PIE

This is not a local recipe: it was given me by a friend who lived on Cape Cod where the cranberries grow. Because it's so pretty, red, and deliciously different, I'm letting you have it.

Pastry for a 9-inch pie, single crust, unbaked

1 cup whole cranberries	1 cup water
1/2 cup seeded raisins, cut fine	1 good tablespoon flour
	1 tablespoon vanilla
1 cup sugar	1 tablespoon butter

Boil all the ingredients together in a heavy saucepan until very thick, then turn burner on the lowest setting on your stove and let the filling "stew" for about 15 minutes. Cool thoroughly before putting it in the unbaked pie shell. Bake for half an hour at 350 degrees. Let cool and refrigerate over night—it seems to need that refrigeration to give it its special flavour.

PEACH PIE

Could anything be more melliferous than a fresh, juicy peach pie with rich pastry crusts, top and bottom?

Pastry for a double-crust 9-inch pie

3 cups sliced peaches	3 tablespoons cornstarch
1/2 cup white sugar	3 tablespoons butter

Mix the sugar and cornstarch together; then stir the mixture into the sliced peaches and pour them into the pie shell. Dot with butter, or melt the butter and dribble it on. Cover with the top crust—or a lattice—seal and flute the edge, slit a pattern to let out steam and bake at 425 degrees for 15 minutes, then at 350 degrees for half an hour or longer—till the filling has that glazed, transparent, honey-like look.

MAGGIE'S PEACH PIE

Maggie Moyer, a wiry little old spinster who lived on a farm near Bloomingdale and for years sold vegetables at the Kitchener market, once took a ride down the Grand River in a barrel; and often she donated one of her own special peach pies to Blooming-dale church socials, where everyone wanted her recipe.

Pastry for a one-crust, 9-inch pie

14 or 15 peach halves, peeled
3/4 cup white sugar
1/4 cup flour
2 tablespoons butter

1/4 cup peach juice (if peaches are canned; water, if peaches are fresh)
2 tablespoons lemon juice
1 cup cream, whipped and sweetened

Make crumbs of the sugar, butter and flour and spread half of them in the unbaked pie shell. Place peach halves prettily in shell with the cut side down. Cover with the remaining crumbs. Sprinkle the peach juice and lemon juice over the crumbs. Bake at 375 degrees for 40 minutes. Cool; before serving heap pie with whipped cream sweetened with sugar and almond extract.

THICK CREAM PEACH PIE

Is it possible to make comparisons while using superlatives—as anyone must who is writing about peach pies?

Pastry for a one-crust, 9-inch pie

14 or 15 peach halves, peeled
1 cup white sugar

1 cup thick (or sour) cream
2 eggs (or 1/3 cup flour)

Place the peach halves tightly together in circles in the unbaked crust. Beat the eggs, add the sugar and sour cream; mix thoroughly. (If you use flour instead of eggs, mix it with the sugar then stir in the cream.) Pour the mixture over the peaches and bake at 425 degrees for 15 minutes and at 350 degrees for 35 minutes. Cool and don't let your conscience spoil your enjoyment.

RASPBERRY PIE

My sister Norm has raspberries growing in her garden and while they're ripening she makes a pie every day.

Pastry for a two-crust, 9-inch pie

3 or 4 cups raspberries
3/4 cup sugar
2 tablespoons cornstarch

Pinch of salt
2 tablespoons butter

Mix the sugar, cornstarch and salt and spread 1/4 of it over the bottom of the pie shell. Fill the shell with raspberries, sprinkle the rest of the sugar mixture over the fruit, dot with butter and cover with the upper crust or a lattice. Bake at 450 degrees for 15 minutes, then at 350 degrees for 30 minutes—or until the crust is delicately browned.

CHERRY PIE

Norm also has a sour-cherry tree in her back yard and when the cherries are ripe she goes out and picks a bowlful and in no time makes the best cherry pie I've ever tasted.

Pastry for a lattice-top 9-inch pie

3 cups pitted sour cherries	2 tablespoons flour
1/2 cup white sugar	2 tablespoons butter
1/2 cup brown sugar	

She mixes the sugar, flour and butter, then the cherries and pours the mixture into the pie shell. Sometimes she puts on a top crust but usually she crisscrosses narrow strips of pastry across the top; occasionally she sprinkles the top with crumbs made of:

1/2 cup flour	1/8 cup butter
1/2 cup brown sugar	1/4 teaspoon vanilla

She bakes the pie at 350 degrees for 40 minutes.

PLUM PIE

Norm has a plum tree in her back yard too and she makes the plum pies in the same way as she does her cherry pies but with a sprinkling of cinnamon added.

CONCORD GRAPE PIE

Made in exactly the same way as Norm's cherry pie except that I use all white sugar and a crumb topping. To get rid of the seeds I pop the grapes out of their skins into a sauce pan, boil them just long enough for the seeds to come free of that green pulpy stuff, then I strain them through a colander and combine the juice with the grape skins.

BLUEBERRY PIE

This is a sweetie—with a lattice top, white or brown sugar, flour and butter.

BLACK CURRANT PIE

We had this only once in a summer because of its very strong flavour.

RED CURRANT PIE

Mother's red currant pies were a beautiful colour, little red jewels, tart and sweet, using an extra half cup of sugar and no top crust.

ELDERBERRY PIE

Mother even canned elderberries to make this pie during the winter. I've always thought elderberries a bit gravelly because of the seeds; I might have been prejudiced because when I was young Mother made me help pick the pesky little berries off the stems.

Pastry for a deep pie, double crust

3 cups elderberries	**1 cup white sugar**
4 tablespoons flour	**2 tablespoons butter**

Mix the sugar, flour; sprinkle $1/3$ of the mixture on the pastry. Put in half the berries. Sprinkle with $1/2$ remaining sugar mixture. Put in remaining berries and sprinkle remaining sugar on top. Dot with butter, put on top crust with vents for steam. Bake for 45 minutes in a 350-degree oven.

ELDERBERRY CUSTARD PIE

A seedless elderberry pie that, in my opinion, is worth eating.

Pastry for a one-crust, 9-inch pie

1 cup elderberry juice drained from a jar of canned elderberries. (You can use the drained berries in muffins)	**$1/4$ cup flour** **1 cup white sugar** **1 egg, separated** **1 cup milk** **$1/4$ teaspoon salt**

Bring the juice to the boiling point. Combine the sugar, flour and salt, add $1/4$ cup milk and stir it into a paste. Add the paste to the juice and cook until the mixture is thickened. Take it from the heat and add the egg yolk stirred into the rest of the milk. Fold in the stiffly beaten egg. Pour the mixture into the unbaked pie shell and bake at 350 degrees for 30 minutes—or till a knife comes out clean when inserted into the middle of the pie.

You could make this pie with other fruit juices as well.

SQUASH PIE

This is another golden memory of my well-fed childhood. Made only in the fall when Mother could buy squash at the market; it has a finer texture and more delicate flavour than pumpkin.

Pastry for a one-crust, 9-inch pie

2 cups boiled squash	**2 eggs, beaten slightly**
2 cups milk	**1 teaspoon salt**
1¹/₂ tablespoons flour	**Nutmeg or cinnamon**
1¹/₄ cups white sugar	

Mother would cut the squash into long slices, peel the segments, cut them into pieces ¹/₂ inch thick and cook them till they were soft. She'd rub the cooked squash through a colander—(till ricers were invented and she got one). It would have been so much easier for her if she'd baked it in the oven till it was soft and then scooped it out and mashed it—but Mother's grandmother had always boiled it so Mother boiled it too. *Work* was revered in those days. When the squash was slightly cooled she added the sugar, flour, salt and eggs, then gradually the milk. She poured the mixture into the unbaked pie shell, sprinkled the top with cinnamon and a bit of nutmeg, then baked it at 350 degrees for 40 minutes till it was set. I wish I could have a piece right this minute.

FLUFFY PUMPKIN PIE

This is one of my favourite pies in the world: it is light, golden and delicate—unlike the solid pumpkin pies that are soggy and so grey with spices that you'd hardly guess they were pumpkin.

Pastry for a one-crust, 9-inch pie

2 cups cooked and strained pumpkin (I use the tinned kind)	**1 teaspoon vanilla**
	¹/₂ teaspoon cinnamon
	¹/₈ teaspoon cloves
1 cup milk	**¹/₈ teaspoon nutmeg**
3 egg yolks, beaten	**3 egg whites, beaten stiff**
1 cup sugar	

Mix the pumpkin and milk, beaten egg yolks, then the sugar mixed with the spices, salt and vanilla. Fold in the stiffly beaten egg whites, turn the mixture into the unbaked pie shell and bake about 45 minutes in a 350-degree oven.

I have a fairly deep pie plate but I find that the filling sometimes fluffs up to more than I need to fill it; if that happens I quickly roll out a bit more pastry and make another small pie— or I put the overflow into a buttered custard dish to be baked and served as a pudding.

Of course I prefer seeing whipped cream heaped over the top of the pumpkin pie when I serve it—but I find it is safer to put a bowl of whipped cream on the table to let people help themselves. It is unlikely that you'll have any pie left over but if you do it's better not to have the cream melting on top—especially if you might like to have the pie for breakfast next morning, or —as I often do—two healthy wedges for lunch. After all pumpkin is a vegetable.

KARRUPS PIE MIT SCHNAPPS (Whisky Pumpkin Pie)

Can you resist trying this?

Pastry for a large deep pie

2 cups cooked pumpkin	1 tablespoon cornstarch
4 eggs, separated	$^1/_2$ cup butter, melted
1 cup sugar	$^1/_3$ cup cream
$^1/_2$ teaspoon cinnamon	1 cup whisky

To the pumpkin add the sugar, yolks of eggs, cinnamon; beat for several minutes. Quickly add the cream, butter and whisky; mix well. Sprinkle the cornstarch over the stiffly beaten whites of eggs and fold into the first mixture. Pour into a pastry-lined pan about $2^1/_2$ inches deep and bake for an hour in a 375-degree oven. Try to let it cool before you demolish it.

LOTVARRICK PIE (Apple Butter Pie)

You'll savour every mouthful of this pie's tangy, flavourful, custard.

Pastry for a 9-inch pie

$^3/_4$ cup sugar	$^1/_4$ teaspoon cream of tartar
$^1/_2$ cup apple butter	$^1/_4$ teaspoon soda
2 eggs, beaten	2 cups milk
4 tablespoons butter, melted	$^1/_4$ teaspoon nutmeg
1 tablespoon flour	

Mix the sugar, flour, soda and cream of tartar; blend in the melted butter, add the beaten eggs, apple butter, then the milk. Pour into the pie shell and sprinkle with the nutmeg. Bake at 425 degrees for 10 minutes, then at 350 degrees till the custard is set.

FRUIT CUSTARD PIES

Mother made so many good fruit pies when we were youngsters that it's hard for me to say which kind was my favourite. Sometimes I think it was raspberry custard—or strawberry custard—

or any of her fruit custard pies. They were more delicate than pies made of masses of fruit.

RASPBERRY OR STRAWBERRY CUSTARD PIE

Pastry for a one-crust, 9-inch pie

$1/_2$ to $3/_4$ cup fruit	$1/_2$ cup sugar
$2^1/_2$ cups milk	$1/_2$ teaspoon salt
3 eggs, beaten	1 teaspoon flour

Combine the sugar, flour, and salt; add the beaten eggs. Bring the milk almost to boiling point and add gradually to the egg mixture Pour into the unbaked pie shell and dot the berries over the top. Bake at 350 degrees for about 45 minutes—or until a silver knife stuck into the middle comes out clean. In exactly this way you can also make

CHERRY CUSTARD PIE

MULBERRY CUSTARD PIE

BLUEBERRY CUSTARD PIE

RED OR BLACK CURRANT CUSTARD PIE

RHUBARB CUSTARD PIE

RAISIN CUSTARD PIE (soak the raisins first)

DRIED CURRANT CUSTARD PIE (soak the currants first)

Sometimes Mother made a PLAIN CUSTARD PIE, using $1/_2$ cup more milk and sprinkling the surface with nutmeg and cinnamon.

GWETCHA PIE (Prune Custard Pie)

Bevvy is proud of this recipe from a Mennonite friend in Pennsylvania.

Pastry for a one-crust, 9-inch pie

$2^1/_2$ cups cooked prunes, chopped	2 eggs, beaten
5 tablespoons white sugar	$1/_2$ cup cream
1 rounded tablespoon flour	$1/_2$ cup prune juice
	Cinnamon

Combine sugar and flour and sprinkle half the mixture in the bottom of the unbaked pie shell. Combine beaten eggs, cream, prune juice and the remaining sugar and flour mixture; add the chopped prunes and pour into the crust. Sprinkle cinnamon over the top. Bake at 350 degrees for about 40 minutes—till custard is set.

COTTAGE CHEESE PIE

"They sometimes pour maple syrup or fruit over this," Bevvy says. "That makes it real tasty."

Pastry for a one-crust, 9-inch pie

1¹/₂ cups cottage cheese	2 tablespoons flour
¹/₂ cup sugar	1 tablespoon butter
¹/₄ teaspoon salt	2 eggs, separated
Flavouring—lemon, or vanilla, or cinnamon or nutmeg—or whatever you like	2 cups milk

Combine the cheese, sugar, salt, flour, butter, beaten egg yolks and flavouring. Mix well. Add the milk slowly to make a smooth mixture. Fold in the beaten egg whites, then pour into the pastry shell and bake at 350 degress for 40 minutes, till set.

LEMON SPONGE PIE

This is light as a feather and one of Bevvy's family's favourites.

Pastry for a one-crust, 9-inch pie

1 cup white sugar	¹/₂ teaspoon salt
2 tablespoons butter	Juice and grated rind of
3 eggs, separated	1 lemon
3 tablespoons flour	1 cup milk

Cream the butter, add the sugar and egg yolks and beat well. Add the flour, salt, lemon juice, rind and milk. Fold in the stiffly beaten egg whites. Pour into the unbaked pie shell. Bake at 350 degrees for 45 minutes.

WALNUT CUSTARD PIE

Bevvy makes this with black walnuts from the tree that grows by the fence in the orchard—it's good too with pecans.

Pastry for a one-crust, 9-inch pie

1 cup brown sugar	²/₃ cup molasses or corn
2 eggs	syrup
2 tablespoons flour	1 cup chopped nuts
³/₄ cup water	

Mix the sugar and flour, add the beaten eggs, molasses, water and nuts. Pour into the pie shell and bake at 350 degrees for 40 minutes or slightly more.

THICK MILK PIE

When Bevvy talks about "thick" milk she means sour milk that is not *too* sour. Her eyes gleam with delight when she talks of this pie: it is one of her favourites.

Pastry for a one-crust, 9-inch pie

2 cups thick milk	4 tablespoons flour
1 cup brown or white sugar	Cinnamon and nutmeg
¹/₂ cup molasses, maple	
syrup or apple molasses	

Bevvy deftly blends all the ingredients, pours the mixture into the pie shell and sprinkles the spices over the top. She bakes it at 425 degrees for 15 minutes, then at 350 degrees for 25 minutes —or until it is set.

VANILLA PIE

The Mennonite ladies of Waterloo County made dozens of these delicious pies to sell at the New Hamburg Mennonite auction and the Elmira Maple Syrup Festival.

Pastry for a one-crust, 9-inch pie

Bottom part:	Top part:
¹/₂ cup white sugar	¹/₂ cup brown sugar
2 tablespoons flour	¹/₄ cup shortening
1 egg, well beaten	1 cup flour
1 cup maple syrup	¹/₂ teaspoon soda
1 cup water	¹/₂ teaspoon baking powder
1 teaspoon vanilla	

Blend ingredients for bottom part and cook until thickened. Set aside to cool. Combine ingredients for top part into crumbs. Pour bottom part into pie shell, top with crumbs. Bake at 350 degrees for 45 minutes or until delectably browned.

FRENCH CREAM PIE

Bevvy doesn't know why this is French—unless some of the Mennonites who came from Alsace brought the recipe with them two hundred years ago.

Pastry for a one-crust, 9-inch pie

<table>
<tr><td>³/₄ cup granulated sugar</td><td>Pinch of salt</td></tr>
<tr><td>2 eggs, separated</td><td>¹/₂ teaspoon baking soda</td></tr>
<tr><td>1 cup sour cream</td><td>1 cup currants</td></tr>
<tr><td>¹/₂ teaspoon cinnamon</td><td></td></tr>
</table>

Blend the sugar, egg yolks and cream, add the cinnamon, salt, baking soda and currants. Pour into the pie shell and bake at 350 degrees for half an hour—or until it is set. Cover baked pie with meringue made with the 2 egg whites, 4 tablespoons sugar, 1 teaspoon vanilla and ¹/₄ teaspoon cream of tartar; put in 300-degree oven for 12 minutes.

GRAVEL PIE

Bevvy says this is a good pie to dunk in your coffee at breakfast.

Pastry for a one-crust, 9-inch pie

<table>
<tr><td>1¹/₄ cups brown sugar</td><td>1 egg, separated</td></tr>
<tr><td>2 cups flour</td><td>¹/₂ teaspoon salt</td></tr>
<tr><td>¹/₄ cup butter</td><td>¹/₂ teaspoon soda</td></tr>
<tr><td>¹/₄ cup lard</td><td>1 teaspoon baking powder</td></tr>
<tr><td>²/₃ cup milk—or enough to
    make a nice batter</td><td></td></tr>
</table>

Sift flour, sugar, salt, baking powder into a bowl; add butter and lard and mix until crumbly. Take out ¹/₂ cup of the crumbs. To the rest add the blended egg yolk, milk and flavouring. Beat the egg white till stiff and fold it into batter. Pour into unbaked pie shell and sprinkle the ¹/₂ cup of crumbs over the top. Bake in a 350-degree oven for about 45 minutes.

SHOO-FLY PIE

Whenever people talk about Mennonite food they mention shoo-fly pie—which is rather like a cake baked into a pie shell. It is a favourite with busy farmers' wives because it keeps moist in the cellar.

Pastry for a one-crust, 9-inch pie

Bottom part:	Top part:
1/2 cup molasses	1 1/2 cups flour
1 teaspoon soda	1 cup brown sugar
1 cup boiling water	3/4 cup butter or lard
Pinch salt	1/2 teaspoon cinnamon

Dissolve the soda in the molasses and stir until it foams; add the boiling water. Mix the flour, cinnamon, sugar and butter into crumbs. Pour one-third of the liquid into the unbaked crust; sprinkle one-third of the crumbs over the liquid and continue alternating layers, putting the crumbs on top. Bake in a 375-degree oven for about half an hour until the crumbs and crust are golden.

SHOO-FLY PIE WITH A WET BOTTOM

I once had this kind of pie for breakfast in Lancaster, Pennsylvania—with an inch of whipped cream on top, a pie to remember.

Pastry for deep, one-crust, 9-inch pie

Bottom part:	Top part:
3/4 cup boiling water	1 1/2 cups sifted flour
1 cup dark molasses	1 cup brown sugar
1/2 teaspoon soda	3/4 cup shortening
	1/4 teaspoon salt

Pour boiling water over soda in a bowl and stir in the molasses. Pour into the pie shell. Mix ingredients for crumbs and sprinkle over the molasses mixture. Bake in a 350-degree oven for 30 to 40 minutes. Let cool and slather it with whipped cream.

CANDY PIE

This was my Mother's adaptation of shoofly pie. Oh boy, and did we love it!

Pastry for one-crust, 9-inch pie

Bottom part:	Top part:
1 1/2 cups maple syrup	1 cup flour
1/2 teaspoon soda	1 cup brown sugar
	1/2 cup butter

Dissolve the soda in the maple syrup and pour the mixture into the pie shell. Spread the crumbs over the top and bake in a 350-degree oven for about half an hour. But watch it—this bubbling, sticky, luscious thing has a tendency to run over and make a mess of the oven. Mother made candy pie recently and I found I could just eat a sliver—it was so excessively rich and sweet; my slender young nieces and nephews cleaned it up and wanted more.

BOTZELBAUM PIE

Botzelbaum means somersault: you put the dough in the bottom of the pie shell and it comes out on top when it's baked.

Pastry for a one-crust, 9-inch pie

Dough part:	Juice part:
1 cup sugar	$1/2$ cup sugar
$1/4$ cup lard	1 teaspoon cloves
1 egg	1 teaspoon cinnamon
$1/2$ cup sour milk	1 tablespoon flour
$1 1/4$ cups flour	1 egg, beaten
$1/2$ teaspoon soda	$1/2$ cup molasses
	1 cup water

Mix both parts in the order named. Put the dough part into the pie shell first, then carefully pour in the liquid part. Bake at 350 degrees for 35 to 40 minutes.

PIES MADE IN BAKED SHELLS

All those lovely pies cooked in a double boiler and poured into a ready-baked shell! Fine for an emergency because the fillings can be made in a jiffy; the shells baked—or bought ready-made—can be kept on hand and warmed in the oven to freshen them when you are ready to use them.

PLAIN CREAM PIE

$1/2$ cup white sugar	Yolks of 2 or 3 eggs
Pinch of salt	$2 1/2$ cups whole milk
2 tablespoons cornstarch	Lump of butter
	1 teaspoon vanilla

Mix the ingredients in the order given and thicken the mixture in a double boiler or in a heavy saucepan, stirring almost constantly.

Add the butter and vanilla. Cool it before you put it into the pie shell and cover it with meringue.

MERINGUE

> **2 or 3 egg whites beaten stiff**   **Pinch of cream of tartar**
> **4 tablespoons sugar**   **1/2 teaspoon vanilla**

Gild the meringue slightly in the oven or under the broiler—but watch it!

BANANA CREAM PIE

Make the filling for Plain Cream Pie and arrange banana slices in the shell before you pour in the filling; put some slices on top too before you pile on the meringue. But remember—it must be eaten before the bananas turn brown.

COCONUT CREAM PIE

Same basic Cream Pie recipe plus $1^1/_4$ cups shredded coconut. When the filling is cool stir in $^3/_4$ cup of the coconut and sprinkle the rest over the top of the meringue to be toasted golden brown in the oven.

COFFEE CREAM PIE

Add 1 tablespoon of instant coffee powder to the basic Cream Pie recipe or substitute 1 cup strong coffee for 1 cup of the milk. Omit the vanilla.

RAISIN CREAM PIE

Soak 1 cup of raisins in warm water till they are plump. When you've made the filling for Plain Cream Pie stir the drained raisins into it, pour it into the shell and cover it with meringue.

SPICE CREAM PIE

Stir $^3/_4$ teaspoon each of cinnamon and ground cloves into the basic cream filling.

BUTTERSCOTCH PIE

You might substitute brown sugar for white in the Basic Cream Pie recipe and call it butterscotch—but it's pretty pallid. This is Bevvy's better way.

First part:
1/2 cup brown sugar
3 tablespoons boiling water
1 tablespoon butter
1/2 teaspoon salt
1/2 teaspoon vanilla
1/8 teaspoon soda

Second part:
2 egg yolks
1/3 cup flour
1/2 cup white sugar
1 1/2 cup hot milk

Combine the first part—all but the soda—in a saucepan. When the mixture begins to boil add the soda. Boil until the syrup forms a hard ball when a drop is put in cold water—it doesn't take long. Combine the egg yolk, flour and white sugar; slowly add the hot milk. Add the second mixture to the first and cook till it thickens. Pour the cooled filling into the baked pie shell, cover it with meringue and bake at 325 degrees for 12 minutes, or put it under the broiler till golden.

MAPLE SYRUP PIE

1 1/2 cups maple syrup
Pinch of salt
2 tablespoons cornstarch

Yolks of 3 eggs
1 cup milk
Lump of butter

Mix in the order given and thicken in a double boiler, stirring constantly. Cool before you put it into a baked pie shell and cover it with meringue; put it under the broiler till the meringue is golden—not long.

CHOCOLATE PIE

Sometimes I think this is my favourite of favourites.

1 baked pie shell
3 heaping tablespoons flour
1 large heaping tablespoon
   cocoa
1/2 teaspoon salt
1 cup white sugar

a little cold water
2 cups boiling water
   (or hot milk)
Butter the size of an egg
1 teaspoon vanilla

Blend the flour, cocoa, salt and white sugar in a little cold water. Add this to 2 cups boiling water in a heavy pan or double boiler and cook till it is really thick—it takes 10 minutes. Remove pan from stove and stir in the butter and vanilla until well blended. Let the filling cool before you put it into the pie shell; serve with a mound of whipped cream or meringue on top of each piece. If you're not going to serve the pie immediately, pour the filling into a bowl and keep it until you're ready for it. There's nothing more pitiful than a pie with a soggy bottom.

This chocolate filling can also be used as a pudding, or put into tart shells.

BLACK BOTTOM PIE

This is one of Wende Machetzki's recipes; she says, "You have never eaten a really good dessert until you have tried Black Bottom Pie."

1 nine-inch baked pastry shell	**1 cup semisweet chocolate pieces**
1/2 cup sugar	**1 envelope unflavoured gelatine**
1 tablespoon cornstarch	
2 cups milk, scalded	**1/2 cup cold water**
4 beaten egg yolks	**4 egg whites**
1 teaspoon vanilla	**1/2 cup sugar**
2 to 4 tablespoons rum or bourbon to taste (Wende comes from Tennessee.)	

Combine sugar and cornstarch, slowly add milk to beaten egg yolks. Stir sugar mixture then cook and stir in top of double boiler over hot but not boiling water till custard coats a spoon; remove from heat, add vanilla to 1 cup of the custard, add the chocolate pieces and stir till melted. Pour into the bottom of baked, cold pastry crust.

Next, soften the gelatine in cold water and add to remaining hot custard; add the rum, stir well and chill until slightly thick. Beat the egg whites, gradually add 1/2 cup of sugar and continue beating until stiff peaks form. Fold in the custard-gelatine mixture, pile on top of chocolate layer in pie shell. Chill. Just before serving cover the whole thing with a layer of thick whipped cream and decorate with chocolate shavings.

LEMON MERINGUE PIE

No cookbook would be complete without this standard recipe; it seems to please everybody—especially the men.

1 baked 9-inch pie shell	1^1/$_2$ cups boiling water
1^1/$_4$ cups white sugar	3 egg yolks, beaten
3 tablespoons cornstarch	Grated rind and juice of
3 tablespoons flour	1 lemon (^{1}/$_3$ cup)
^{1}/$_4$ teaspoon salt	3 tablespoons butter

MERINGUE

6 tablespoons sugar	3 egg whites, beaten stiff
1 teaspoon lemon juice	

In the top of a double boiler or heavy pot mix the sugar, cornstarch and salt. Add slowly the 2 cups of boiling water and bring to a boil, stirring constantly; reduce heat and keep on cooking and stirring till the mixture is quite thick. Now stir a small amount of the hot mixture into the beaten egg yolks; stir in more of the hot mixture — about a cupful — then blend it with the rest of the hot mixture and keep stirring and heating for 5 minutes. Remove from heat, add butter and lemon rind; then slowly stir in the lemon juice. Cool. Pour into the baked pie shell just before serving. Pile the meringue lightly on top and let the peaks become golden under the broiler—watching every second.

TARTS

Since most tarts are miniature pies, almost any pie filling could be dropped by spoonfuls into tart shells; they're a little more bother to make but easier to eat than a pie if you have a big crowd that's not for a sit-down meal.

BUTTER TARTS

The best tarts in the world: rich, gooey and a bit runny.

Rich pastry for 8 or 10 tarts

1 cup brown sugar	Butter the size of an egg, melted
1 cup raisins	1 tablespoon water
1 egg, beaten	1 teaspoon vanilla

Beat the egg, add the sugar and beat again; add the water, vanilla, raisins and butter. Drop mixture into tart shells to almost half-full and bake in a 450-degree oven for about 15 minutes.

TAFFY TARTS

Even richer and gooier.

Rich pastry for 12 tarts

1¹/₂ cups corn syrup	4 tablespoons melted butter
1 cup brown sugar	2 eggs, beaten

Dissolve the sugar in the beaten eggs, add syrup and melted butter. Bake at 450 degrees for 15 minutes.

MAPLE SYRUP TARTS

Pastry for 8 tarts

1 cup maple syrup	Butter the size of an egg,
2 tablespoons flour	melted
1 egg, beaten	1 teaspoon vanilla

Make a thin paste of the flour and some of the maple syrup, add the rest of the syrup, the beaten egg, melted butter and vanilla. Drop into tart shells and bake at 450 degrees for 15 minutes.

MOM SWALLOW'S LEMON HONEY

These were Mom's specialty—and they were certainly special. The filling keeps indefinitely in a jar and can be used to fill *baked* tart shells.

1¹/₄ cup sugar	2 beaten eggs
Juice of 2 large lemons	1 tablespoon butter
Rind of 1 lemon	

Cook sugar and lemon juice and rind in double boiler till clear—stirring all the time. Add beaten eggs, stir till thick; take off stove and add butter. Spoon the lemon honey into tart shells or stash it away.

BEVVY'S SOUR CREAM TARTS

Everybody likes these.

Rich pastry to fill 8 large, 12 small tart shells

1 egg, well beaten	1 cup sour cream
1 cup white sugar	1 cup raisins
	Nutmeg

Mix the ingredients in the order given, sprinkling the nutmeg over the top. Spoon into tart shells—two-thirds full—and bake at 400 degrees for 20 minutes—but watch them.

COCONUT TARTS

These are really for fancy.

2 dozen baked pastry shells	yolks of 3 eggs
1 cup white sugar	1 quart milk
2 tablespoons cornstarch	$^1/_4$ pound coconut

Heat milk in double boiler, slowly pour in the other ingredients mixed together and cook till thick; stir in the coconut. Cover with meringue, sprinkle with coconut, and put in 325-degree oven for 10 minutes to delicately gild the top.

Desserts

When we were all skinny little girls living at home Mother never served a meal without fresh fruit for dessert in summer, bananas and oranges or canned fruit in winter, and always cookies or cake. Sometimes she made puddings, on Saturday and Sunday we had pie, and for company there was always a choice of fruit, cake and cookies, pie, cheese, pudding or something soft, luscious and loaded with calories—like maple mousse or home-made ice cream. And we didn't get fat.

The choices at Bevvy's table are no less generous. Though pie, fruit and cake are Mennonite favourites, Bevvy's little notebook has recipes for custards, dumplings baked in brown-sugar sauce, and dozens of puddings—most of them steamed.

David and the children smile broadly when they come in from the cold on a bleak winter's day as the steamed pudding emits its fragrance of spices and fruit from the top of Bevvy's ever-burning black wood stove; steaming for two or three hours, it gently humidifies the air as well.

Salome makes a sauce for the pudding and puts a pitcher of thick sweet cream on the table "for those who like either or both."

Lyddy goes down to the basement, brings up a jar of canned peaches and empties them into Bevvy's tall pressed-glass compote. She then cuts a cake into generous slices and puts fat molasses and date cookies on a plate.

"I feel real bad that we haven't got pie yet," Bevvy apologizes to me, "but sometimes, like now at the end of the week, they are all; and I just stir up a pudding."

I assure her that because of the calories I sometimes don't have any dessert at all.

"Ach no!" she exclaims in amazement. "Without dessert at the back part of a meal we'd feel we weren't finished."

Amsey says, "We would all get up from the table starving to death."

APPLE SPONGE PUDDING

From Eliza Gingerich's grandmother, handed down because it's so good.

6 medium-sized apples	1 teaspoon baking powder
2 eggs, separated	1 cup water
1 cup sugar (white)	1 teaspoon vanilla
1 cup flour	2 cups brown sugar
1/2 teaspoon salt	1/4 cup butter

Peel and slice the apples. Beat the egg yolks, add the white sugar and beat until light. Sift the other dry ingredients and add alternately with the water and vanilla to the sugar-egg mixture. Fold in the stiffly beaten egg whites.

In the bottom of a greased baking dish melt the butter and brown sugar; spread the sliced apples over the mixture. Pour the batter over the apples and bake at 350 degrees for about 45 minutes. Serve warm with whipped or ice cream.

This should serve eight people but it probably won't.

FRUITY APPLE PUDDING

Fresh and fruity in a mince-pie sort of way. Can be eaten hot or cold.

3 cups flour	1 lemon, grated rind and
1 cup butter	juice
1/4 cup sugar	2 egg yolks
	1/4 cup cold water

Blend the butter and flour. Beat the egg yolks and add the water to them. Combine the mixtures, adding grated lemon rind, juice and sugar. Pat into a baking dish—1/2 an inch thick, keeping some dough to cover the dish after it's filled with fruit.

2 quarts apples, diced	1 cup seeded raisins
1 cup sugar	1/2 cup currants
1/4 cup almonds, blanched and chopped	1/4 cup red or white sweet wine
1 lemon, rind and juice	

Mix and pour into dough in baking dish; criss-cross remaining dough over the top. Bake 50 or 60 minutes at 400 degrees.

APPLE DUMPLINGS

Don't eat too much before you have these, you're sure to want more than one.

2 cups flour	4 or 5 apples pared, cored
4 teaspoons baking powder	and cut in half
1 teaspoon salt	Sugar
4 tablespoons shortening	1 teaspoon cinnamon
1 cup milk	

Sift the dry ingredients, cut in shortening, add milk and mix to a smooth dough. Turn onto a floured board and divide into 8 or 10 portions; roll out each portion large enough to cover one half-apple. Place apple on each piece of dough, fill core-hollow with sugar and cinnamon. Wet edges of dough and press together over apple. Place on a greased baking sheet and bake in a 350-degree oven until the apples are tender—about half an hour. Serve with a boiled brown-sugar sauce or put the dumplings into a baking dish, pour the uncooked ingredients for Brown Sugar Sauce into the pan around them and bake till the dumplings are done and the sauce is thick.

BROWN SUGAR SAUCE

2 cups of water, 2 cups of brown sugar, 3 tablespoons of butter; combine and cook together for 5 minutes; or simply pour uncooked sauce around dumplings and bake.

DUTCH APPLE PUDDING

You could make this with other fruit as well.

2 cups flour	Butter, the size of an egg
1/2 teaspoon salt	1 egg, beaten light
1/2 teaspoon soda	2/3 cup milk
1 teaspoon cream of tartar	

Sift dry ingredients, work in butter; combine egg and milk and blend with dry mixture. Spread 1/2 an inch thick in a pan. Pare and cut 4 apples into eighths; stick them into the dough in rows; sprinkle with sugar and cinnamon. Bake 20 minutes in a 400-degree oven. Serve hot with sweet cream or ice cream, or Brown Sugar Sauce.

APFELSTRUDEL

A German specialty, often served in Kitchener and Waterloo, it has many variations—some of them pretty dull and dry. I'll never forget the Apfelstrudel a German woman served me warm from the oven; she told me how to make it.

2¹/₂ cups flour	1 cup brown sugar
1 teaspoon salt	¹/₂ cup seedless raisins
2 tablespoons shortening	¹/₂ cup chopped nuts
2 eggs slightly beaten	5 tablespoons melted butter
¹/₂ cup warm water	¹/₂ teaspoon cinnamon
5 cups sliced apples	Grated rind of 1 lemon

Sift the flour and salt together. Cut in the 2 tablespoons of shortening and add the eggs and water. Knead well, then throw or beat the dough against a board until it blisters. Stand the dough in a warm place under a cloth for 20 minutes. Cover the kitchen table with a small white cloth and flour it. Put the dough on it and pull it out with your hands very carefully to the thickness of tissue paper. Spread with a mixture of the fruits, sugar, melted butter, cinnamon and lemon rind. Fold in the outer edges of the dough and roll like a jelly roll about 4 inches wide. Bake in a very hot oven (450 degrees) for 10 minutes, reduce the heat to 400 degrees and bake about 20 minutes longer. Let it cool. Cut in slices about two inches wide. It should be flaky, moist, and one of the best things you've ever tasted.

APPLESAUCE

The moment the first green Harvest apples appear at the market I buy a six-quart basket of them and immediately make the most wonderful applesauce in the world.

I wash the apples, cut out the blossom ends and stems, cut the apples into quarters and plunge them into boiling water in a big kettle—enough water to cover three-quarters of the apples. Boil the apples till they are soft, puffy, and their skins have fallen off; stir them occasionally so the top ones will go down to the bottom and they'll all cook evenly. While it is hot put the whole mass through a food mill or colander to remove the skins, cores and seeds. Then while still piping hot, add sugar—about 1 cup to 2 quarts of applesauce—more if the apples are very sour (taste till it seems just right—not too sweet). Sprinkle liberally with cinnamon, cool it, then try to find enough covered containers and enough space in your fridge to keep it—it's too good to be kept very long. (By boiling the applesauce after you put in the sugar and cinnamon and then pouring it into sterilized jars you can keep it as you would any canned fruit—but I don't think it tastes as good.)

I like this Harvest or Yellow Transparent applesauce to be quite thin and cold. I'll eat it every day till it's "all." With home-made bread toast in the morning, and as a dessert with a nut loaf, gingerbread, molasses or oatmeal cookies it "can't be beat."

APPLE CRISP

A delicious old stand-by.

8 apples, sliced and peeled	**Topping:**
1/2 cup white or brown sugar	**3/4 cup flour or rolled oats**
1 tablespoon flour	**1 cup brown sugar**
1 teaspoon cinnamon	**1/4 cup melted butter**
1/4 teaspoon salt	

Combine the sugar, flour, cinnamon and salt and mix with the sliced apples. Put all in a greased baking dish and cover with the topping mixture which you have rubbed into the crumbs. Bake in a 375-degree oven for about 30 minutes—or until the top is nicely browned and the apples are soft. Serve with sweet or whipped cream.

FRESH WINTER FRUIT

All my life I've been eating this fresh winter fruit and I've never tired of having it several times in a week—with various cookies or cake. It's so simple; all you do is cut up oranges, grapefruit, slice a banana, slice an apple or two, cut up a few maraschino cherries for colour if you like, and grape halves. Sometimes my combination of fruits has been limited to just bananas and oranges.

After cutting, I mix them in a bowl, sprinkle them with sugar and serve. If I want to be a bit more subtle—and to create more juice—I add a tablespoonful or two, or more, of muscatel, sherry, or apricot brandy.

STRAWBERRY OR PEACH SHORTCAKE

Years ago I should have mimeographed copies of this old-fashioned biscuit-dough shortcake recipe—it would have saved me the time I've spent giving it to all the people who've eaten it at my table.

4 cups flour	1 teaspoon salt
2 tablespoons baking powder	1 cup shortening
1 teaspoon soda	2 cups sour milk or buttermilk
1 cup sugar	

Mix the dry ingredients and the shortening till the mixture is crumbly. Add the sour milk and mix just enough to make sure the dry part is moistened. Spread the dough out in a greased cake pan—quite a large flat one—or you can use half the recipe and put the batter into a 9 x 9-inch square one. Sprinkle white sugar over the top and bake in a 400-degree oven for about 20 minutes, or a bit longer—prick the centre to be sure. Serve warm and smothered with sugared berries or sliced peaches. You don't need to split it and butter it or slather it with whipped cream. This one stands on its own.

FRESH STRAWBERRIES, LEMON, AND WINE

At dinner one May night in Italy we were appalled to see our waiter sprinkle perfect, ripe strawberries with sugar, then lemon juice. But when we ate, we found that the strawberry flavour had been heightened by the lemon. Try this with your strawberry shortcake—or strawberries served alone: from 2 quarts of berries pick out the most perfect ones, sprinkle with sugar; mash the imperfect berries with the juice of a small lemon—or half a lemon —slightly less than $1/2$ a cup of sugar and add 1 cup of light sweet red wine. Pour this purée over the whole berries, stir well together and serve with the shortcake or in a dish with scones or cake on the side. Use raspberries in the same way.

COUSIN LUCY'S MERINGUE PEACH PIE

When we ate this at Cousin Lucy's place in Grand Rapids, Michigan, we thought it was the most delicious thing we had ever tasted in all our lives. (I was fourteen.) I still think it's one of the most glamorous party desserts to be made throughout the fresh fruit season. If you have an electric mixer, it's a cinch;

Cousin Lucy had to beat the eggs with a wire whisk. Try it with fresh strawberries or raspberries too.

4 egg whites	**$^1/_4$ teaspoon cream of tartar**
1 cup sugar	**$^1/_2$ teaspoon salt**

In a large bowl, let the egg whites warm to room temperature. Beat the egg whites with the cream of tartar and salt until they are stiff, but not stiff enough to form peaks. Gradually beat in the sugar a bit at a time and keep on beating and beating until the meringue is very firm and the peaks very stiff, shiny and moist. Spread the meringue over the bottom of the large, well-greased pie plate, about $^1/_4$ of an inch thick; cover the sides an inch deep and as high as the meringue will stay. Bake at 275 degrees for an hour—it should be light beige and crisp. Don't put it too near the floor of the oven or its bottom might burn. When it is cold—and you can keep the baked meringue for several days (or weeks)—fill the hollow of the pie shell with about $^3/_4$ of an inch of ice cream and over that, and nicely filling the whole thing, pour in coarsely sliced and lightly sugared peaches—or strawberries, or raspberries.

This one is really ambrosial. And what are you going to do with those egg yolks? Make a sponge cake, or noodles, or custard sauce—or simply lose them in an omelette or scrambled eggs.

FRUIT CRUNCH

Here is a versatile, easy dessert that everyone raves about. You need four cups of any fruit you'd like to try, but it's especially wonderful with rhubarb.
Mix until crumbly:

1 cup flour	**Combine the following:**
$^3/_4$ cup rolled oats	**1 cup sugar**
1 cup brown sugar, packed	**2 tablespoons cornstarch**
$^1/_2$ cup melted butter	**1 cup water**
1 teaspoon cinnamon	**1 teaspoon vanilla**

Press half the crumbs into a greased 9-inch baking pan—pyrex preferred. Cover with 4 cups of cut-up rhubarb—or what have you. Cook the second mixture till it is thick and clear and pour over the rhubarb. Top with remaining crumbs. Bake at 350 degrees for 1 hour—or slightly less—it should be golden and rich. Cut into squares and serve while warm—as is or with plain or whipped cream. When peaches are in season I use them instead of rhubarb. One day I tried it with apples—also "delish"; another time I mixed 2 cups of sweetened applesauce with 3 tablespoons of butter and the yolks of 2 eggs, the stiffly beaten whites folded in (instead of the cornstarch mixture). The result was creamy and wonderful. I'm sure it would be equally super with raspberries or blueberries or any other berries.

RASPBERRY PUDDING

A company dish, sweet and pretty, with a crisp, almost meringue-like top covering the moist goodies underneath. It can be made with a variety of fruits.

2 or 3 cups fresh raspberries (or 1 frozen package)	1 teaspoon baking powder
2 cups sugar, plus 2 extra tablespoons	$^1/_2$ teaspoon salt
	5 tablespoons butter
2 or 3 tablespoons butter	$^1/_3$ cup milk
1 cup flour, plus 2 extra tablespoons	1 egg

Spread your fruit on the bottom of a buttered and floured cake pan—preferably pyrex, 9 by 9. Sprinkle the 2 extra tablespoons of flour and sugar over the fruit. (If you use frozen fruit let it thaw first and blend the juice with the sugar and flour before pouring it over the fruit in the pan.) Cut the 2 or 3 tablespoons of butter over the fruit in paper-thin slices.

Now, in a bowl, cream the 5 tablespoons of butter and 2 cups of sugar; blend in the egg; sift the cup of flour, baking powder and salt and add to the creamed mixture alternately with the milk. Beat well. Drop the batter in spoonfuls over the fruit. Bake at 350 degrees for about half an hour—longer if you have used frozen berries. Serve warm or cold with whipped or ice cream, topping with a few whole, especially nice berries. And be prepared to hand out the recipe.

GINGER OR CHOCOLATE WAFER DESSERT

For a good reason this recipe has been popular for a long time. Buy a package of very thin ginger or chocolate wafers. Whip some cream, add sugar and flavouring then slather whipped cream over the wafers and stack them in neat little piles that will be enough for individual servings. Ice each stack with the whipped cream and serve. I like my wafers crisp but Mother used to let them stand till the cream had softened them slightly.

TRIFLE

Sometimes Mother made a Daffodil Sponge Cake, light, high, and pretty to look at, but uninteresting after a day or two; none of us ate much because we so greatly preferred the trifle Mother made with what was left over.

Half a sponge cake, lady fingers, or any other dry cake	Custard sauce:
	2 tablespoons flour
1/2 cup red jelly or jam	1/2 cup sugar
1/3 cup sherry or brandy or rum	Pinch of salt
	2 eggs
1/4 cup chopped nuts	2 cups milk
1 cup whipped cream	1 teaspoon vanilla

To make custard sauce: Mix flour, sugar and salt. Beat the eggs lightly and blend with the sugar. Scald the milk and gradually add it to the other mixture. Cook over hot water, stirring constantly until the sauce thickens and coats a wooden spoon. Cool, add vanilla and chill.

To combine trifle: cut the cake in strips and spread jam generously on the pieces. Criss-cross 1/4 of the pieces of cake in a pretty bowl, sprinkle them with sherry—enough to moisten the cake but not make it soggy. Sprinkle on nuts and 1/4 of the custard sauce. Repeat this performance till all the cake, jam, sherry, nuts and custard are used up—the custard on top. Chill a few hours; then, before serving, top with whipped cream and chopped nuts.

TWENTY-MINUTE DESSERT

Worth trying. It's really good—dumplings in caramel sauce.

1 1/2 cups brown sugar	2 tablespoons butter
2 cups boiling water	

Stir all together in a cooking pot till sugar has dissolved; add butter and simmer while you mix the dumplings:

1/2 cup sugar	1 1/2 cups flour
1/2 teaspoon salt	3 teaspoons baking powder
1 tablespoon butter	1/2 cup milk

Cream butter, salt and sugar; add sifted flour and baking powder alternately with milk to make a stiff batter. Drop by tablespoonfuls into boiling sauce—or maple syrup—cover and let boil gently for about 15 minutes. Serve with or without whipped cream.

DEVIL'S FOOD PUDDING WITH ICE-CREAM SAUCE

This is terrific, the sauce is divine; the recipe came from a local friend's grandmother.

3 squares of chocolate	1 cup milk (2nd amount)
1/2 cup sugar	2 cups flour
1/2 cup milk	1/2 teaspoon salt
1/2 cup vegetable shortening	1 teaspoon vanilla
1 cup sugar (2nd amount)	1 teaspoon soda mixed with
2 eggs	1 tablespoon water

Melt the chocolate in a saucepan, add the 1/2-cup of sugar and the 1/2-cup of milk. Cook until thick; cool. Blend shortening with 1 cup of sugar and the eggs; stir in the chocolate mixture. Add 1 cup of milk alternately with the flour sifted with salt. Add vanilla, then soda, mixed with water. Bake in a tube pan at 325 degrees for almost an hour—or steam for 40 minutes, then bake at 325 degrees for 10 minutes. Serve with Ice-Cream Sauce.

ICE-CREAM SAUCE

3/4 cup sugar	1/3 cup melted butter
1 egg	(or Crisco)
1/8 teaspoon salt	1 teaspoon vanilla
	1 cup cream, whipped

Beat together the sugar, egg and salt. Add the melted shortening and beat well. Add the vanilla. Fold in the whipped cream—and that's it—devilishly tempting you to eat far more than you ought to.

CREAM PUFFS

Here is Mother's recipe:

1 cup boiling water	1 cup sifted flour
1/2 cup butter	4 eggs

Put butter and water into a saucepan and boil until the butter is melted. Stirring rapidly, add flour and cook until mixture is thick and smooth. Scrape into a mixing bowl and when lukewarm add one egg at a time, beating after each addition until the mixture is very smooth. Drop by spoonfuls on a greased baking sheet at least 1 1/2 inches apart. Bake in a 400-degree oven about 35 minutes. When cool make a slit in the side of each great puffy thing with a pair of scissors and fill with sweetened whipped cream.

LOTTIE RITTINGER'S SNOW BALLS

¹/₄ cup butter	1¹/₈ cups flour
¹/₂ cup sugar	2 teaspoons baking powder
¹/₄ cup milk	Whites of 2 eggs

Cream butter and sugar, stir in the milk and beat until sugar is dissolved. Sift in flour and baking powder, and beat thoroughly. Fold in the beaten egg whites. Put into buttered moulds and steam 35 minutes. Serve with chocolate sauce.

BREAD PUDDING

Mother told me a thousand times that bread pudding was delicious, healthful, economical, and I must eat it.

1 quart stale bread cubes (or even stale cake)	2 eggs, well beaten
2 cups milk	¹/₄ cup seeded raisins
¹/₂ cup sugar, white or brown	¹/₄ teaspoon nutmeg
	¹/₂ teaspoon cinnamon

Beat the eggs, add the sugar, spices and milk. Butter a baking dish, arrange bread or cake and raisins in the dish and pour the liquid over it. Let stand until bread has been thoroughly soaked. Bake in a 350-degree oven for 25 minutes.

Knowing how much I liked chocolate, Mother sometimes put in 2 tablespoons of cocoa instead of the spices and served the pudding with a chocolate sauce instead of the usual custard sauce. I was never fooled; it still was bread pudding.

COTTAGE PUDDING

1 cup brown sugar	2 cups flour
3 tablespoons melted butter	2 teaspoons cream tartar
¹/₂ teaspoon salt	1 teaspoon soda
2 eggs, beaten	1 cup sour milk

Blend the sugar and butter and salt; beat in the eggs, then add alternately the milk and the dry ingredients sifted together. Bake at 350 degrees for about half an hour. Serve with any sauce that you like.

MAPLE PUDDING

This is a dandy little pudding to make in a hurry. Heat 1 cup of maple syrup to boiling and pour it into a buttered baking dish. Combine the following in the order given:

1 tablespoon lard	1/2 cup milk
3 tablespoons white sugar	1 cup flour
2 teaspoons salt	2 teaspoons baking powder
1 egg	

Pour the batter into the hot maple syrup and bake in a 350-degree oven till it is done.

BANANA SPONGE

This won't keep long. For two reasons.

2 tablespoons gelatine	4 tablespoons lemon juice
1/2 cup cold water	1 1/3 cups mashed bananas
2/3 cup boiling water	4 egg whites
1 cup sugar	

Soften gelatine in cold water. Dissolve sugar in boiling water; boil a minute. Remove from fire, add gelatine and dissolve. Add lemon juice and banana. When partly set, beat; then add stiffly beaten eggs. Chill. Serve with whipped cream or custard sauce made with egg yolks.

JELLO FRUIT PUDDING

Always appreciated.

1 package of jello—any flavour or colour that goes with your decor	12 dates, seeded and chopped
1 pint boiling water	1 banana, sliced
1/4 teaspoon salt	1/4 cup nuts, chopped
1/2 cup seeded raisins, chopped	

Dissolve the jello in boiling water, add salt, then chill. When slightly thickened, fold in the fruits and nuts. Turn into a mould and chill until firm. Unmould, serve with whipped cream or Ice-Cream Sauce (see Index).

LEMON SNOW

Wonderfully tart and light after a heavy dinner.

1 tablespoon gelatine	**¹/₄ teaspoon salt**
¹/₄ cup cold water	**¹/₄ cup lemon juice**
1 cup hot water	**Whites of 2 eggs, beaten**
Grated rind of 1 lemon	**stiff**
³/₄ cup sugar	

Dissolve the gelatine in cold water, add hot water, sugar and salt and stir until dissolved. Add lemon juice and grated rind of one lemon. Cool and, when quite thick, beat until frothy; add whites of eggs beaten stiff and keep on beating mixture until stiff enough to hold its shape. Put into a pretty serving dish and chill. Serve with custard sauce; decorate with maraschino cherries.

CHOCOLATE SOUFFLÉ

Calorie counters be consoled when you eat this that a lot of it is just egg fluff.

2 ounces of bitter chocolate	**Dash of salt**
³/₄ cup sugar	**4 eggs, separated**

Melt the chocolate and stir in the sugar. Beat the whites of the eggs until they are stiff, adding a dash of salt to help them along. Then beat the yolks until they thicken and fold them into the whites; fold in the chocolate mixture with a little vanilla added to it. Turn into a greased baking dish, set the dish in a pan of hot water in a 350-degree oven and bake until the soufflé is firm.

PRUNE WHIP

We never wanted plain prunes again after Mother had treated us to this.

3 egg whites	**2 tablespoons lemon juice**
¹/₄ teaspoon salt	**2 cups finely chopped**
¹/₂ cup sugar	**prunes (cooked)**

Beat the egg whites with salt until stiff—but not dry. Add the sugar gradually, beating it in. Add the lemon juice to the prune pulp and gradually beat it into the egg mixture until the whole thing is fluffy. Pile lightly into individual serving dishes and chill.

Or pour into a greased baking dish, set in a pan of water and bake at 325 degrees until it is firm.

Serve with whipped cream or custard sauce.

Other fruits may be used instead of the prunes—apricots, peaches, strawberries, bananas—but not baked.

BAKED CUSTARD

So good for the children—and you.

3 eggs, beaten	**¼ cup sugar**
2 cups milk	**1 teaspoon vanilla**
½ teaspoon salt	**Cinnamon**

Scald the milk; beat the eggs, adding the salt and sugar to them; stir in the hot milk slowly, add vanilla and pour into a baking dish. Dust the top with cinnamon and bake at 350 degrees for almost an hour. Test by putting a silver knife into the middle; if it comes out clean the custard is done.

MAPLE CUSTARD

Can be made the same way, putting in ⅓ of a cup of maple syrup and 1⅔ cups of milk.

CARAMEL CUSTARD

In Spain they call this *flan*; it was the only dessert we got there except fruit. Instead of using plain sugar, spread half a cup of sugar over the bottom of a heavy, flat pan and heat it over low heat until a light brown syrup has formed. Mix this very gently into the scalded milk and heat until all the sugar is dissolved—then make the custard in the usual way.

CHOCOLATE CUSTARD

Add an ounce of bitter chocolate to the milk when it is put on to scald and be sure it is all melted before you mix in the eggs. You might want more sugar.

MOTHER'S CORNSTARCH PUDDING

For one of those days when you need some blandness.

3 cups milk	**½ teaspoon salt**
4½ tablespoons cornstarch	**¾ teaspoon vanilla**
¾ cup sugar	

Scald 2¹/₂ cups of milk in the top of a double boiler. Mix corn-starch, sugar and salt with the remaining ¹/₂-cup of cold milk. Stir until smooth. Pour a little of the scalded milk on the mixture and blend. Add gradually to the hot milk, stirring constantly. When smooth, cover and cook for 25 minutes, stirring occasion-ally to prevent lumping. Add vanilla and pour into a mould. Cool, then place in fridge to chill. Unmould on a large plate and garnish with fresh fruit, preserved fruit, or serve with a chocolate or butterscotch sauce, or maple syrup—or anything else you can think of that might pep it up.

CHOCOLATE DESSERT

This is a smoothie that will quickly win warm approval.

1 heaping tablespoon cocoa	2 cups boiling water
3 heaping tablespoons flour	1 teaspoon vanilla
¹/₂ teaspoon salt	Butter the size of an egg
1 cup white sugar	A little cold water

Blend the flour, cocoa, salt and sugar in a little cold water. Add the boiling water and cook until thick—it takes a little over 10 minutes. After it is taken from the stove, add the butter and vanilla. Stir until smooth. Pour into a serving dish and chill. Serve with a mound of whipped cream on top and perhaps a few nuts, but don't keep on tasting (and diminishing) it before it reaches the table!

MAPLE MOUSSE

Mother makes this often—so smoooooth, and rich and delicate; we love it.

1 dessertspoon plain gelatine	2 eggs, beaten
¹/₄ cup cold water	1 cup maple syrup
	1 cup cream, whipped

Soak the gelatine in the cold water. Beat the eggs and add the maple syrup, cooking the mixture in a double boiler for about 2 minutes, stirring constantly. While the maple–egg mixture is still hot, add the gelatine and stir in well. Let cool till it is almost thick, then fold in the stiffly whipped cream. Put the mousse in an ice tray in the refrigerator to chill thoroughly. Mother says, "It's good to give it a stir with a fork before it sets."

MARSHMALLOW-COCOA ICE CREAM

We always thought Mother's ice cream was smoother, and more chocolatey than the boughten kind—and more easily available for the little stolen tastes!

12 marshmallows	Pinch of salt
2 tablespoons sugar	$^1/_2$ cup milk
2 tablespoons cocoa	1 cup cream, whipped

In a double boiler, stir till dissolved: the marshmallows, sugar, salt, cocoa and milk. Cool—but before it sets, add whipped cream. Put the mixture in the fridge, in an ice tray, stirring with a fork before it gets hard.

CREAMY RICE PUDDING

When I was eight years old I visited my Aunt Nellie for three weeks and I'm sure we had rice pudding for dessert every meal —dry, baked, flavourless rice. I wished Auntie Nellie could cook rice nice and creamy like Mother's. This way:

$^1/_2$ cup uncooked rice	$^1/_4$ teaspoon salt
2 cups whole milk	1 teaspoon vanilla
2 eggs, separated	$^1/_2$ cup raisins
$^1/_2$ cup sugar	A sprinkling of cinnamon

Put the rice, salt, and milk in a double boiler and cook until the rice is tender—about $^3/_4$ of an hour. If it seems dry, add more milk. At half-time put in the raisins. Beat the egg yolks, add the sugar, stir some of the hot rice into the mixture, then add to the rice in the double boiler and cook for 2 or 3 minutes, stirring all the time. Remove from heat, stir in vanilla and a generous sprinkling of cinnamon. Add more milk (or cream), if it is dry; it should be moist.

Let it cool a bit—but not be quite cold when you serve it topped by a perky mound of the egg whites beaten stiff, with four teaspoons of sugar and a couple of drops of vanilla.

TAPIOCA PUDDING

Fish eyes and glue we used to call the half-cooked, large-grained, starchy tapioca without flavour that we were served every week in our residence at university. How I longed for the creamy pudding Mother used to make.

¹/₄ cup quick tapioca or big tapioca soaked in water overnight
¹/₂ cup sugar
¹/₂ teaspoon salt
1 egg, separated
1 teaspoon vanilla
3 cups milk

Scald the milk in a double boiler and add tapioca, sugar and salt. Cook until the tapioca is clear, stirring often. Pour some of the tapioca mixture over beaten egg yolk, stirring rapidly; return to double boiler and cook until mixture thickens. Remove from fire, add vanilla and fold in the stiffly beaten egg white—or make a meringue of the egg white to serve with the tapioca after it has been chilled.

CHOCOLATE TAPIOCA PUDDING

Add melted one and a half squares of unsweetened chocolate; or blend ¹/₃ of a cup of cocoa with the sugar before adding to hot milk in the recipe above.

CHRISTMAS PLUM PUDDING

Too bad Christmas comes only once a year.

2 pounds raisins
2 pounds currants
1 pound mixed peel, cut-up
1 pound brown sugar
1 pound breadcrumbs
1 pound beef suet, chopped fine
¹/₂ pound dates
¹/₂ pound almonds, chopped
1 pound flour
2 tablespoons baking powder
1 teaspoon nutmeg
1 teaspoon ginger
1 teaspoon cloves
1 teaspoon cinnamon
1 teaspoon salt
2 medium-sized apples
2 carrots, grated
4 eggs
1 pint milk
1 cup molasses

Sift flour, baking powder, salt and spices together. Chop the suet finely and add chopped dates, raisins, currants and cut-up peel, apples, carrots and almonds; mix thoroughly and combine with flour mixture. Soak the bread crumbs in the milk, add sugar, well-beaten eggs and molasses; combine with first mixture. Turn into well-greased moulds, cover and steam for six hours. Serve with brandy or wine sauce (see Index).

CARROT PUDDING

While I'm eating this I usually think I like it better than real plum pudding.

2 cups cooked and mashed carrots	Grated rind of ¹/₂ lemon
1 cup finely chopped suet	¹/₂ cup flour—or enough to stiffen batter
1 cup molasses	1 teaspoon allspice
1 egg	1 teaspoon cinnamon
1 teaspoon baking soda, dissolved in ¹/₄ cup hot water	1 teaspoon cloves
	1 teaspoon nutmeg
2 tablespoons brown sugar	¹/₂ cup raisins
¹/₂ teaspoon salt	¹/₂ cup currants
	¹/₂ cup citron peel, cut fine

Mix all ingredients together, adding the dissolved soda last. Put into a buttered mould and steam for 3 hours. Serve hot with a brandy, wine, or whisky sauce (see Index).

Now Bevvy's Dessert recipes:

QUICK PUDDING

This was baking in Bevvy's oven while we were eating our supper; I wished I'd saved more room for it.

¹/₃ cup white sugar	1 cup flour
¹/₂ cup milk	1 teaspoon baking powder
1 cup raisins	

Mix in the order given and put into greased baking dish. Over it pour: ¹/₂ a cup of brown sugar, dissolved in 1 cup of boiling water, and a piece of butter the size of an egg. Bake ¹/₂ an hour. The dough part comes to the top and is surrounded by rich brown sauce.

KING GEORGE PUDDING

1 pint breadcrumbs	¹/₂ teaspoon each of cloves, nutmeg and cinnamon
¹/₂ cup butter	
¹/₂ cup brown sugar	1 teaspoon soda
2 eggs, beaten	2 cups flour
1 cup sour cream	1¹/₂ cups currants

Combine the crumbs, sugar and butter; add the eggs beaten into the cream, then the flour sifted with the soda and spices and with the currants added to them. Steam 2 hours. Serve hot with a sauce.

RAW CARROT PUDDING

1 cup sugar	1 cup raisins
1/2 cup lard	2 cups flour
1 cup grated carrots	1 tablespoon soda
1 cup grated potatoes	

Blend the sugar and lard, add the raw carrots, potatoes and the raisins, then the flour sifted with the soda. Steam 1¹/₂ hours. Serve hot with a sauce or maple syrup.

CUP PUDDING

1/2 cup butter	3/4 cup milk
1/2 cup sugar	1¹/₂ cups flour
1 egg, beaten	2 teaspoons baking powder

Blend butter and sugar; add the egg; then, alternately the milk and flour sifted with the soda. Spoon the batter into greased cups and steam for 1/2 an hour. Serve with a sauce or maple syrup.

STEAMED JAM OR MARMALADE PUDDING

A good way to get rid of that bit of jam in the bottom of the jar.

2 tablespoons shortening	1¹/₂ cups flour
1/4 cup sugar	1 tablespoon baking powder
1 egg, beaten	1 tablespoon milk
6 tablespoons jam or marmalade	1/2 teaspoon salt

Cream shortening and add sugar. Add egg and marmalade. Sift baking powder and flour into the mixture. Add milk if needed to moisten. Put in mould or bowl and steam for 2¹/₂ hours. Serve hot with brown sugar or brandy sauce (see index).

SUET PUDDING

1 cup suet, finely chopped	1 cup raisins
1¹/₂ cups molasses	2 cups flour
1 cup sour milk	1 teaspoon soda
1/2 cup brown sugar	

Mix in the order given and steam for 2 hours. Serve with your favourite hot sauce.

BLAUMA PUDDING (Plum Pudding)

Made with plums.

2 cups stoned plums, cut in half	1/4 teaspoon nutmeg
1/2 teaspoon salt	1 tablespoon melted shortening
2 teaspoons soda	1/4 cup honey
1 1/3 cups flour	1/3 cup hot water
1/4 teaspoon allspice	Grated rind of 1 lemon

Sift the dry ingredients and add the plums. Combine the shortening, honey, hot water, and lemon rind and add to first mixture, blending well. Pour the batter into a well-greased mould, cover and steam for 2 1/2 hours. Unmould and serve hot with a sauce.

KASCHA ROLLS (Cherry Rolls)

Made with canned cherries; these are really "for nice," Bevvy says.

2 cupfuls flour	Sauce:
3/4 teaspoon salt	1/3 cup brown sugar
1/4 teaspoon soda	1/3 cup white sugar
2 1/2 teaspoons baking powder	1 1/2 tablespoons cornstarch
1 teaspoon cinnamon	1 1/2 cups cherry juice (with enough water to make
2 tablespoons sugar	up the amount)
2 tablespoons soft butter	1/2 teaspoon almond flavouring
1 egg, beaten	1 1/4 tablespoons butter
3/4 cup sour cream	Red colouring
2 cups cherries, pitted and drained	

Mix and sift dry ingredients; beat egg and sour cream together and blend with the flour mixture. Roll dough 1/4 of an inch thick on a floured board. Spread lightly with soft butter and cover with cherries. Sprinkle with cinnamon and two tablespoons of sugar. Roll like a jelly roll and cut into 1 1/4-inch slices. Put into a greased baking pan. Pour over the slices the sauce—previously prepared: mix sugars, cornstarch and juice; boil till slightly thickened. Add the butter, flavouring and red colouring. Pour over the rolls and bake at 375 degrees for 25 minutes. Serve hot or cold with whipped or ice cream—or just plain.

LEMON SOUFFLÉ

The page in Bevvy's note-book is badly spattered over this one.

1 tablespoon melted butter	2 eggs, beaten separately
1 cup white sugar	Juice and rind of 1 lemon
2 heaping tablespoons flour	1 cup milk

Stir together the sugar and flour, blend in the butter, egg yolks, lemon and milk; lightly fold in the stiffly beaten egg whites. Pour into greased baking-serving dish and set the dish in a pan of water. Cook in a 350-degree oven for about half an hour—there will be a tender, spongy part on top and a lemony sauce underneath. Perfect after a heavy dinner.

ST. JAMES PUDDING

3 tablespoons butter, melted	1 cup dates, cut in pieces
1/2 cup bran	1/2 teaspoon soda
1/2 cup molasses	1/2 teaspoon salt
1/2 cup sour milk	1/4 teaspoon each of cloves,
1 1/2 cups flour	allspice and nutmeg

Combine butter, bran, molasses and milk. Sift flour, soda, salt and spices; add to first mixture, with dates, stirring only until combined. Fill greased mould about 2/3 full. Cover tightly and steam 3 hours. Serve hot with sauce.

BLUEBERRY MUSH

This can also be made with other berries, apples, or peaches.

1 quart of berries	2 cups flour
2 cups sugar	4 teaspoons baking powder
1 teaspoon lemon juice	1 teaspoon salt
1 tablespoon butter	3/4 cup milk

Sift flour, baking powder and salt together and work in the butter. Add the milk and blend thoroughly. Combine the sugar, berries and lemon juice. Mix with batter. Pour into a buttered mould, cover tightly and steam for 45 minutes. Serve with plain or whipped cream.

SEVEN-CENT PUDDING

Those were the days!

1 cup sugar
1¹/₂ cups flour
1 teaspoon soda
¹/₂ teaspoon baking powder

1¹/₂ cups oatmeal
¹/₂ cup cream
¹/₂ cup buttermilk

Sift dry ingredients, add oatmeal; mix; add cream and buttermilk. Bake in 350-degree oven. Serve wth crushed fruit as a sauce.

PUDDING SAUCES

CUSTARD SAUCE

1¹/₂ cups milk
3 egg yolks
¹/₄ cup sugar

¹/₈ teaspoon salt
¹/₂ teaspoon vanilla

Scald milk in double boiler. Beat yolks, add sugar and salt and beat until light. Pour scalded milk over mixture, blend and return to double boiler. Cook till sauce coats wooden spoon, stirring constantly. Chill and add vanilla.

LEMON SAUCE

¹/₂ cup white sugar
1¹/₂ tablespoons cornstarch
Grated rind and juice of
    1 lemon

¹/₄ teaspoon salt
2 tablespoons butter
1¹/₂ cups boiling water

Combine sugar, salt, and cornstarch. Slowly add the water and cook in a double boiler until mixture thickens and is clear, stirring constantly. Remove from heat and stir in the butter until melted, then stir in the grated lemon rind and juice until well blended.

The juice and rind of an orange could be used if you want *Orange Sauce.*

FOAMY SAUCE

2 tablespoons butter
2 tablespoons flour
¹/₂ cup sugar
1 egg yolk

¹/₂ cup water
1 teaspoon vanilla
1 egg white

Cream butter and add flour mixed with sugar; gradually, while stirring constantly, add egg yolk, well-beaten, water and vanilla.

Cook in double boiler until mixture thickens, stirring constantly at first, then occasionally. Cool and, just before serving, add egg white beaten until stiff.

CARROT OR PLUM-PUDDING SAUCE

1 cup brown sugar
1/2 teaspoon salt
2 cups boiling water
2 jiggers of sweet wine,
    brandy, whisky or rum
    —or 2 teaspoons vanilla

2 tablespoons cornstarch
4 tablespoons butter

Mix sugar, cornstarch, salt; add water gradually, stirring, constantly. Boil for 5 minutes—till thickened and clear; remove from fire, add butter; let it melt as you stir, then add liquor or vanilla.

BROWN SUGAR SAUCE—ONE

1 1/2 cups brown sugar
2 cups boiling water

4 tablespoons butter

Boil all together for about 10 minutes.

BROWN SUGAR SAUCE—TWO

1 cup brown sugar
2 cups boiling water
2 tablespoons butter

3 tablespoons flour or 1 1/2
    tablespoons cornstarch
1 teaspoon vanilla

Melt the butter, add the flour and stir until smooth. Add the sugar, keep stirring and cook until it becomes a darker brown. Slowly add the water and cook until thick, then add vanilla.

NORM'S SHERRY SAUCE

1/2 cup white sugar
1 tablespoon cornstarch
1 cup boiling water
2 tablespoons butter

1 tablespoon vanilla
Pinch of salt
1 jigger sweet sherry

Mix sugar, cornstarch, salt; add water gradually, stirring constantly as you boil it for 5 minutes. Remove from fire; add butter, vanilla, and wine.

CHOCOLATE SAUCE

2 squares unsweetened
    chocolate (or ¹/₂ cup
    cocoa)
1 cup sugar
1 cup hot water

1 tablespoon cornstarch
1 tablespoon butter
¹/₄ teaspoon salt
1 teaspoon vanilla

Melt chocolate in top part of double boiler. Gradually add hot water and stir until smooth. Dissolve cornstarch in a little cold water and add to chocolate mixture with sugar and salt; stir frequently until mixture is thick and smooth—about 10 minutes. Remove from heat and add butter and vanilla.

BUTTERSCOTCH SAUCE

Mother writes in her little black book, "This is very good, even on cake."

1¹/₂ cups brown sugar
¹/₂ cup corn syrup
4 tablespoons butter

¹/₂ cup sweet cream
1 teaspoon vanilla

Bring sugar, syrup and butter to a boil and cook until soft ball forms when a bit is dropped in cold water. Remove from fire and cool. When cold add vanilla and cream.

THIN CHOCOLATE SAUCE

Or for a milk drink. This is not thick or rich—but delicious on ice cream.

1³/₄ cups water
1 cup cocoa

1¹/₂ cups sugar (white or
    brown)
¹/₂ teaspoon salt

Stir all together and boil 5 minutes. Keep in a sealed container in a cool place. Serve hot or cold on ice cream—or add 1 tablespoon to a cup or glass of hot or cold milk.

Candy

Like all Old Order Mennonite children Bevvy's family are sheltered from knowledge of the wicked ways of the world by being denied the ownership of radios, TV sets, telephones and cars. They may not go to movies or any entertainment that might fascinate or corrupt them.

Yet I've never heard them complain of not having anything interesting to do. After school they weed the garden, milk the cows, feed the chickens, do chores in the barn and the fields, or go fishing. In addition the girls learn from Bevvy how to sew, cook and keep their house and clothes clean.

In the evening they study and read or play crokinole. As a special treat Bevvy often lets them make candy. Lyddy and Amsey like taffy best because it's so much fun to pull it; Salome prefers brittles and popcorn balls; Bevvy likes to experiment with chocolate creams and soft fudges.

I haven't tested any of Bevvy's candy recipes but, because I have very often yielded to the temptation of eating too many of their results in her warm friendly kitchen, I agree with what Amsey says: "If she could make humbugs and licorice whips yet, I'd think Mom's candy is better than in the store."

BEVVY'S FAVOURITE FUDGE

1 cup white sugar	$^1/_4$ cup melted butter
1 cup brown sugar	2 heaping tablespoons cocoa
$^1/_4$ cup corn syrup	1 teaspoon vanilla
$^1/_2$ cup sweet milk	

Boil the first five ingredients for $1^1/_2$ minutes, then add cocoa; boil 5 minutes longer, take from stove and add vanilla. Beat till creamy, pour into buttered pan and mark in squares.

FUDGE FROM ELLA

2 cupfuls white sugar	2 tablespoons butter
²/₃ cup milk	1 teaspoon vanilla
2 squares chocolate, chopped	2 tablespoons corn syrup

Combine the sugar, milk, and corn syrup; add the chopped chocolate and cook slowly, stirring until the chocolate and sugar are melted; then stir occasionally. Boil until 238 degrees (or the softball stage) is reached. Remove from fire, add butter without stirring. Cool until lukewarm, or 110 degrees. Add vanilla and beat until it loses its shiny look. Pour into a buttered pan and mark in squares.

BEVVY'S CHOCOLATE CREAMS

Two cups white sugar, ¹/₂ cup cold water, scant ¹/₃ teaspoon cream of tartar.

To keep from sugaring set on stove and cover; dissolve slowly, then boil slowly till soft ball can be formed in cold water (238 degrees). Don't stir or this will be sugary. Let it cool a little (but don't let it get cold). Stir until it forms a nice cream, then roll into balls—if it is too soft a little powdered sugar may be added. Coat neatly with: ¹/₂ cup cocoa, butter the size of a large egg, ¹/₃ block paraffin wax, 2 dessert spoonfuls powdered sugar—melted together but not boiled.

GRUMBARA CANDY (Potato Candy)

1 medium hot baked potato	¹/₂ cup chopped walnuts
3 tablespoons butter	3 to 4 cups icing sugar
4 tablespoons cocoa	

Scoop out the potato from the skin and beat with butter until creamy; add sugar and cocoa gradually, then add nuts. Knead until it will mould, pack into a buttered pan and cut into squares.

DATE CHOCOLATE DROPS

¹/₂ cup mashed potatoes	¹/₂ cup chopped dates
¹/₂ cup chopped walnuts	¹/₄ teaspoon vanilla
Icing sugar to thicken	Sweet chocolate

Mix all together with enough icing sugar to make it thick but pliable. Take small lumps and roll to size desired. Let stand over night, then coat with melted sweet chocolate.

EASY-TO-MAKE CHOCOLATE DROPS

Take a little powdered sugar, add the white of an egg, $^1/_2$ teaspoon water, $^1/_2$ teaspoon milk. Add more powdered sugar till the mixture is so stiff that it won't stick to the fingers, then make into forms. Melt a sweetened chocolate bar with a little paraffin wax, dip the drops into it and set on a buttered tin till hard.

CANDY COPPER ROCKS

2 coconuts, shelled and sliced on cabbage cutter	$^1/_2$ cup cold water
2$^1/_2$ cups white sugar	1$^1/_2$ cups golden corn syrup

Mix all together and let stand overnight. In the morning boil to soft-ball stage (238 degrees), stirring often. Add enough extra shredded "store" coconut to thicken it well. Turn out in a buttered pan and let cool enough to handle, then roll into balls.

COATING: Boil 2 cups of brown sugar, $^1/_2$ cup corn syrup, 1 cup milk, to soft-ball stage (238 degrees); add 1 teaspoon vanilla, then beat until nice and creamy, and thick enough to set. Keep warm while dipping. Place on buttered tins and set out to cool.

MRS. ANANIAS FREY'S CRUNCHY BARS

1 cup sugar	2 cups rice crispies
1 cup corn syrup	2 cups salted peanuts
1 cup cream	1 cup chopped walnuts
5 cups corn flakes	

Cook sugar, cream and syrup to soft-ball stage (238 degrees). Remove from heat and pour over the cereals and nuts; mix thoroughly and pack into well buttered pans. When cool cut in squares.

PUFFED RICE CANDY

$^1/_2$ cup water	2 tablespoons butter
1 heaping cup brown sugar	3 cups puffed rice
A pinch cream of tartar	Flavouring to taste
1 tablespoon vinegar	

Boil water, sugar, vinegar for 10 minutes, stir in the butter and continue boiling till it forms a hard ball in cold water (265 degrees). Add cream of tartar and flavouring; lift from fire and add puffed rice. Press into buttered pan and cut in squares or form into balls.

POPCORN CAKE OR BALLS

1 cup brown sugar
1/2 cup maple syrup
Butter the size of an egg

Nuts and coconut (if you like)
1 pound of popcorn, popped
  to about 3 gallons

Boil sugar, syrup and butter till it strings. Put the popcorn through the food chopper or roll it with a rolling pin and mix it with as many nuts or coconut (or both) as you like. Pour the syrup over the popcorn mixture, stirring briskly. When all is mixed, press into a buttered dish or form into balls.

WALNUT CANDY

Spread whole walnuts evenly over a deep buttered platter. Mix together:

1 1/2 pounds brown sugar
1 pint molasses

1/4 pound butter
1 tablespoon vinegar

Let boil without stirring until brittle (265 degrees). Pour over walnuts and cool.

SEAFOAM CANDY

3 cups brown sugar
1 cup cold water
1 cup nuts

1 1/2 teaspoons vinegar
2 egg whites, beaten stiff
1 teaspoon vanilla

Boil sugar, water and vinegar to hard-ball stage (265 degrees). Add slowly to beaten egg whites, beating all the while; add nuts and vanilla; then beat till quite stiff and pour into a buttered dish and cut into squares.

TOFFEE

1 1/2 cups brown sugar
1/4 cup vinegar

2 tablespoons butter
1/2 cup water

Cook sugar, water and vinegar till the mixture forms a hard ball in water (265 degrees). Add butter and pour onto greased pan. Nuts or raisins may be added.

MOLASSES CANDY

1 quart molasses
Butter size of an egg

1 cup brown sugar
1/2 teaspoon soda

Stir the mixture of molasses, butter and sugar until it boils (to prevent burning). Add soda when the toffee becomes brittle in cold water or breaks between the teeth (265 degrees). Pour into buttered pans.

WHITE PULLING TAFFY

2 cups granulated sugar	2 tablespoons vinegar
1 cup water	1 teaspoon butter

Boil the mixture until it forms a hard ball in water (265 degrees). When it cools, butter your hands and pull the taffy between them —or two people may pull it back and forth.

DADDY'S PULLING TOFFEE

We thought our father was the most wonderful man in the world when he made pulling toffee—and without a recipe. Unfortunately I don't know how he made it except that he did put in honey which he said would ward off a cold or cure one. And after he pulled and we pulled the toffee it was chewy and honey-coloured and the best candy we had ever tasted.

BEVVY'S DELICIOUS CREAM CANDY

5 cups white sugar	1/2 cup sweet cream
1/2 cup boiling water	1/2 teaspoon vanilla

A deep saucepan should be used to make this candy as it boils up to a considerable height, Bevvy says. First dissolve the sugar in boiling water, using a whipping motion, until there is no trace of the grain of sugar. Do not stir after placing on fire. Cook the mixture until it forms a soft ball in cold water (238 degrees), then add the cream. Cook until it forms a hard ball when tested (265 degrees). Add vanilla just before taking it from the fire. Pour into buttered plates and, when cool, pull the candy. Cut into pieces of desired length. This candy should be set aside for about 24 hours—then it becomes flaky and will simply melt when put into the mouth, according to Bevvy's little black book.

MAPLE SYRUP CREAM CANDY

1 cup brown sugar and	1 tablespoon butter
1 cup maple syrup	1 teaspoon vanilla
1 cup milk	

Mix together all but the flavouring. Do not boil too fast and do not stir. Boil till a soft ball may be formed in water (238 degrees). Beat and pour onto buttered plate when thick and creamy.

MAPLE CREAM

4 cups brown sugar	1 cup top milk or thin cream
2 tablespoons flour	4 tablespoons butter
2 teaspoons baking powder	Pinch salt

Mix all together; cook, stirring constantly until soft-ball stage (238 degrees); add vanilla and beat, adding nuts when the candy becomes thick and creamy.

GINGER CREAMS

My friend Lillian Y. Snider of St. Jacobs gave me an airtight box of her own homemade candy. By allowing myself to eat only one piece after dinner each day I finished it in three weeks, when it was as soft and creamy as on the day she made it.

2 cups white sugar	2 tablespoons butter
1 cup brown sugar	1 teaspoon vanilla
$3/4$ cup milk	$1/4$ cup preserved ginger
2 tablespoons corn syrup	

"First of all," Lily says "if you are going to use preserved ginger, drain it well; if you have candied ginger wash the sugar from it in the milk, dry the ginger and chop it finely."

Now, stir the sugar, milk and syrup over a hot fire until the sugar is dissolved; then cook it slowly to the soft-ball stage (238 degrees), stirring often. Add the butter, and vanilla; remove the pan from the stove, cool and beat the candy until it begins to thicken. Lily says she let her electric mixer do the work; then she added the ginger, stirred it in with a spoon, poured the candy onto a buttered plate and cut it into squares before it hardened (only it didn't harden but remained firm and deliciously creamy).

LILY'S LIGHT CREAMY CANDY

I shared some of Lily's candy with my neighbour, a testy connoisseur; she tasted, rolled her eyes heavenward and emphatically pronounced, "Perfect!"

2 cups sugar	2 tablespoons corn syrup
$3/4$ cup rich milk	1 teaspoon vanilla
1 cup rich cream	1 cup walnuts or pecans
$1/8$ teaspoon salt	

Put all but the vanilla and walnuts into a pan and stir until the sugar is dissolved. Cook and stir over slow heat till the soft-ball stage (238 degrees) is reached. It takes from ³/₄ to one hour to reach it, Lily says. Remove from the fire, cool and add the vanilla. Beat the mixture until it is creamy. Lily says she uses her electric mixer at high speed and it usually takes about 5 minutes—sometimes more, sometimes less. Add the nuts and pour into a buttered pan. When it is cold cut into squares, and place in an airtight container. This candy improves with age, Lily says, but I doubt if age would ever overtake it.

A Variety of Things

SAUSAGES, CHEESES, SOAP, AND HOME REMEDIES

SAUSAGES

Bevvy's little book has recipes for summervascht, schwadamahga sausages, liverwurst, and head cheese, but you and I can't have them unless we butcher a pig or a cow. Or buy them at the Kitchener market.

SUMMER SAUSAGE

This is my favourite, on bread and butter or with potatoes. I'll give you its ingredients:

Sixty-six pounds of beef ground very fine; 33 pounds sidemeat; 4 pounds salt, 1/2 pound pepper, 1/2 pound saltpetre, 3 pounds sugar. Mix well; stuff solidly into long, firm cotton bags the size of a lady's stocking. Hang where they won't freeze for a few days, then smoke with maple smoke.

CHEESES

Unfortunately you'll no longer be able to buy schmierkase at Kitchener's market. The last black-bonnetted Mennonite woman who made it has told me she can't get the buttermilk curd that is needed to produce its rich creamy smoothness.

Bevvy tells me the cheeses she makes must have whole, fresh, unpasteurized milk. And where can you get that unless you have your own cow? You can still buy kochkase at the Kitchener market, and in local groceterias they have some in tins imported from Germany. I'll give you Bevvy's recipes in case you know a friendly cow-owner who can supply you with milk.

EASTER CHEESE

The Mennonites make this delicate, custard-like cheese at Easter for a special treat, to be eaten with fresh maple syrup.

4 cups fresh sweet milk	1 teaspoon salt
2 cups buttermilk or sour	1 teaspoon sugar
milk that isn't very sour	4 eggs

Scald the sweet milk but don't boil it. Beat the eggs till almost frothy; add the buttermilk, salt and sugar, and beat again; then pour the mixture into the hot sweet milk. Cover and let stand for about 10 minutes then stir slowly until it separates. Remove the solid part from the liquid by draining through a colander. Put it into a bowl to set—it will be soft, but solid enough to cut. It is lovely.

SCHMIERKASE (SPREADY CHEESE)

The name of this cheese isn't attractive but the cheese itself is delicate and delicious; spread on homebaked fresh bread with apple butter, or spooned into a dish with maple syrup poured over it and served with slightly warm doughnuts, it's fit for a king— but what king would ever be lucky enough to get schmierkase?

Bevvy says on the same day that you make butter you pour boiling water over the buttermilk and let it stand till the water makes the buttermilk curdle and the curds sink to the bottom of the bowl or kettle. Pour off the liquid and add cold water. Pour that off and strain the curd into muslin bags. Put a string around the top of the bag and suspend it from a broom handle over a bowl to let it drip through the night. Next morning put it in a dish—it will be kind of lumpy at first; work it with a spoon till it's fine, add salt and sweet cream till it's the consistency of soft ice cream or whipped cream. It has a slightly sour taste that is complemented deliciously by the maple syrup or apple butter.

COTTAGE CHEESE

Try this and you'll be surprised how much milk is needed to make a bit of cheese. Let skim milk get sour—the more milk you have the better. Put your pail of milk on the stove—preferably an old-fashioned iron wood-stove that has a section that is always warm but never hot. Keep turning the pail so the warmth of the stove is distributed evenly. When the milk becomes thick put your hands through it and keep working it to make sure the consistency is right. (If you use your hands the milk can't become too hot or your hands and arms wouldn't stand it—that's the best way to test it.) When the consistency seems right—something a natural-born cheesemaker knows instinctively—you strain it through a cloth till all the liquid has dripped out. And that's it—cottage cheese.

I had a Yorkshire landlady once who made it every Friday when she also baked bread; all any of us boarders ever wanted for supper on Friday night was still-warm buttered bread and fresh cottage cheese with plenty of salt and freshly milled pepper sprinkled over it.

SCHWEITZER (SWISS) CHEESE

A mild firm cheese that Bevvy makes often.

1 pail fresh milk, unskimmed   **Cheese colouring to give**
2 pails skim milk   **yellow tint**
1 tablespoon rennet

Heat the milk to 85 degrees, put in colour and rennet and stir well. Let stand half an hour; then cut and stir with hands and heat to hand temperature. Skim off whey as fast as it gathers, till it is nearly all off. Salt it and keep it moving so it will not settle in a lump. Get into a cheese press as quickly as convenient.

LIMBURGER CHEESE

The rose by any other name would smell as sweet.

1 pail fresh whole milk   **1³/₄ dessert spoons rennet**
1 pail skim milk   **¹/₂ teaspoon cheese**
                                               colouring

Heat milk to 110 or 112 degrees; take from fire, add rennet and colouring, stirring well. Let stand about 20 minutes, stirring slowly once in a while. When cheese is rubbery take off whey and put the cheese in a box. Let stand for 4 hours then turn upside down till next morning. Rub with salt on 3 mornings, then wrap in cloth and put away to ripen. As it ages it will soften and develop the strong aroma and delicate flavour for which it is notorious.

BELLE'S SOAP

In the cupboard under my kitchen sink I keep a tin into which I pour all the bacon fat or any meat dripping I don't want to use. When the can is filled I give it to my neighbour who uses it to make soap that is gentle, yet powerful enough to remove spots that have resisted other soaps and detergents.

5½ cups fat
11 cups water
3 cups cold water
½ can Gillette's lye

2 tablespoons powdered borax
1 cup detergent

Boil the grease in the 11 cups of water; let stand until grease hardens, then skim off grease. Melt the grease in an enamel saucepan until lukewarm. In another enamel pan slowly empty the ½-can of lye into the 3 cups of cold water; add powdered borax and stir occasionally until dissolved. When the lye mixture is lukewarm pour slowly, carefully, into lukewarm grease and add the detergent. Stir thoroughly for 10 minutes. Pour into a glass or enamel pan. Keep in a warm place for 2 days and then cut into cakes. Let the soap ripen for a month before using it.

BEVVY'S LOTION FOR CHAPPED HANDS

5 cents' worth quince seed
10 cents' worth glycerine

10 cents' worth rose-water
1 pint boiling water

Scald quince seed with boiling water, let stand on back of stove for 24 hours but don't let it simmer. Keep it hot. Add glycerine and rose-water when it is cold.

HOME REMEDIES FOR THINGS THAT MIGHT AIL YOU

Even at eighty-seven my mother considers sickness an affront; she has no patience with it at all. When we were young she fed us so well and took such good care of us that we had no reason or right to be sick. If we complained she would say, "There's nothing wrong with you, march off to school and forget about it." And we did; we got no children's diseases but measles.

HOT LEMONADE

If any of us had a sniffle Mother gave us hot lemonade and sent us to bed.

Juice of 1 lemon **1 cup boiling water**
2 tablespoons honey

Heat the water in a pan, spoon in the honey, add the lemon juice and heat the mixture but don't let it boil. Pour the lemonade into a mug, get into bed and drink it steaming hot and strong enough to screw up your face.

HONEY

Daddy always said honey was good for us. He said honey and horseradish would ward off a cold.

RAW ONIONS

To our genteel teen-age disgust, Daddy used to slice raw Spanish onions, sprinkle them with brown sugar, cover them with cider vinegar, then a few hours later eat them on slices of buttered bread while he tried to persuade us to do likewise. He would say, "If you eat onions like this you will never be sick." We took our chances.

MUSTARD PLASTER

If a cold ever got down into our chests Mother went after it with a mustard plaster. She would mix equal parts of mustard and flour with enough warm water to make a paste, then she'd spread it on a cloth, cover it with another cloth and slap it on an ailing chest, covered by a bath towel. She'd leave it there for about fifteen minutes—till the skin showed signs of redness.

FOR MINOR BURNS OR SCALDS

A wet tea bag held on the burned spot will take out the sting and might keep it from blistering.

BEVVY'S REMEDIES FOR A COLD

A drink of hot sage tea with honey to sweeten it.

A mixture of one-third turpentine and two-thirds goose grease heated to blood warmth and rubbed on the chest for a cold or cough. "And how the children giggle when you rub it on," Bevvy says. Cover the chest with flannel.

COUGH MIXTURE

This sure-cure is in a local I.O.D.E. cookbook.

1 pint Jamaica rum   **Juice of a lemon**
3 ounces glycerine   **1 pound rock candy**

There are no directions for making or taking it.

MORE REMEDIES

When Mother and Daddy were in the United States on their honeymoon they bought *The Every Day Cook Book* by Miss E. Neil, published in 1884. Mother says she didn't find it very useful —despite the following suggestions:

FOR LEANNESS

First restore digestion, take plenty of sleep, drink all the water the stomach will bear in the morning on rising, take moderate exercise in the open air, eat oatmeal, cracked wheat, Graham mush, baked sweet apples, roasted and broiled beef, cultivate jolly people and bathe daily.

FOR ASTHMA

Sufferers from asthma should get a muskrat skin and wear it over their lungs with the fur side next to the body. It will bring certain relief.

FOR FEVER AND AGUE

Four ounces galangal-root in a quart of gin, steeped in a warm place; take often.

TO RESTORE FROM STROKE OF LIGHTNING

Shower with cold water for two hours; if the patient does not show signs of life, put salt in the water and continue to shower for an hour longer.

FOR CONSTIPATION

One or two figs eaten fastly.

DIARRHOEA

For any form of diarrhoea that, by excessive action, demands a speedy correction, the most efficacious remedy that can be employed in all ages and conditions of childhood is the tincture of kino, of which from ten to thirty drops, mixed with a little sugar and water in a spoon, are to be given every two or three hours till the undue action has been checked.

THE QUININE CURE FOR DRUNKENNESS

Pulverize one pound of fresh quill-red Peruvian bark; and soak it in one pint of diluted alcohol. Strain and evaporate down to one-half pint. For the first and second days give a teaspoon every three hours. If too much is taken, headache will result, and in that case the doses should be diminished. On the third day give one-half a teaspoonful; on the fourth, reduce the dose to fifteen drops, then to ten, and then to five. Seven days, it is said, will cure average cases, though some require a whole month.

And Finally

For almost two years I have been collecting, testing and writing these recipes. If the results you achieve when you try them are anything like Bevvy's and Mother's I'm sure you'll be pleased and your family will love you.

Don't take any of the recipes too seriously—have fun while you try them, substitute ingredients you like for ones that you don't; experiment, improvise, be a little bit reckless.

And kindly remember, if you make any bloopers, that I warned you I am strictly an amateur cook with no qualification for writing a cookbook except that I was brought up and well-fed in Waterloo County where we boast that our food really *schmecks*.

Index

grape conserve, 115
jewel jam, 115
mock maple syrup, 116
plum conserve, 115

Kale, 82
Kohlrabi, 73

Leftover Dishes
bye-bye shortcake, 124
casserole for Carol and Paul, 123
chicken dish, 123
ham loaf, 126
ham and noodles, 125
handy cottage pie, 126
kartoffelkrapfen, 88
meat casserole, 122
meat roll, 122
pork pie, 124
Quiche Lorraine variation, 118
leftover roast, 125
stuffed squash, 125
Lemon bread, 164
butter icing, 212
butter sauce for fish, 67
lemonade, 20
hot, 280
in-a-hurry, 20
filling, 216
meringue pie, 242
pudding sauce, 266
snow, 257
soufflé, 265
sponge pie, 234
Lettuce salad, 92
in tossed salad, 94
Liver and bacon, 41
in sour cream, 41
Liver sausage, headcheese or
levavascht
burgers, 129
hot, 47
in pahnhass, 134
Lunches, Suppers, Brunches,
Leftovers, 117

Macaroni, 121
Maple Syrup
cake, 196
candy pie, 237
cream candy, 273
custard, 258
with fat cakes, 212
icings, 215
mock maple syrup, 116
mousse, 259
pie, 240

pudding, 256
vanilla pie, 235
Meats, Fowl, Fish and Meat
Accompaniments, 31–68
see Bacon
see Beef
bologna, breaded, 130
hot rings, 129
see Chickens, 55
duck, same as Turkey, 61
with apple or sauerkraut
stuffing, 57
Dutch beef pie, 39
see Fish
gallrich, 46
goose with gooseberry stuffing, 62
with sauerkraut stuffing, 57
see Ham
hamburgers with gravy, 39
headcheese or liversausage
burgers, 129
hot melted, 47
in pahnhaas, 134
heart, stuffed, 32
kartoffelkrapfen, 88
kraut wickel (cabbage rolls), 45
see Leftover Dishes
liver and bacon, 41
liver in sour cream, 41
meat balls, 52
meat loaves
beef, 38
gallrich, 60
ham and fresh pork, 52
ham and pineapple, 52
ham leftover, 126
stuffed beef loaf, 39
veal, jellied, 33
veal loaf, 38
meat pies
crusty chicken, 60
Dutch beef, 39
handy cottage, 126
pork pie, 124
mock duck, 37
pahnhaas, 134
pigs' feet, 45
hocks, gallrich, 46
knuckles, 46
tails, 42
see Pork
potpie
chicken (hingle), 59
crusty chicken, 60
veal, 60